BUYING A BUSINESS
AND
MAKING IT WORK

*A step-by-step guide to purchasing
a business and making it successful*

MARK BLAYNEY

howtobooks

Published by How To Books Ltd,
3 Newtec Place, Magdalen Road,
Oxford OX4 1RE, United Kingdom.
Tel: (01865) 793806. Fax: (01865) 248780.
email: info@howtobooks.co.uk
http://www.howtobooks.co.uk

British Library Cataloguing in Publication Data
A catalogue record for this book is available from the British Library

Cover design by Baseline Arts Ltd, Oxford
Produced for How To Books by Deer Park Productions, Tavistock
Typeset by TW Typesetting, Plymouth, Devon
Printed and bound by Bell & Bain, Glasgow

NOTE: The material contained in this book is set out in good faith for
general guidance and no liability can be accepted for loss or expense
incurred as a result of relying in particular circumstances on statements
made in the book. The laws and regulations are complex and liable to
change, and readers should check the current position with the relevant
authorities before making personal arrangements.

Dedication

To Pat, as ever, and my parents.

Contents

Acknowledgements   xiii

Important Notice   xiv

Introduction   1
Who are you and how can this book help?   5

PHASE 1: THE PLANNING PROCESS

1   Deciding You Want to Buy   11
    Undertaking research   11
    You as a business buyer   12
    Who are you and why do you want to buy?   14
    What buying a business will not do   16
    The qualities you need (or why you shouldn't buy a business)   17
    And what happens if it all goes wrong?   23
    Alternatives to buying for expansion   25

2   Deciding What to Buy   27
    The importance of focus   27
    What type of business do you want to buy?   28
    What types of business are there?   34
    Other characteristics to consider   42
    Researching the business   44
    Where should you buy a business?   45
    When is the best time to buy a business?   48

3   Beginning Your Planning and Appointing Advisers   55
    Having a plan   55
    Doing it as a group   56

Purchasing vehicle   60

Acquisition plan   63

Who you will need   64

Appointing advisers   66

Managing your advisers   68

The need for due diligence   69

PHASE 2: THE SEARCH PROCESS

4 Starting Your Search   75

What are you looking for?   75

Who are sellers?   77

Why do sellers sell?   78

Why sellers don't sell   83

Family businesses   88

Who are you competing with?   93

5 Finding a Business to Buy   95

Search tactics   95

Businesses for sale and not for sale   98

Finding businesses that are formally for sale   99

Financial promotion   110

Finding businesses that are not for sale   112

MBO specific issues   116

Franchising   118

PHASE 3: APPROACHING AND SCREENING

6 Before You Approach   123

Desktop reviews and screening   123

Sources of non-financial information   124

Financial information   128

Having faith in numbers   129

Understanding accounts   131

How are accounts prepared?   132

What is in each part of the accounts?   133

What should you look for in the accounts?   136

Understanding profitability   137

Understanding financial stability 145
Understanding financial efficiency 147
Summary 153

7 **Approaching the Business** **156**
The importance of first contact 156
Approaching the business 157
Approaching a business that is not for sale 159
The first meeting 161
Understanding the business beyond the numbers 164
Review checklist 166
Confidentiality 177

8 **What is it Worth?** **180**
The importance of realistic valuations at the outset 180
How does price relate to risk for each side? 182
Valuations are valueless 184
The value of valuations 187
What if the seller has set a high asking price? 189
It's rude to talk about money 190
Bases of valuations 191
What is for sale? 192
Is it really a buyable business? 194
Dealing with a mixed bag 196

9 **Valuation Techniques** **199**
Do you need to know about valuations? 199
Restatement of earnings 199
In the black 201
Asset valuation 203
Market valuation 206
Discounted cashflow 208
Return on investment 213
Sector specific 214
Earnings multiples 215
What you should not pay for 216
Summary 217

10	**Financing the Deal**	**219**
	What does the money need to cover?	219
	Where do you get the money?	221
	What form of external finance is right?	223
	Equity	226
	Borrowing against personal property	229
	Grants	231
	Debt	234
	Management buy-out financing information checklist	236
	How much can you borrow?	244
	Vendor finance	246
	Financial assistance rules	248

PHASE 4: NEGOTIATING THE PURCHASE

11	**Negotiating the Price**	**253**
	The negotiation process	253
	What if negotiations run into difficulties?	256
	Structuring the deal	258
	How certain is payment going to be?	260
	How much is the seller financing?	262
	How certain is the price?	263
	Other key terms	265
	Heads of terms	266

12	**Due Diligence**	**269**
	What is due diligence?	269
	Legal due diligence	271

13	**Financial Due Diligence**	**280**
	Why financial due diligence is important	280
	More than just ticks in boxes	287
	Contents of due diligence report	288

14	**Commercial Due Diligence**	**296**
	Why commercial due diligence is important	296
	Assessment of the management team	298
	What about the old owner?	302
	Problem due diligence	304

15	**The Sales Contract and Completion**	**307**
	The twin track process	307
	The sales contract	308
	So what are representations, warranties and indemnities?	310
	Covenants	318
	Closure	319
	Typical share purchase agreement	321

16	**Trouble with the Taxman**	**323**
	The importance of tax	323
	Value added tax	323
	Stamp duty	324
	Capital gains tax	325
	Income tax	325
	Interaction of income and capital gains taxes	326

PHASE 5: MAKING IT WORK

17	**Taking Control**	**331**
	The timescale and need for speed	331
	Fast or slow integration?	334
	Your plan	340
	Communications	342
	Change management	348
	Managing people and the process of change	352
	How can you make change happen?	353
	Managing and motivating staff to change	358
	Redundancies	361

18	**Financial Management**	**364**
	Managing by the numbers	364
	Group structure	364
	Cleaning up the group structure	366
	Management information	369
	Profit improvement	376
	Cashflow management	381
	Cashflow improvement	392

19 Buying a Business to Turn Around   397
   Why buy a business in difficulties?   397
   So how and why do businesses start to fail?   399
   Finding a business to turn around   404
   Buying a business before insolvency   407
   Buying from a receiver or administrator   410
   Making a turnaround work   414

The Golden Rules   418

Useful Contacts   421

Glossary of Acronyms   423

Appendix A: Sample Confidentiality Agreement   424

Appendix B: Sample Legal Due Diligence Questionnaire   432

Appendix C: Sample Financial Due Diligence Checklist   452

Appendix D: Summarised Sample Share Purchase Agreement   462

Index   479

Acknowledgements

I would like to thank Robert Thompson of Ward Hadaway, George Moore of Resolution Inc, and Alistair Aird of Baker Tilly for their assistance, and Baker Tilly and Ward Hadaway for the use of sample documents.

Important Notice

The sample documents included are provided only for the purposes of illustration. As with all legal documents, actual agreements should only be drafted by professional advisers sufficiently qualified and experienced to understand all the issues arising from them and from any particular factual situation. You should always seek specific advice for all specific situations and neither the author, the publisher, nor Baker Tilly who have kindly supplied the two due diligence sample documents, or Ward Hadaway who have kindly supplied the legal due diligence document and sample legal agreements, can be responsible to you and accept no responsibility for any loss suffered by anyone as a result of action or omitting to act as a result of the material contained in the sample documents provided here and elsewhere in the book.

Introduction

When you think about buying a business, what sort of image comes to mind?

Is it late nights in smoke-filled rooms with solicitors struggling through closure meetings? Is it the ruthless corporate raider Gordon Gekko in *Wall Street* planning the financial strategy? Is it teams of accountants crawling all over the books, doing due diligence in trying to find any hidden problems before it's too late?

All these images capture the excitement, thrills and suspense of the buying process which, in truth, is one of the riskiest business decisions you may ever make. But they also reflect only a relatively small part of the process of buying a business since doing the deal is only one part of an overall process.

As it is one of the largest financial transactions you'll ever undertake, in many ways the best way to think about buying a business is like buying a house.

Unless you make a completely impulse purchase, the process that you go through when house hunting (leaving aside any need to sell your existing house) is generally:

◆ You decide that you want to move.

1

◆ Taking into account the price your current house will fetch and how much you are likely to be able to raise as a mortgage, you decide how much you can afford to spend. You might have a preliminary discussion with a lender at this stage just to confirm how much you can borrow but until you have actually found a property that you want to buy, you normally cannot do very much more than this.

◆ You think about what's important to you about your next house and therefore what you're looking for.

◆ You start to look for houses that match your criteria by studying the adverts and sending for details of those that interest you. Perhaps you will also contact the estate agents who seem to sell the types of houses that you are interested in, to be put on their lists to receive details of appropriate properties when they come up for sale.

◆ You make arrangements to visit houses that seem to match your criteria for an initial viewing.

◆ If you decide to make an offer on a property, you negotiate a price with the owner.

◆ Once your offer has been accepted, you need to arrange your mortgage, engage a solicitor and have a survey done. Your mortgage lender will also arrange their own survey.

◆ Once you've agreed which fixtures and fittings are staying, you exchange contracts and commit to a completion date.

◆ On the day of completion you receive the keys to your new home and move in. You have to arrange practical matters such as transferring utility bills to your name. Immediately after you move in there is generally quite a lot of upheaval as you unpack all your belongings.

♦ It's only really in the weeks and months after the immediate completion that you can really start to relax and enjoy the property and to take steps to make any longer term changes that you are planning such as building a garage or putting up a conservatory.

In many aspects the process of buying a business follows a very similar pattern to that of buying a house outlined above.

Because buying a business is not an event, it is not simply doing the deal, however involved, pressurised and complex that might feel at the time. It is a process that you have to go through to achieve the objective that you want to achieve. You do not buy a business simply to buy a business. You buy a business to become the owner of a successful business that achieves your personal or business goals for you thereafter.

And the process that gets you to that objective is one that has at least five parts:

1. **The planning phase** – deciding to buy and what you want.

2. **The search phase** – finding the business to buy which is the right one to enable you to achieve your objectives.

3. **The approach and screening phase** – narrowing your search down to businesses you want to speak to, opening contact with the owners, making a judgement as to whether you want to buy and making an initial offer.

4. **Doing the deal** – carrying out the detailed checking of the business you're going to buy so that you know what you are

getting, and negotiating the detailed structure of the deal through to completion.

5. **Making it work afterwards** – because as pointed out above, you don't buy a business just for buying a business's sake, you buy it to provide you with the future stream of income, the lifestyle or the security that you are seeking for your future or the increased market share you want for your company.

In short, a successful business acquisition is not just a matter of successfully buying a business, but it is also making a success of the business that has been bought.

So the process doesn't begin with deciding to buy the business and doesn't end with doing the deal, and unfortunately buying a business is more complicated than simply buying a house.

Yes, the process is similar and yes, some of the checking that you need to do is very similar in nature to the checks that you need to undertake when buying house. Just as you might obtain a survey of a house, so you also need to check the business structure is sound in how it operates.

◆ Does it have the right plant and machinery?

◆ Does it have the right systems?

And just as you need a solicitor to check the local planning permissions for things that will affect a property's value, so you also need to check that there are no significant changes happening or likely in the business's market that will significantly affect its market position.

While the five-phase process outlined above mirrors the process of buying a house, it's important to remember that the process of buying a business is inevitably much more complex and stressful than buying a house simply because a business is a more complicated thing than a house.

Remember that a business is not simply bricks and mortar or plant and machinery. It is also people; both employees inside, and relationships with customers and suppliers outside. It is also more abstract things which are equally as important such as knowledge, know-how, reputation and image.

It is also not a static thing like a property but is part of an ever changing business environment in which there are new customers, new suppliers, new competitors, as well as new products and ways of doing business, all of which the business has continually to be anticipating, planning and reacting to successfully to remain on track.

The degree of complexity of the work you have to undertake in respect of any phase will vary with the scale of complexity of the business you're looking to buy, but whether it's a corner shop or a large PLC the fundamental principles will be the same. This book is therefore structured around the five phases outlined above.

WHO ARE YOU AND HOW CAN THIS BOOK HELP?
The nature and skills of buyers can vary enormously from:

♦ a management buy in (MBI) team of experienced executives backed by a venture capital house

♦ a business owner seeking to expand market share by making an acquisition

♦ an experienced businessperson looking to go it alone for the first time; to

◆ someone looking to buy a retirement business.

All buyers will, however, have something in common; they will all want their purchase to be a success. At the same time, they will also obviously differ significantly in the scale and complexity of the business they are looking to buy, from the household name to the corner shop, and the resources they have available to help them, from phalanxes of advisers to their own common sense and commercial judgement.

Given these differences, for sake of clarity in my approach to writing this book I have assumed that you are an individual, with a reasonable level of general business knowledge, looking to buy a business for the first time; and that you are looking for a business that is more than simply a lifestyle, one of a size to have a number of employees.

It is of course true that whatever the size and complexity of the deal, from the sub post office to the PLC subsidiary, these will all still have many issues in common, from finding the right business to buy to negotiating the right terms, from understanding the staffing issues to raising the cash.

Where significantly smaller or larger deals will have different characteristics I have therefore simply indicated these in the text, while I have also tried to flag up issues such as post-acquisition integration that are more applicable to an existing business making an acquisition than an individual purchaser.

Additionally, at various points within the book the need for specialist expert advisers is stressed, from corporate finance accountants and lawyers, through to asset finance brokers, independent financial advisers and surveyors. I am always pleased to help as far as possible any readers who are in need of such professionals with an introduction to capable advisers in their area, so please feel free to contact me on the email below for this or with any queries about any aspect of this book.

Good luck.

Mark Blayney

(mark@theoss.freeserve.co.uk)

GOLDEN RULES

1. Realise that this is a process – it's not doing the deal, it's making the deal work.
2. You are not buying a business for the sake of buying a business, you are doing it to achieve your objectives, whatever they may be.

Phase 1: The Planning Process

① Deciding You Want to Buy

UNDERTAKING RESEARCH

Buying a business is likely to be a long drawn-out, stressful and expensive affair. So before embarking on such a project, it's worth taking a while at the outset to think through a number of key questions, both to ensure that if you do buy a business, it is as successful as possible; and to ensure that you are making the right decision in looking to take this step.

It is vital therefore to start the process with some thorough research to help you decide what sort of business you might want and what issues you will need to consider, including whether you ought to be buying a business at all.

The areas you need to cover are broadly:

Personal questions

◆ Are you already in business?

◆ What is motivating you to buy a business? What are you looking to get out of it? The lifestyle? An opportunity to turn your hard work into a financial killing? An investment? Or an expansion of your existing business?

◆ What facilities, housing, schools and local amenities will you need in any area that you live in and how does this affect whether you can move to buy a business?

- What skills do you have that are appropriate for running a business?

- How much cash are you and your family or your business willing to risk?

- Are you prepared for what's involved in buying and running a business?

Business questions
- What sort of business should you buy?

- How can you find out more about it?

- What locations are appropriate?

- When is the best time to buy?

Planning your approach
- How are you going to go about finding a business?

- What advisers or help are you going to need?

The result of your research should be an outline plan setting out what you're looking for and how you intend to go about getting it. The importance of this part of the process in minimising the risks and giving the best chance of success cannot be overemphasised and evidence of sufficient thorough preparation is the first step in establishing credibility with the lenders and advisers who may be the key to allowing you to complete a deal at all. The chapters in this section are set out to cover these three issues.

YOU AS A BUSINESS BUYER
The starting point for research is your own background. You should therefore consider carefully two questions.

Your motives

Firstly, why do you want to buy a business? People's motives in buying a business can differ significantly from seeking a challenging opportunity to build and then sell a highly valuable business in a very competitive environment; to seeking to downshift from the rat race or acquire a stable retirement income. You might want the opportunity to really focus on some particular skills you have developed, or you may be feeling stale and are seeking an opportunity to try something different. In contrast, existing business owners will normally be interested in an acquisition as a way of achieving a step change in growing their business.

Whatever your personal circumstances and desires it is important that you think carefully about what you are looking to get out of buying a business, as this will be critical in setting your objectives in searching for a business and the criteria you apply in screening targets that you find. Just by considering this point, you will hopefully already see that any decision to buy a business is far from a simple financial or commercial one and must take into account a whole range of personal and emotional factors.

Your personal attributes

And secondly, it also follows that you need to consider what personal characteristics, skills and experience you have that you can draw on to make the process a success. Are you experienced in buying or running a business or will this be your first time? Are you confident that you have the full range of skills needed to run a business, from selling and operations through to managing staff and the books? How deep is your knowledge of the sector or industry that you are thinking about or are you coming into it afresh? What sizes of business have you been involved in running before? Have you got the drive and determination to get through the setbacks and make whatever you buy a success? How much risk are you prepared to take in buying a business? How supportive is your family of your plans?

Only by thinking through the answers to these questions can you start to decide what sort and size of business might suit you.

And since both the process and the result of buying a business will have such a significant impact on your life if this is your first time, it is also worth testing the question whether you really do want to buy a business or not.

WHO ARE YOU AND WHY DO YOU WANT TO BUY?

There are many types of people who consider buying a business and the characteristics and scale of business that they will be interested in will differ significantly dependent upon their motivation. Are you any of these?

The retiree

Many people do not wish to fully retire at the end of their 'normal' working life and are therefore interested in buying small but steady lifestyle businesses such as shops or bed and breakfasts as a way of both continuing to work and generating a retirement income.

The MBO

At the other end of the scale, there may be the divisional director of part of a large listed organisation who is interested in buying it out or indeed the chief executive who would like to take the company from public to private ownership. These will be 'big ticket' deals funded by venture capitalists (VCs) and driven by expectations of creating significant value.

The first time entrepreneur

This is the person looking to get into business for the first time who takes the view that it will be safer to buy an existing business rather than starting one from scratch. In addition to exploring a normal sale, such buyers might well also consider looking at buying a franchise as a way of achieving this objective (although you do need to be careful when looking at franchises to ensure that you find good evidence to show that the business model really works for franchisees).

The serial entrepreneur
Then there is the recent seller, who has already successfully built and sold at least one business, and is now looking for a new challenge.

The downshifter, the frustrated entrepreneur and/or the self realiser
Sadly, many people seem to find themselves trapped in careers that do not satisfy them and buying your own business is one way of achieving a significant career change.

This is the group amongst whom actual motivation varies most widely. For some it is a major lifestyle change such as a divorce or serious illness that leads to a reassessment of priorities and a desire for change. Others simply find that their creativity is frustrated by their existing employment, or the current trends towards flat management structures mean that there is a lack of opportunity to progress in their current job. In some cases people want to be able to take the broader view, to be their own boss, to be in charge and run things the way they want to run them, to have full overall responsibility for a business.

Some people are motivated by a desire to follow a particular line of work or to take the opportunity to turn what was a hobby into a living. Some are simply motivated by desire to reap the rewards of their own work rather than earning for other people. Some want the status; some want the challenge so that they can prove they can do it.

The family buy-out
This is a case of the next generation ensuring an orderly
succession and avoiding the confusion that often lingers in such
businesses, by clearly taking over the business and allowing the
previous owners to formalise their pension arrangements.

The expanding business
Then there is the small business owner who is looking to acquire
further operations as a bolt-on acquisition to their existing
company. This is typically in order to expand by entering new
markets or building on turnover, as an acquisition can provide
step growth for an existing business by:

◆ adding more customers

◆ taking out a competitor

◆ accessing new products for existing customers

◆ providing new channels to market

◆ giving access to new technology

◆ allowing entry to new markets.

The investor
The investor is not looking to run the specific business that is
being bought; they are interested in building a chain of
businesses or a portfolio of interests that they can manage.

WHAT BUYING A BUSINESS WILL NOT DO
So if these are some of the reasons that people buy businesses,
it's worth tackling some of the myths by saying the things that
buying a business generally will not do. Two of the most

important of these for individuals looking to run their own business for the first time are:

- You cannot rely on it to give you a better lifestyle in qualitative terms, certainly not in the short term, as you will find that the commitment required by you to run your own business means that almost every thing else is sacrificed to it.

- It will also not generally give you more time with your family. Running a small business or buying a business is an all-consuming activity for the first few years. You will eat, drink and sleep your new business, think of nothing else and talk of little else to your loved ones. Irrespective of the financial issues involved, the personal commitment required of you is likely to severely test your relationships.

THE QUALITIES YOU NEED (OR WHY YOU SHOULDN'T BUY A BUSINESS)

The buying process is going to be a long haul. You will need the time, the money and the commitment to push through successfully to complete the purchase. Before going to this trouble, however, you need to take stock of your most valuable resource – yourself – to see whether you are likely to make a success of both buying a business and running it thereafter.

You should therefore review the resources, skills and experience you are bringing to the situation and make an honest assessment as to your strengths and weaknesses and how these are likely to affect the success of your venture.

Characteristics important to getting the deal done include:

- **Stamina** to keep going through a long fraught process. If you are going to become discouraged and give up when negotiations run into difficulties or problems arise in the paperwork, then you can save yourself a lot of heartache by not starting.

◆ **Self-confidence** and the **decisiveness** to press the button and do the deal. When the moment of truth comes, will you actually sign on the dotted line or pay over equity raised by borrowing against your house to acquire the business in question? Because if not you'd be wasting your time and your money in pursuing the search.

◆ An **open mind** but also a **commercial mind**, remembering that whatever your objectives and reasons for being interested in buying a particular business, your overall objective is to buy a business and make a success of it. This means that you mustn't allow yourself to get emotionally attached to any one opportunity or focused exclusively on one deal. Remember that until completion these are only opportunities, and you should therefore whenever possible be pursuing a number of opportunities to find the one that is going to pay off, even if this inevitably means that you will end up having wasted some time, if not some cash in the process.

◆ Enough **cash** to buy the size of business that you are looking for. Even if you can finance much of the deal by borrowings against the assets (as outlined in Chapter 10) and receive vendor financing for much of the rest, you are still going to need to put some cash out yourself by way of equity. Additionally, you will need some cash on which to live whilst you are in the process of finding and negotiating a purchase, which could well take over a year, unless of course you continue to work during your search.

You will also need to pay fees to professional advisers during this period, although you may be able to negotiate that a significant amount of these are charged on a contingent fee basis and are therefore only payable on success. This is likely, however, to increase the overall cost as the advisers in question will load the rates to compensate for the risk and uncertainty of being paid.

And don't forget that once you have actually bought the business you will also need **funding** to meet its ongoing working capital requirements, as well as any restructuring costs or investment required. This funding will again have to come from either your equity or from borrowing against the assets purchased. So you need to have a realistic look at how much equity you will be able to raise to put into the project from your own resources such as by borrowing against your house.

◆ An appropriate **attitude to risk** that is going to enable you to see the process through to a successful conclusion. Are you prepared to spend the time and cash required to pursue the idea of buying a business with no guarantees of success? What happens if you do not find a business that you want to buy? How much of a disaster will this be?

  – Are you really prepared to take the risk of investing significant sums in buying a business even if you have checked it out?

  – Are you really prepared to take the risk of losing all your investment (or more in some cases) if it doesn't work out?

  – Are you prepared to buy a business, warts and all?

◆ The **credibility** in terms of experience, commitment and financing to persuade professional intermediaries and business sellers that you are serious about buying a business and worth dealing with.

– Have you been involved in previous business acquisitions?

– Have you run a business before?

– Have you a serious and credible acquisition plan, targeting businesses and industries with which you have some experience?

– Can you demonstrate that you have a substantial amount of personal cash readily available to invest in the purchase?

– Are you willing to agree to pay a lead adviser to conduct the search for you?

◆ The ability to get the appropriate **licensing or regulatory approvals** to conduct the business you are looking to run. It doesn't matter how thriving the pharmacy is that you are thinking about buying, if you are not a pharmacist, you will not be able to operate the business. There is not much point in thinking about buying a successful pub if there is no prospect of you being able to apply for a publican's licence.

But it's not just doing the deal that's important. You also need to be able to run the business afterwards.

◆ Do you have all the **skills and knowledge** needed successfully to run the business once you have bought it? Can you 'sell' as well as 'do'? Can you manage all the functions needed to make the business work – its marketing, finance and operations, as well as the back office administration? Can you manage staff as well as dealing with the ongoing and ever increasing burden of regulation?

◆ Do you have all the **personal characteristics** needed to make a go of it? Are you a self-starter with self-discipline and able to get things done? Can you manage your own time? Can you get along with people; are you happy to work with them, able to persuade and lead? Can you work hard? Will you be dedicated enough to work the hours that will be needed, planning menial jobs and detail, sometimes for very little apparent reward? Do you have sufficient self-reliance and bloody-minded stick-at-it-ness to see whatever is needed through?

◆ To help you with some self-analysis, you (and any members of your team) should consider taking some psychometric tests to help you better understand your strengths and weaknesses and to give you some objective insight into how these might impact on your ability to manage other people. Two types of psychometric test that are particularly useful are:

– Belbin – a set of tests designed to show your preferred 'team roles' from 'ideas person' through 'networker' to 'completer finisher'. The point being that a balanced team needs people undertaking a number of different functions in order to work properly.

– PPA – a set of tests which give insight into your preferred personal operating style (do you seek constant change or stability, are you focused on achieving goals or being the centre of attention?). The point here is that your personal operating style will significantly affect both your style of management and the way that you communicate with others, and that awareness of your natural tendency will allow you to modify this to become more effective depending upon your audience.

◆ Will you have your **family's support**?

◆ Are you in **good health** and will you be able to manage stress?

◆ Have you experience of running a business in the sector ('**sector experience**') you are considering? Venture capitalists are in many ways the professionals at buying businesses as they do so regularly. When VCs are looking to back a management buy in team (an 'MBI') they generally look for individuals with a high degree of experience and contacts in the industry, as from bitter experience of failed deals they have learnt that having a good contact network in the industry can be vital for getting over the inevitable wobbles in the early years of any such buyout. And if the professionals put such a premium on industry experience then shouldn't you?

◆ Have you experience of running the **size** of business you are considering? That running a small business may not completely qualify you to run a very large one is an idea that seems obvious to most people. However many people from large business environments automatically assume that they will be well-equipped to run a small business. This can be a very dangerous assumption and some such buyers suffer a severe culture shock in the small business environment. If you are used to the way of working where a strong support network was in place for you from secretaries to an IT support department, running a small business where you are 'it', and you have to buy your own stamps, make your own coffee, do your own photocopying, empty the bins and troubleshoot your own laptop, can come as a great shock.

◆ Can you learn from your mistakes? Are you willing to seek and **take advice**?

◆ Are you prepared for the full range of **responsibilities** that you may be taking on and their personal consequences? When buying a business you are not simply taking straightforward commercial financial risks but becoming responsible for a whole raft of other issues, as the tendency in many areas of legislation such as environmental issues and health and safety is increasingly to make directors personally liable for defaults. If your business hasn't dealt with its responsibilities under, for example, the new laws concerning asbestos risk assessment, then it is you as director who faces jail.

◆ Are you prepared to **persevere** and take the long view? And while we are on the long view, don't forget that you are going to need to organise your own pension arrangements once you are working on your own.

◆ Are you confident that you **know the risks**?

This is obviously quite a list of attributes to consider; so you should take the time to reflect whether you have sufficient strength in everything listed above to look seriously at buying a business.

If not, you should consider very seriously whether you should be going ahead with buying a business.

And if you think I am trying to put you off, you are absolutely correct. Buying a business will be a huge emotional and financial investment, and one to which not everyone is suited. So if you do wish to proceed you need to be doing so with your eyes clearly open to the risks as well as the rewards.

AND WHAT HAPPENS IF IT ALL GOES WRONG?

If you haven't had experience of running a business before, if everything so far hasn't been enough to put you off, are you prepared for the fact that people's ability to pay their mortgages, their livelihoods, their futures will become your responsibility?

If the business you buy hits rough times and you need to cut costs, could you make some of the people working for you redundant?

What are you going to do if it gets to the end of the month and you don't have enough cash for the payroll? Could you cope with the fact that if the business goes down, you may end up having cost many suppliers, be they companies or sole traders, real money, that might push some of them in turn into financial difficulty?

And if the potential impact on relative strangers worries you, how you going to feel if the business goes wrong and you have asked your family or friends to put money into it?

Example

A retired professional put £300,000 of his pension fund into buying into a business developing a new process. As the business got into difficulties, he then persuaded his brother, who had no involvement with the business, to invest £25,000 to meet the wage bill and some pressing creditors. Despite this funding, the business still failed a month or so later with the investors losing everything.

The point is that once you have bought into a business, the buck really does stop with you. You will be completely responsible for the business and how it operates. There is nowhere to hide, no one else to blame. It is completely down to you whether this business succeeds or fails.

Personal financial risk

And beyond the personal and emotional pressure there will also be financial ones as your assets are likely to be on the line. Banks and other lenders will not want to be the only people with a financial exposure to the business. Irrespective of their position with regard to security, they will often expect you to give personal guarantees for the company's borrowings to ensure that you cannot simply walk away if it all goes wrong leaving them with a problem. So if the business does fail and they face a potential deficit, they will be in a position to look to you for the repayment of some of the company's debts, at a time when you have lost your income from the business. Are you really prepared to put your family's house on the line to buy this business?

Legal risks

And then there are the legal risks. If the business becomes insolvent, as a director you could also face the risk of action against you personally by a liquidator for wrongful trading (so you will need to take careful professional advice should your business start to get into this position). In every case of failure you will of course also be subject to a report by the appointed insolvency practitioner under the Company Directors Disqualification Act, as a result of which the DTI may choose to take action to ban you from being a director in future.

ALTERNATIVES TO BUYING FOR EXPANSION

A particular word of warning if you are looking to buy a business as an acquisition to your existing operation.

The process of buying and then integrating a new operation with your existing business will be extremely time-consuming and difficult. In fact the making of an acquisition is one of those big projects, absorbing cash and management time and distracting you from the day-to-day ongoing running of your main business, that can in some circumstances lead to the failure of the original business.

When considering an acquisition you should think very clearly about whether you have the time and management resources to devote to not only doing the deal but to managing the business afterwards. Will you need to move one or more of your key personnel across to manage the new business's affairs? If so, what impact is that going to have on your ongoing operation?

How difficult will the cultural issues be to manage? How far will the acquisition stretch the original business's financial resources?

You should always ask yourself before you start: would you be better off investing the money in your own organisation? Can you, for example, increase profits by cutting costs, more safely than by buying a bolt-on business?

GOLDEN RULES

3. Go in with your eyes open, and make an honest appraisal of your reasons for buying a business and your strengths and weaknesses.

Task
Prepare a CV setting out your:

◆ strengths and weaknesses

◆ relevant transferable skills.

2

Deciding What to Buy

THE IMPORTANCE OF FOCUS

Unsurprisingly, once you begin to approach the intermediaries who represent business sellers, or seek to engage an adviser to search for a business for you, the obvious first question that they are going to ask you is: 'What sort of business are you looking to buy?'

Response 1

'I am interested in buying a nice profitable business that I can make my million on/run in retirement' (delete as applicable).

This is an aspiration not a search criteria; and professionals can't do much for you with your dreams. They will also try not to waste their time dealing with someone who is so obviously unprepared.

Response 2

'I am interested in buying a widget manufacturer based in Yorkshire or Humberside with a stable turnover of £3m to £5m, that is currently profitable, makes its own branded products, and has the basis for expansion.'

This is a search profile that demonstrates that you are serious and with which a professional can work with you to find, fund and buy a business.

At first sight it might appear that the more flexible you are about the type of business that you want to buy, the more choice you will have. And in some parts of the market such as for small shops, bars, pubs, restaurants, and hotels where there are plenty of businesses turning over that can be easily identified from advertising by the specialist brokers, this may well be the case.

However, the market for most other types of business is relatively inefficient and as discussed in Chapter 5, a key part of your effort will need to go into finding appropriate businesses for sale. So while it will pay to be flexible about the details of business that you looking to buy, if you're looking for a larger business it is important to identify and then keep focused on a particular target market. This will allow you to:

◆ effectively communicate what you are looking for to the various parties who may be able to introduce appropriate targets to you

◆ persuade potential introducers and lead advisers that you are serious in your search

◆ focus your search so that it is as efficient as possible.

Having said that, you will also undoubtedly find that as you review the details of businesses for sale and screen potential targets, you will at the same time refine your criteria and improve your targeting.

WHAT TYPE OF BUSINESS DO YOU WANT TO BUY?

Before looking at the different types of businesses that you might consider, you first need to think about your motivation for buying a business, as you will want to buy one that is most likely to allow you to meet your personal or business objectives.

For individuals, the starting point in assessing what type of business you should be looking for is to decide what is most important to you about buying a business. Ask yourself, are you looking at this step principally as:

♦ a chance to change significantly your **lifestyle** by either taking more control or by downshifting?

♦ a financially driven **entrepreneurial or commercial opportunity** and a chance to make significant amounts of money either in ongoing earnings or by building a business to sell?

♦ an **investment decision** in the way that you might buy any other financial asset, and where you might in fact want no role in running the business once you have bought it?

Lifestyle businesses

Business professionals often refer to some businesses as 'lifestyle' ones. These are typically those where the business can be run at such a level as to support the chosen lifestyle of the owner, but which generally have little opportunity to build significant capital value.

Lifestyle businesses generally divide into property-based businesses such as shops, post offices, pubs or guesthouses; or service-based businesses such as freelance work or self-employed consultancy, and tend not to involve employing significant numbers of staff.

Property-based lifestyle businesses can be easily bought. However, in many service-based lifestyle businesses, despite having a powerful niche presence or well-known name in their industry, there is in practice no real business to be sold. This is because the owner is the business and the business has no life outside of them and their skills and contacts. Without a significant amount of work to 'institutionalise' these relationships and knowledge into some business structure outside of the individual, the business has no value, as on the principal's retirement the customers will have no reason to deal with any new owner.

Lifestyle businesses are particularly appropriate for buyers who are more interested in their lifestyle and work-life balance than in pure financial return, perhaps because they have other sources of income.

So if your reasons for being interested in buying a business are focused around the following then you might consider buying a lifestyle business:

◆ working for yourself without office politics

◆ organising your own time and avoiding a nine to five routine

◆ working in a pleasant environment and choosing your working conditions to suit yourself

◆ working on your own without the need to manage staff

◆ living and working where you want rather than commuting to an office.

Given these priorities which a lifestyle business will tend to satisfy, there is a view that these businesses are only of interest to people seeking a more relaxed lifestyle. In fact the owners of many lifestyle businesses work extremely hard and can generate a very good income from their business.

However, to make a success of a service-based lifestyle industry requires very strong self-discipline and time management as without a supervising 'boss' you need to avoid a number of dangers:

◆ As your working and domestic lives merge and you are able to work outside the confines of normal business hours set by others, it may be difficult to avoid being sucked into other domestic activities when you should be working (as you are at home and dressed in casual clothes it can be difficult for other family members to remember that you are actually working).

◆ You may also find that your natural working rhythm lies outside of the normal nine to five of office hours. This is fine and may allow you to work in a way that is more efficient for you, but beware of the danger of having your working time drift too far out of kilter with that of your clients. One self-employed person I know works very efficiently from noon through into the early evening. However, his clients' perception is simply that he is never available in the mornings and this undoubtedly damages his business.

◆ In contrast, without the formal structure of a normal working week you may also find that you end up being able to work 'whichever seven days a week you choose' and are unable to switch off your working life in order to have clear periods of domestic life.

◆ In managing your time you need to remember to set aside some of it to reinvest in the business. One of the key mistakes owners of lifestyle businesses make is to rely on an existing network of contacts or knowledge base they have either acquired in buying a business or have brought with them from their previous employment. The problem is that in some cases over surprisingly short periods of time, contacts will gradually fade away as they meet new suppliers, move on within their organisations or retire; and any body of knowledge will become out of date. To maintain the value of a lifestyle business you will need to work in a structured way at continuously renewing its *raison d'être*.

And finally, if you are buying a business for lifestyle reasons, you must make sure that you have really understood what the business lifestyle really entails. For example, many people dream of running a pub. However, the reality of running a pub is that most need to be open from 11 a.m. through to 11 p.m., seven days a week, 52 weeks a year, after someone has thoroughly cleaned the public areas. The scope for any time off is extremely limited. The work can be extremely hard and put a great deal of pressure on any partnership running it including marriage partners; and alcoholism resulting from the stress and continual requirement to perform as the host and authority figure night after night is a real risk.

Commercial businesses

A **commercial** business in contrast is one where the business can be run to generate profits in excess of those needed simply to support the owner's lifestyle and where the business can either be expanded or developed to generate a real capital value.

So if your reasons for buying a business are much more financially focused you are likely to be looking for a commercial business that offers you the opportunity to:

◆ grow the business, which is likely to involve employing staff if the business does not already do so; and

◆ work towards a sale of the business to give you a capital return.

This type of business will demand a higher level of commitment from you as owner than a lifestyle business, and you will have to trade your lifestyle and work-life balance in terms of hours worked in the business or being continually on call, for the greater returns that may be available.

Investors and businesses

You may, however, whilst wanting to build capital value, not be looking to work specifically in any one particular business. Instead you may be looking to buy a number of businesses, normally in a related area, so as to be able to build up a portfolio of investments, or perhaps a chain of similar businesses where the whole is more valuable than the sum of the parts. Each individual business within your empire is therefore an **investment** as far as you are concerned, to be either retained or disposed of as part of your management of your portfolio.

This approach to owning businesses can lead to high returns if managed properly but will require you to take on and manage appropriate staff in order to run each of the businesses, while you will need to focus on the questions of strategy and managing the acquisition process. It will also require you to think through how you are going to manage a number of separate business units within the group. Some groups are in practice very 'hands off', allowing each unit to operate with a high degree of independence and simply manage on the basis that each business unit is responsible for hitting its financial targets. Other groups are highly centralised and seek to impose consistent standards of operations and approaches on all businesses that they buy through a thorough post-acquisition integration process.

From this it can be seen that a critical characteristic of a business to be bought for investment purposes is that the business can clearly support the cost of paying for its own management and provide over and above this an investment return to you as the investor.

Buying a share in a business

As a last point on the subject, if you are simply looking for an investment you might consider whether you want to buy the whole of the business, that is 100%; a controlling share, 51% or above; or simply a minority stake, less than 50%.

Obviously buying a minority stake which does not allow you to control the business except with the cooperation of some of the other shareholders, leaves you exposed to the risk that the controlling shareholders will cause the company to act in ways you don't want it to. Against this, a minority stake will presumably have cost you less than buying a controlling share or the whole of the business, so financially you may have less at risk than had you bought a larger stake.

WHAT TYPES OF BUSINESS ARE THERE?

Once you have decided what you are looking to achieve from buying a business and therefore what you are looking for in a business, you need to consider what area of business you want to buy.

Before going into the characteristics of the main broad groups of businesses, it is worth saying at the outset that the best business for you to buy will be the one that you already know the most about. In other words, wherever possible seek to buy a business within which you have already worked or in an industry that you know. In doing so you are:

◆ reducing the risks significantly

◆ improving your chances of engaging high-quality professional advisers as you will be a more credible purchaser

◆ improving your probable credibility with the seller which as we will see can be important in helping deals to go through

- improving your chances of obtaining funding from backers who will be more prepared to believe that you will know what you are doing once you buy the business.

There are obviously many different ways of categorising businesses into groups. For simplicity's sake I will divide them into five main classes with a limited number of significant sub-groups as follows:

Production

Production covers a wide scope of manufacturing activities that result in the physical production of goods to be sold. The best-known manufacturers will be those that produce their own branded products (often referred to as **original equipment manufacturers** or OEMs) such as cars or domestic appliances.

But of course these manufacturers will generally only have produced some of the components in-house and will actually be **assemblers** of a mix of their own products (the car's engine and body shell) with those purchased from subcontractors (the windscreen and tyres) to make the finished product.

The levels of work undertaken by **subcontractors** can range from the creation of bespoke one-off orders to match a client's specific requirements, to the production of large batches or continuous product runs on behalf of large manufacturing customers. In some cases the parts produced will be specifically to the customer's design and unique to their product (a plastic moulded bumper or a particular shaped headlamp lens). In other cases the subcontractor will be producing a range of their own standard products (such as tyres, light bulbs or car radios) as an OEM in their own right, which the customer has then decided to specify for use in their product.

In some cases such subcontractors may also have much of the subassembly work outsourced to them by the customer, or the customer may engage specific subcontractors to finish components (such as machining rough castings to the tolerances required) and to produce subassemblies.

As companies seek to concentrate on their core skills and to outsource secondary activities to specialists who should be able to undertake them more efficiently, it is rare these days to find a fully **integrated** manufacturing business which produces completely finished goods for supply to the consumer directly from raw materials.

The largest exception to this general rule is in the area of **agriculture**, which I would tend to class within the broad category of manufacturing, although the financial characteristics of agriculture are significantly different from most other forms of manufacturing.

The other activity which should be included in manufacturing but which differs significantly from other types is the production of **raw materials** such as quarrying and mining (sometimes referred to as primary production). In some ways this activity has more in common with agriculture than other forms of manufacturing in that it is largely based on the acquisition and efficient exploitation of property assets.

Manufacturing businesses tend to have significant physical and financial assets in terms of plant and machinery, premises, stock and a debtor book. They can therefore be easier to finance than retail or service businesses. As materials will form a major part of their cost base, the labour element of their costs and in some cases the criticality of labour overall will also be lower than in service and retail businesses.

Those looking for a commercial or entrepreneurial opportunity often find manufacturing businesses to be of most interest and particularly those which produce their own branded products for sale to OEMs or direct consumers, not least because of the perception that the market risks inherent in a transfer of ownership will be lower than for a service business based on personal relationships.

Distribution

Distribution companies may either be acting as:

◆ **transporters** offering a service to manufacturers in taking their goods to market; or

◆ **wholesalers** offering a service to both manufacturers as a channel to market, and to retailers as a way of packaging industrial quantities of goods into amounts convenient for a retailer to stock.

As facilitators, margins are generally low since the existence of a high margin would incentivise manufacturers to expand downstream into undertaking its activity and capturing its margin for themselves. Distribution businesses therefore rely on:

◆ high levels of turnover

◆ effectively sweating the assets, so for a transport business for example, utilisation of the trucks and ensuring that return runs are always fully loaded is critical to profitability

◆ negotiation of volume discounts and rebates – these are areas that are notoriously difficult to police and quantify (they were for example the issue underlying the accounting scandal at Wickes) and will be an area of real uncertainty for any purchaser requiring significant due diligence work.

The strength of the distributor's contacts with both the suppliers and customers are therefore critical and the degree to which these can be successfully transferred will be a key issue in considering a purchase.

The nature of distribution businesses means that they are unlikely to be attractive as a lifestyle purchase, while the margin pressure also tends to make them unattractive commercial or entrepreneurial prospects, unless you can identify some significant level of underperformance that you will be able to address or significant scope to develop the business, such as by adding on extra lines.

Retail

Retail might be considered a subset of distribution as retailers are acting as a 'mini wholesaler' between the wholesaler or manufacturer and the end-user consumer. In fact some retail outlets such as motor main dealers are really in effect franchised extensions of the manufacturer's own distribution chain and have to operate in many ways as dictated by the manufacturer as the franchisor (e.g. use of standardised accounting packages and marketing materials).

Retail differs from pure distribution in that the retailer is always dealing direct with the end-user and is therefore having to market direct to, and interact directly with, consumers.

Gross margins in retail businesses are generally high, with 50% being not untypical. This is, however, in order to cover a correspondingly high level of overheads of which the major components are property costs and staffing.

Retailers are generally very site dependent, although the development of e-commerce gives both an opportunity to retailers to expand easily beyond the confines of their bricks and mortar sites, but also acts as a threat in that it enables manufacturers to more easily deal direct with consumers, bypassing traditional distribution and retail networks and generally offering goods at a lower cost as a result of not having to carry the high property and staffing overheads of a retail network. The exception to this is generally the 'tied' outlets such as motor dealers, where the majority of profit can come from ancillary services such as servicing and spare parts, and from volume overrides tied to the level of new car sales.

In addition, unless they are able to negotiate supplies on a sale or return basis, retailers take significant risks in the degree to which they have to buy and hold stock. The ability to forecast customer tastes and requirements and to stock appropriately so as to neither lose sales (because you have run out of stock), nor be left with unsold goods is critical to the success of a retail business. If you are considering buying a retail business you will have to be very sure of your abilities in this area.

Single-sited retail businesses often offer potentially attractive lifestyle business. They are, however, obviously limited in their scope to expand without you having to take on good management to run any larger number of outlets.

As service and the ability to give the customer an attractive shopping experience is often critical to the success of a retail business, you will need to be confident of your abilities to successfully 'front' the business, as well as managing the 'theatre' of the shop's décor, layout, lighting and ambience so as to make it a success.

Services
Service businesses divide into **business services** such as advertising, consultancy, recruitment, or professional firms through to banking, as well as outsourced suppliers of

administration and services such as telemarketing, software support or call centres; and **leisure and consumer services** which can range from hairdressers and landscape gardeners through to vets and travel agencies, and on to holiday operators, publicans, restaurateurs and hoteliers.

Despite the fact that service businesses do not produce a solid product in the way that manufacturing companies do, service businesses that establish and maintain a good reputation for value and service may be extremely solid businesses.

The key to a successful service business is the strength of its relationships with customers; which in turn is normally dependent upon the quality and commitment of its staff and the efficiency of the business systems in supporting staff to deal with customers.

The new owner's ability successfully to take over and continue the customer relationships, as well as to manage staff so as to provide the required level of service, will be critical in any purchase of a service business. Providing you believe you have the necessary personal characteristics that will be required for the type of business you are looking at, such businesses can be a reasonable lifestyle or commercial opportunity.

Given the vital importance of transferring the customer relationships and the difficulty of valuing most service businesses because of the uncertainty as to how successful this will be, retaining the old owner for a period on a consultancy basis – tied into payments by way of an earn-out dependent upon the future performance of the business – is normal in such situations.

Construction
Construction businesses can either be:

◆ the equivalent of manufacturers operating in their own right, acquiring land as their raw material and converting this into property for sale or lease; or

◆ providers of services to others in carrying out projects on their behalf.

There are a number of specific issues affecting the construction industry, such as:

◆ The standard form of contract with its structure of payment on applications. This leads to restrictions in the ability to finance working capital and also to disputes and claims, which mean that there is a tendency to conflict and legal wrangling between main and subcontractors throughout the industry. There is also still the tendency of larger contractors to 'subbie bash' or stretch payment terms to subcontractors.

◆ The highly cyclical nature of the business from boom to bust which closely tracks the overall level of economy. This effect is magnified by the relatively low barriers to entry which tend to reduce the levels of achievable profit (as in any period when the market picks up, there is little to prevent new contractors starting up, resulting in increased price competition), while at the start of any boom there always tends to be a shortage of skilled labour which drives wage costs up and tends to make it difficult to retain skilled employees. Another result of large numbers of entrants into the market is inevitably a large number of failures at the end of each boom.

◆ The criticality for developers of holding an appropriate 'land bank' for the stage in the cycle.

In other respects the characteristics of a construction business will tend to mirror those of either manufacturer or a service businesses as appropriate.

Mixed characteristics

With each of these categorisations, there can be a high degree of overlap.

For example, a manufacturing workshop that acts solely as a subcontractor producing sub-components for other manufacturers, is in many ways supplying a business service in that it is 'renting out' its machining capacity to those who want to hire it. Many such manufacturing businesses will also have a significant role in helping customers to design the goods or components to be manufactured, or being involved in assembling components into subassemblies, again supplying services to their customer.

At the other end of the scale, an integrated supplier producing own branded goods may well have its own distribution network to take them to market and even in some cases its own dedicated retail outlets.

OTHER CHARACTERISTICS TO CONSIDER

Size

The size of business you look at will be influenced by both the type of business you want and the funding you have available. Those interested in lifestyle businesses tend to look for smaller businesses, with less staff to manage and a lower purchase price so that the owner is under less financial stretch. Those looking for commercial opportunities may be more prepared to take on larger businesses with more staff and higher financing requirements.

The levels of financing that you are likely to be able to raise against the assets being bought is discussed in detail in Chapter 10. The difference between this and the purchase price of the business will have to be met from either vendor finance (the seller allowing you credit or time to pay) or from the cash of your own that you put into the deal. So the level of equity that you are able to raise (e.g. by borrowing against your house) will have a direct impact on the size of business that you are going to be able to buy.

Underperformance

Most people looking to buy a business will be looking for one that is as profitable and low risk as possible. However, some entrepreneurial buyers will be deliberately interested in finding businesses that are loss making or in difficulties despite the higher risks involved. This is because you might be able to buy such a business relatively cheaply, while if you are able successfully to turn it around to be a stable, profitable and growing business you may then be able to realise a substantial capital gain.

Buying an under-performing business to turn around can, however, be a very risky business and the issues involved are covered in detail in Chapter 19.

Franchises

There are also of course businesses which are operated on a franchise basis. These will generally be in the services and retail sectors and will require the franchisee to have bought the franchise for the area. There will then generally be a requirement to purchase the bulk of goods from the franchisor and/or to pay some form of commission or royalty on sales. In return, the franchisee should expect to receive a business that is a proven model and normally a degree of ongoing management and marketing support to make the business a success. The franchisor will usually retain some rights to approve any subsequent purchaser of the business.

Whilst there are a number of successful businesses that have been franchised, there can be risks in buying a franchise business, as discussed in Chapter 5.

RESEARCHING THE BUSINESS

If you are interested in buying a business in an industry that you don't know well (and even if you do know the industry well) you should conduct research into the sector and its trends and developments. Sources of information that you can use include:

- **Publicly available data** produced by government departments, business directories, local authorities, local libraries, business associations, Chambers of Commerce and so on, much of which will be available either on the web or through a decent local library. If you are having difficulty obtaining information at your library, try visiting the business library of your nearest university which is likely to have more extensive sets of reference books than an ordinary lending library. If you're in London try the Business Information Library on London Wall.

- **Trade associations and publications**. Most industries have some form of trade association that produces material and information about the sector as well as a publication to which you may be able to subscribe. Similarly, most industries will have some form of trade press which may alert you to trade exhibitions and shows that you can attend.

- **Bankers and professional advisers**, who may be able to provide information, with some banks producing ranges of leaflets or briefings for potential customers on different types of business.

- Any **personal contacts** that you have who may be involved in the industry or have connections to people who are.

Perhaps the most valuable source of information, if you are able to tap into it, is owners and managers currently in the industry, some of whom may be prepared to talk to you if approached in the right manner. These are people who will be able to give you the inside track on what it's really like in the business and they may even be able to point you towards businesses that are likely to be for sale.

The sorts of questions you could ask (many of which you might also usefully ask of the owner of any business you are considering buying) are:

◆ What was your motivation for getting into the business? Has it fulfilled your expectations? Has it given you the lifestyle or financial return you were expecting? What impact has it had on your family life?

◆ What are the key skills that you have needed to make a success of it? Did you learn these on the job or did they come from your previous experience?

◆ Did you set the business up or did you buy it? If you bought it, how did you go about finding a business? Where did you raise the finance? What advisers did you use?

◆ Have you any particular rules for success? Is there anything you wish you'd known before you bought?

◆ What is changing in the industry? Are there any particular issues to do with regulation, customers or suppliers to be aware of?

◆ Would you buy a business in this industry now? If not, why not? Do you know any that may be for sale?

WHERE SHOULD YOU BUY A BUSINESS?

After thinking about what you want to achieve by buying a business, and the types of business that might enable you to do this, the next question that you need to consider is: where do you want to buy a business?

Do you want to buy something local to where you currently live or do you want to, or are you willing to, move to buy the right business? Obviously if you are simply an investment buyer and not interested in working directly in the business to be bought then the impact of the business's locality will be much less than on a buyer who is intending to work in it.

Family and lifestyle issues

This is a major decision for both you and your family and raises a whole range of issues, such as:

◆ Do you have family commitments that will prevent you moving, such as responsibilities for older relatives, or children at critical periods of their schooling?

◆ Does your partner work? If so how will any move affect this and what impact might any change have?

◆ Are there any factors that will be critical in any new area that you might move to, such as schooling for your children?

◆ What sort of housing will you need in any new area and how likely is it to be available at a price you can afford?

◆ How important to you is your current social life? How easy will this be to maintain if you move away from your current area? How easy will you find it to create a new social life in your new area?

Differences in culture

If you are considering a move to a very different type of area, such as from town to country or vice versa, ask yourself if you have a realistic appreciation of the differences in lifestyle that this will involve. Do you feel you (and all your family) are suited to this type of change?

You should also bear in mind that different areas of the country will have different cultures and ways of life. So even though both might be rural, buying a business in Wales may be significantly different from doing so in East Anglia.

Locality and service industries

And of course the importance of locality to the success of the venture varies across the different types of business. For a pub, shop or other supplier of local services, the nature of the local marketplace is obviously critical, as the business's customer base will be determined by whether the locality is:

◆ rural, suburban or urban

◆ rich or poor

◆ a place people retire to such as the south coast (so has a more aged population than normal) or an educational centre such as a university city which might have a higher number of young people

◆ a centre of high-tech industries or traditional ones

◆ up and coming or in decline.

Locality and manufacturing businesses

By contrast, for a manufacturing business supplying into a national or even international market and which is not therefore simply relying on serving the local marketplace, the locality will, however, still have an impact in a variety of ways, such as the:

- availability of skilled and qualified staff

- transport infrastructure for getting the goods to market

- planning rules that may impact any plans to expand

- level of grant support available.

Property issues

Whilst on the subject of locality, the type, precise location and tenure of property should be part of the criteria you consider.

Again, the importance of the property issues will vary significantly between different types of business. A small manufacturing or printing business, say, may be able to operate from almost any industrial unit and you can therefore have an open mind towards the business's existing property when searching for targets.

The location of a shop or hotel will generally, however, be absolutely critical to the success or otherwise of the business, as will its state of repair and decoration.

Many purchases of small retail and leisure businesses are in effect purchases of property with a business element, rather than purchases of the business with a property element. The state of the buildings and the tenure available (freehold or leasehold) will therefore be critical to the value of the deal and you should form a view as to your preferences in putting together your criteria.

WHEN IS THE BEST TIME TO BUY A BUSINESS?

All businesses, sectors and industries go through cycles of growth (A), stabilisation (B) and eventual downturn and contraction (C), before hopefully being reinvigorated into new growth by some change in economic climate or the introduction of some new technology. These tendencies are known as business life cycles and are overlaid in turn by the general cycle of growth, stability or downturn of the economy as a whole. The conditions at any point will tend to affect the valuation of businesses based on the anticipated future continuation of the trend.

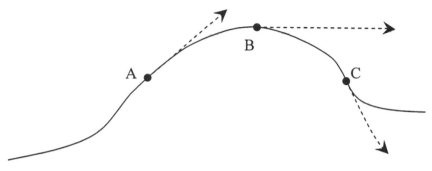

Figure 1. Business life cycle

The safest advice concerning the best time to buy a business is therefore:

◆ **Don't buy into a rising market** – as valuations are based on a multiple of earnings that takes into account an expectation of future growth, it is very easy to overpay in a market that is growing significantly. The thing to remember about any period of growth is that at some point it will come to an end. The faster the rate of growth, the more attractive it will have been for businesses to pile into the area and to create capacity, and the greater the fall out will be when the bubble bursts.

◆ **Don't buy at the top of the cycle** (as growth starts to tail off) – because again there is a significant danger of overpaying. As any market starts to stabilise after a period of high growth there tends to be a lull before the real crash, as all capacity that has been installed by people who have come into the market comes online and fierce price competition ensues as competing businesses try to fill this capacity by buying turnover from each other with discounts.

◆ **Don't buy into a falling market** – as until the market has stopped falling you do not know how much worse things are going to get and how long the shakeout is going to last.

◆ **Don't buy at the bottom of the market** – as once the market is in depression, you do not know how long it is going to be before there will be opportunities for new growth.

The real answer of course is that there are pros and cons of buying at each point in the cycle, which can be summarised as follows:

Market	Pro	Con
Rising	Overall growth in the market can often get you out of trouble. There is a ready resale value to other people wishing to enter the market or other players wishing to expand their market share.	High growth will imply a high growth of the business's requirement for working capital. Will you be able to fund this going forwards? There is a danger of overpaying for the business if the prices are based on current growth trends. How long will current growth trends continue? Increasing levels of competition can be expected from new entrants into the market attracted by the high growth.

Market	Pro	Con
		This will lead inevitably to an eventual shakeout as the rate of market growth must decline at some point, while the growth in number and capacity of players in the market may continue past this point as capacity being built during the boom years continues to come on stream.
Top	Performance trends are easier to see, giving an apparently more stable basis on which to base purchasing decision. Few new entrants coming into the marketplace.	If you are buying at the top of a growth phase you need to consider carefully whether any shakeout and consolidation of the market is complete or is there more pain to come? At this point there is little likelihood of any significant natural growth in the market to get you out of trouble, and the market is only likely to become more competitive as the only route for players seeking to grow their market share is by way of taking it from weaker competitors. If you're fortunate, however, and the market does start to have a second phase of growth, you will be facing the issues to do with

Market	Pro	Con
		working capital requirements outlined above.
		If, as is more normal, the market then shrinks, it will tend to be the stronger businesses in the sector which will be the ones that survive. How comfortable can you be that your newly acquired business will be one of the stronger, better managed businesses in the industry? (If so why did the old owners sell?)
		There will be a limited resale value other than to consolidators looking to strengthen their market share and once the market has fallen there is a significant chance you will have been seen to have overpaid for the business.
Falling or bottom	There will be very little threat to the business from new entrants as who wants to enter into a falling market or one in recession? Businesses may therefore be available at cheap prices due to little demand from buyers. In fact businesses	You're taking a significant risk as you will not be in a position to tell with certainty how far and how fast the fall will continue and what reserves you will need in order to ride out the shakeout. Ironically strong businesses

Market	Pro	Con
	may be under priced as the expectation of further falls in the market may be exaggerated. In addition there will usually be a number of distressed sellers wishing to exit the market because of poor performance of the business or other financial pressures and distressed sellers are in a poor bargaining position.	can do extremely well in a falling or mature market as they can force out or take over the weaker players. Indeed for these stronger businesses, in some ways the longer it lasts the better, as it is sufficient to reduce the number of players to a few dominant ones; these are then in a position to set prices in the market. And they may have little fear of new entrants because their strong brand position, good network of customers and lack of immediate growth potential means there is little to attract new players to invest in the market. By the same token, there is, however, no prospect of growth to get you out of trouble, and you may find difficulty in raising finance as funders will be nervous of the sector.

From the above it can be seen that times of change in the industry or economy as a whole can give increased opportunities, but these will be matched by increased levels of risk.

GOLDEN RULES

4. Decide on your objectives (why you want to buy a business) and stick to them.

Task

List your objectives in buying a business.

$$\overset{\displaystyle\bigodot}{3}$$

Beginning Your Planning and Appointing Advisers

HAVING A PLAN

Finding and buying the right business will not just happen, you need to put in place a plan of campaign, your **acquisition strategy** in order to achieve your objectives.

Some elements of this plan will be immediately obvious and will cover issues already discussed, such as the sort of business you are looking for, which sectors are you interested in and what other characteristics such as geographical location are important to you.

But in setting the plan, you also need to consider a variety of practical issues concerning the process, such as:

◆ How are you going to go about finding a business to buy? Will you be able to pursue the search full-time, or will it need to be a part-time activity? Are you going to undertake the search process on your own or will you engage professional advisers to hunt down the targets for you?

◆ How much professional support are you going to need in checking the business out and completing a purchase?

◆ Where is the finance to do the deal coming from? Is it all going to be raised from your personal or business resources and/or borrowed against the assets being bought? Or are you going to need to find other backers such as a venture capitalist? In which case, do you need to start meeting potential backers early on in the process, before finding a specific target?

◆ How long are you prepared to, or can you afford to, search for?

◆ Should you work on your own or as part of a team?

◆ What sort of corporate vehicle should you use to buy?

DOING IT AS A GROUP

If you are an individual looking to buy a business of any size you might consider getting together with other people to buy it as a group. Doing so can have a number of advantages, as a group of people are likely to have a mix of:

◆ skills covering a variety of functional expertise such as finance, operations, sales and marketing. A team therefore tends to run less risk of having a major hole in the management's skills than an individual

◆ board level experience

◆ industry knowledge and contacts

◆ preferred team roles and personal operating styles.

Analysis of team roles

The most commonly used analysis of team roles is that of Belbin which gives eight main types (or in later versions nine when a technical specialist is included), which are broadly as follows:

◆ **Chairman** – controls the way the team works. They tend to have a strong sense of their objectives and a willingness to bring out the value of potential contributions from all the team members, whilst being able to recognise its strengths and weaknesses.

◆ **Shaper** – the person who 'shapes' the way that the team applies its efforts and sets its priorities. They tend to be focused and certain of their course and push things through with drive and determination.

◆ **Plant** – these are the 'ideas people' who can generate creative and innovative ideas for the business.

◆ **Resource investigator** – the networkers who are also part of the creative resources of a team as they make use of people and contacts to find out what it needs or to achieve objectives. They are good at responding to challenges or exploring anything new.

◆ **Company worker or implementer** – is focused on the good of the company, organised, hard-working and practical. They tend to be the ones you can rely on to get on and do the jobs that no one else wants to do.

◆ **Monitor/evaluator** – the shrewd hard-headed judgement maker, able to coolly assess the merits of any proposal and an antidote to 'seat of the pants' management.

◆ **Team worker** or **team builder** – a critical facilitator, able to respond to people to ensure that all members of the team work together and to promote team spirit.

◆ **Completer/finisher** – a vital member of the team, the one who follows through to ensure that things are taken to a conclusion.

To take advantage of an understanding of team roles, firstly you need to establish each team member's preferred roles by the use of psychometric testing. Then any conflicts need to be resolved so that each member of the team knows which role they should focus on.

Group formation process

In many ways this process can help work through one of the key problems in putting any group together from scratch, in that a group will always take time to 'gel'. Any new group will go through a process of:

- **forming** – selecting the members of the group and bringing them together to meet

- **storming** – having disagreements as to how it is to operate

- **norming** – reaching some kind of agreement as to how it is to operate; before finally

- **performing** – being able to focus on the task that the group is to achieve rather than on how the group is structured.

The process of explicitly discussing and settling on roles can go a long way towards accelerating this process and dealing openly with conflicts such as too many people wanting to take the role of leader so that these are resolved rather than festering.

Financial advantages

Additionally a group is likely to have an increased financial capacity to buy a business as they should be able to raise more equity between them than you will as an individual.

Disadvantages

There are, however, some downsides in working with a group, and you need to think through:

◆ How as a group you will get consensus on whether to buy a particular business, and how will you deal with the situation if some members dissent from a decision to buy?

◆ Do you feel that you have a sufficiently strong relationship or history with each other to make working as a group a realistic prospect, as the search process will be a long and stressful one?

◆ How are you going to deal with a situation where one of the team may have significantly more money to put into a business than the others?

Practical issues

There are also some practical issues to consider. You will be well advised to put in place:

◆ a shareholder agreement that specifies your relationship and covers for example the basis on which any shareholder who wants to retire will be bought out, and whether in the event of the death of any of the shareholders, their shares will be bought out by the others; and

◆ key life policies which can provide the funds with which to buy out a deceased partner shares in the event of their death.

As an individual, you will also have to decide how you feel about having others involved in the business that you want to buy. If one of the reasons for looking to purchase is to be able to run your own show without interference, then this may make working as part of a group contrary to your objectives.

Management buy outs and buy ins

The idea of working in a group is most obviously directly applicable to a management buy out (MBO) team, which will by its nature generally involve a group of senior managers who have worked together as a team before, with skills across the range of disciplines required to run the business, have a good knowledge of the business to be bought, and have experience of the sector/industry.

When looking at a large financial acquisition, venture capitalists will tend to put together a management buy in (MBI) team comprising a number of senior executives. This is in part to ensure there are no holes in the management team upon acquisition in either skill sets or team roles because of the issues discussed above.

As MBIs have historically been more risky than MBOs as a result of the inherently greater risk of dropping a new set of managers into an unknown business, it appears that BIMBOs (Buy In Management Buy Outs) which create a mixed team of new executives with the existing senior management in the company, are increasingly favoured by venture capitalists.

PURCHASING VEHICLE

You have a choice in presenting yourself when you come to buy as to whether you are buying:

◆ in your own name as a sole trader

◆ as a team in partnership (either a traditional partnership or a new limited liability partnership)

◆ as a trading company owned by you solely or by a team

◆ as the holding company of a group of companies (even if the rest of the companies are dormant).

If you are working with a team to buy a business you will normally incorporate a company ('Newco') to act as your vehicle for the purchase early in the proceedings, and as discussed above you should already have in place a shareholder agreement.

As will be demonstrated in the following chapters, establishing your credibility as a buyer with both potential sellers and their agents (as well as with financiers and your professionals) can be critical in both finding appropriate targets and completing deals. As insignificant as it sounds, operating through a pre-established corporate vehicle can help to give you credibility right down to apparently minor things which all help to give the impression of substance to your interest, such as the ability to:

◆ give potential intermediaries your Widget Acquisitions Limited business card that describes you as managing director rather than just acting in your personal capacity as Joe Smith

◆ send a target a letter from Widget Acquisitions Limited asking if the business is for sale, which is likely to be taken more seriously than one from Joe Smith.

Choice of an acquisition vehicle is the first step in packaging yourself as a credible buyer.

Purchasing structures
Your choice of purchasing structure is also important as it will affect the degree of risk that you are taking in buying the business, as well as having tax implications.

The ways in which you can trade are as:

◆ A **sole trader** where you as an individual trade in your own right under either your own or a business name. Essentially there is no distinction between you and your business and so you own the business completely and the business's profits form part of your taxable income. This is, however, a risky way to trade as you are making all purchases for the business personally and are therefore personally liable for all its debts.

◆ **A partnership** – a group of at least two people who are trading together with a view to making a profit. Unless you have agreed a partnership deed which sets out how profits and losses are to be distributed this will be governed by the Partnership Act 1881 under which all profits and losses are shared equally between all partners. In a normal partnership all the partners are liable individually for all the partnership's debts (known as joint and several liability), so if one partner cannot pay their share, the others will still be liable for the full amount due.

◆ **A limited liability partnership (LLP)** where the partnership is a distinct legal entity from the partners and the partners' liability for any debts of the business can be limited to the partnership's assets. In return for this limitation of the partner's risks, LLPs have to file public accounts and returns at Companies House in the same way as limited liability companies.

◆ **A limited liability company** identified by the word 'limited' or the abbreviation 'Ltd' after its name, which is a separate legal entity from its shareholders and directors. This means that the company trades the business in its own right and the company is liable for the business's debts (unless the directors or shareholders have personally guaranteed those debts or are made liable for them as a result of having fallen foul of the rules governing matters such as insolvency). Since the company is able to take credit from suppliers in its own right, the owners and directors are therefore protected from being liable for these. Creditors are in turn protected by the requirement for a company to file accounts and annual returns at Companies House so that the status and profitability of the company is public information.

Companies can be purchased off-the-shelf from a number of suppliers. They are governed by two documents, the **memorandum of association** which sets out the purpose for which the company has been formed, and the **articles of association** which are the company's constitution, and in off-the-shelf companies will be of a standard type.

The company as a legal person in its own right will be liable for tax on its profits under corporation tax and the owners will only be able to obtain the benefit of the profits by way of payments from the company in the form of either salary or dividends. Since dividends do not attract National Insurance payments you should take advice from your accountant as to the most tax efficient way to pay yourself. Be warned, however, that there is an ongoing struggle between business and the Treasury as to the rules governing taxation in this area and the government is continually moving the goalposts.

♦ A **public limited company** (PLC) shares the features of a normal limited liability company but requires a higher level of share capital. The advantage of a PLC is that it will be allowed to be listed on a stock market providing it meets the exchange's criteria.

ACQUISITION PLAN

It is good practice to set out your acquisition strategy in the form of a short business plan, which should cover:

♦ an executive summary

♦ your details (or those of the team if appropriate) setting out why you are a credible business purchaser (you should attach your CV as an appendix)

♦ the type of business sought and your acquisition criteria

- your search strategy

- your strategy for financing a purchase

- your advisers once appointed

- any appropriate references.

This approach achieves several things:

- It ensures that you formalise what you're looking for and summarise it into a coherent and structured set of plans and criteria.

- It enables you clearly to brief your professional advisers.

- Returning to the theme of credibility, it means that you have a document which you can deliver to both your advisers and any potential sources of targets, setting out who you are, what you are looking for and your credentials to be taken seriously.

This obviously implies that the document needs to be finished to a professional standard in the expectation that you will be using it, or parts of it, to sell yourself both to business sellers and professional advisers.

WHO YOU WILL NEED

To buy any size of business you are going to need to obtain some help from professional advisers. The degree of help needed will of course vary depending upon the nature and size of the business you are looking at. As a minimum, in buying a small shop, for example, you are likely to need a professional surveyor to survey the property, some accounting advice on the trading accounts, a finance broker to arrange loans and a lawyer to handle the contracts and conveyancing.

On a larger transaction you will need assistance with all of the above functions but may require correspondingly larger teams to deal with the scale of issues involved. In addition you may need to have engaged professional advisers to assist you in finding a suitable target, approaching potential equity backers such as venture capitalists, and in negotiating the purchase itself. You may also need to engage specialists to deal with aspects of the due diligence process such as environmental risk assessment or health and safety reviews.

The four main sets of professionals that you will be relying on during the deal will generally comprise:

♦ **Lead adviser** – a corporate finance adviser who will act as your main adviser in locating a target and negotiating the sale. Think of them as your partner in making the deal happen. They are your ringmaster, coordinating all the other players into the project of completing a purchase, managing contact with the seller and the many other professionals who will become involved, as well as acting as a cut out between you and the seller who can keep things on a professional basis.

The degree of work that you ask your lead adviser to undertake may vary from simply giving support during the negotiation of the purchase through to a full service involving locating targets, raising finance and managing the initial approach.

♦ **Transaction support** – the accountants who undertake the due diligence work of checking the business over before you buy it. These will usually (but not necessarily) come from the same firm as the lead adviser and buyers will generally look to have the firm that undertake the due diligence stay on to act as the company's accountants and auditors going forwards.

◆ **Lawyer** – the importance of having an experienced corporate finance lawyer involved in undertaking the legal due diligence and drawing up the contracts, including the warranties, representations and indemnities, cannot be underestimated.

◆ **Financiers** – either your asset finance broker who is seeking to arrange finance for you, or your banker who is looking to put together a package to fund your deal. Those involved in arranging the finance for your transaction will need as much time as possible to review cash flows and forecasts and to make an assessment of your credibility and ability to make a success of the deal. You should therefore be seeking to work with financiers as early in the process as possible so that when you need to finalise putting funding in place, this can proceed as swiftly as possible.

In addition you will need a range of other specialists such as a property surveyor as already discussed, through to an insurance broker to make sure that you have all necessary cover in place as you do the deal.

APPOINTING ADVISERS

Of the above, the most critical advisers to appoint initially are your lead adviser and your solicitor.

Lead advisers will generally be found in the corporate finance department of any sizable accountancy firm and for larger businesses in the mergers and acquisitions departments of merchant banks. This is an area where successful individuals often go out on their own, setting up successful small 'boutiques'. Other than as an indication of potential minimum fees, the size of a firm is therefore not necessarily any guarantee of the quality of service you will receive. Indeed, given the need for personal attention and focus, smaller may sometimes be better.

Finding the right person

So how do you find the right adviser for you? Far and away the best way is through personal recommendation. Use your network to find people who have recently bought or sold their businesses. Call them to find out who they saw, who they used and why, and how they performed.

Your own accountant, solicitor or bank manager can also be a valuable source of recommendations from local firms they have dealt with. Treat all such recommendations with a certain degree of caution however, as most professionals, advisers and bankers operate in a local circuit of mutual work referral (known as 'reciprocity') where introductions are currency to be paid, received or banked. I would not suggest your bank manager or accountant would introduce you to someone they did not feel could do the job but you should ask any such referee about the amount of business they have undertaken with the firm being recommended.

Otherwise regional business publications aimed at the mid corporate market will often provide a list of deals done in the region that can show you who is active in the area.

Making your choice

However you find a professional adviser or advisers, you should generally seek to have a presentation made to you by a shortlist of, say, two or three to pitch for your business (a 'beauty parade'). And before engaging any advisers you should check up on their prior work by asking for and taking up references.

So what should you look for in an adviser?

- ◆ A good market reputation and track record. If you want your lead adviser to be successful in finding you credible opportunities, you need a lead adviser who is credible in the marketplace and has the contacts to know or to find out which businesses may be for sale.

◆ Someone with whom you are likely to be able to get on with, as the purchasing process may be long, stressful and complex, and who understands your objectives and critical issues.

◆ Evidence that they will stay committed to you throughout the deal as your key contact point and will not simply delegate the job to junior staff.

Whilst this section has concentrated on lead advisers, all of the above points are equally applicable to corporate finance lawyers.

MANAGING YOUR ADVISERS

Buying a business is a complex long drawn-out affair and one which it is critical to get right. The potential cost of errors in dealing with the process of finding a serious seller, negotiating the best deal available, and structuring the most appropriate terms for your circumstances – before then managing the process of negotiation, due diligence and completion through to a successful conclusion – are so great that they do generally outweigh the very real costs of getting good professional advice.

Letter of engagement

In order to instruct professional advisers you will have to sign a letter of engagement. This is your formal contract with your advisers and your authority for them to act on your behalf. You should review this carefully before signing as it covers such contractual matters as specifying:

◆ the basis of their fees, including how they are to be calculated, and payment terms

- limitation of liability, where your adviser will seek agreement as to their maximum liability in the event of any problem arising as a result of their advice

- the scope of the work to be undertaken for the fees agreed, what information you are expected to be able to prepare and supply for the purposes of the sale, and the basis on which any further fees may be payable by you in respect of any other work needed which is not covered by the description and scope of the assignment.

The letter of engagement should also make clear that the adviser is acting as your agent in any discussion or negotiation, and is empowered to undertake negotiations on your behalf with prospective sellers.

The letter of engagement should also give assurances to you of the confidentiality of any information you provide to the adviser; as well as the basis under which empowered to disclose this information to other parties such as to assist in raising finance.

As it's important to get good advice, do not simply buy your advisers on the basis of the lowest hourly rate. Instead, you should seek to manage costs by agreeing a cap on the level of expenditure with each adviser.

THE NEED FOR DUE DILIGENCE

The due diligence process is covered in detail in Chapters 12 to 14, however it's worth noting at the outset that both you and the seller have a mutual interest in reducing the uncertainty involved in any sale as far as possible, in your case to reduce the risks and in the seller's case to justify a higher price.

You will also find that you are likely to need to have demonstrated that you have undertaken sufficient due diligence to satisfy your potential funders in order to finance the deal.

The degree to which you decide to use advisers is up to you and you may feel that in dealing with a small-business purchase such as a pub there is only a limited scope of work that you would wish to have done. However, acting without an appropriate level of professional advice is dangerous in any business sale.

Example

Purchasers decided to buy a shop that appeared to be extremely cash positive and profitable. As a result there seemed to be few risks and so they decided that they didn't want to pay for any professional advice or for accountants to look at the books.

Following the purchase they found that the level of ongoing business was significantly lower than the books suggested in the past and as a result the shop was significantly less profitable.

Subsequent investigation by their accountants suggested that the shop had in fact been used to launder money for a local criminal and that the apparent turnover and strongly positive cash flow were not related to the shop's actual trading level at all.

Whilst the information uncovered might have been sufficient to enable the buyers to have been warned off in advance and not done the deal, it was however insufficient to prove any wrongdoing after the deal or give them any recourse against the seller.

GOLDEN RULES

5. Get good advisers – and take their advice.

Task
Draft your acquisition plan.

Phase 2: The Search Process

(4)

Starting Your Search

WHAT ARE YOU LOOKING FOR?

In devising profile number two at the beginning of Chapter 2 (p27) the searcher has already identified:

- the **industry** in which they wish to be (widget making) in which presumably they have some knowledge or experience and in respect of which they have presumably taken a view as to the current state and likely prospects of the industry

- the **location** (Yorkshire and Humberside) which presumably fits either where they currently live or where they are happy to move in order to acquire a business

- the **scale** of the business (stable turnover of £3m to £5m) which hopefully will fit the level of experience that they have, and the amount of capital they are going to be able to raise in order to enable the deal to be financed

- the **business performance** (currently profitable) which will provide them with a living and the return which they are seeking as part of the process

- some **particular characteristics** (produces own brand products and capacity for expansion) that they are seeking in a target company in this sector.

Already this straightforward exercise in defining the search has enabled the prospective buyer to focus their efforts quite precisely; they won't be looking at distribution businesses in the West Midlands; they won't be looking at hotels in Scotland; they won't be looking at businesses requiring a major turnaround to achieve profitability; they won't be attempting to bid for a listed PLC.

In other words they have quite clearly defined the key characteristics of the type of business that they would like to buy to the extent needed to commence a search for a business of this type. Chapter 5 sets out how you can go about identifying a selection of such businesses.

Simply carrying out such a search will, however, produce a list of potential targets many of which will still be irrelevant. This is because there is one critical factor missing from these search criteria and one element that has not yet been considered.

You need to add to these criteria something that on the face of it you are unlikely to be able to discover in respect of many businesses from publicly available information – namely the business's owners must be willing to sell.

To have found a realistic target, therefore, you must have found a business that both:

◆ meets your criteria; and

◆ is or may be for sale.

So in this chapter we will consider who sellers are, what motivates them and why a business may or may not be for sale, as well as the specific issues around family businesses.

WHO ARE SELLERS?

Different types of people sell businesses. The person or people you're ultimately dealing with might be any of the following:

- The **owner manager**, who may have founded and built the business from scratch. They may well have a variety of personal issues that are of importance to them in any sale apart from price: ranging from pride in the business and wanting to secure its future going forwards; through wanting to ensure that key employees are looked after; to a desire to have an ongoing role in advising the business in the future. And if these considerations are significant they may have the ability to take their time and be very choosy in who they sell the business to.

- The owner's **executor**, who is dealing with winding up their estate and is simply under a duty to get the best price for the business.

- The **corporate owner**, who has decided that a business unit simply doesn't fit with their current corporate strategy and is therefore disposing of it in order to focus on the rest of the business.

- The **financial owner**, such as a venture capitalist, who is looking to realise their investments as part of their normal business cycle, and who may even be driven by a timetable under which a fund has to be closed by a particular date.

- The **insolvency practitioner**, who has been appointed as receiver or administrator of a business and who will be looking to achieve the best sale possible, usually within a tight timescale, but on the basis of giving no warranties or representations as to the business whatsoever.

Each type of seller will therefore have their own objectives, timescales and key considerations in mind. It would be a mistake to think that the approach to dealing with an owner manager who wants to retire should be the same as the approach to dealing with a venture capitalist, who is looking to exit the business as a normal part of portfolio management. It is too simplistic to think that both will want the maximum sales proceeds as the be all and end all.

Particularly when looking to buy businesses that are not currently formally for sale, you will find it important to understand the psychology and motivation of the seller or potential seller, so as to be able to construct a deal that they will be willing to accept.

WHY DO SELLERS SELL?
You might reasonably ask if a business is doing well, so that it is generating profits for its owner and has good prospects, why on earth would an owner want to sell? And does this mean that businesses are only for sale if there's a problem?

Well thankfully not, there are many reasons that business owners choose to sell their business:

- A desire for retirement or to hand over succession to other family members, business partners or management.

- To acquire money to fund growth, when the opportunities available to a business are greater than can be exploited by the business based on its own financial resources.

- To become associated with a larger firm, allowing access to their developed distribution channels or their particular manufacturing or marketing strengths.

◆ To allow concentration on a particular area of operations without having to worry about 'the whole shooting match'.

◆ To pursue other business interests as individuals, or as corporates to concentrate on or invest in the development of other businesses within the group.

◆ To reduce risk by 'banking' some or all of the cash made in building up the business, thereby reducing some of the personal risks that will come from making future business decisions.

◆ Because, like an executor or an insolvency practitioner, they are under some kind of duty to sell.

The principal reasons that owner managers have for selling divide into a number of personal and business requirements.

Banking the money

Often much of a business owner's personal wealth will be tied up in the company they have created. A sale of the business therefore offers them the principal opportunity to convert this holding into cash which allows them to diversify their investment across a range of different types of asset and investments, thereby minimising their exposure to the particular business's fortunes, and to enjoy the benefits of having created a successful business.

The danger in this case is where the owner thinks that they can get a good capital value for their business and has unrealistic expectations as to what someone will pay.

Reduction of risk

Often in the early days of a business, despite the legal status of limited liability, the owner has found that they have had to put up personal security in order to obtain bank funding, or even have had to give personal guarantees in order to obtain certain supplies, ranging from property leases all the way down to a photocopier. The effect of these personal guarantees is that the owner is liable for the debts of the company in the event of its failure, and such personal guarantees given in the early days of business have often never been fully removed.

In addition, the responsibilities of directors grow ever more onerous with every piece of legislation. There is a risk that in the event of insolvency the directors may face the prospect of potentially being made personally liable for the company's trading losses. It makes sense therefore for owner managers at some point to seek to reduce their exposure to such risks by selling the business to someone who is willing to run it.

Health concerns or retirement
The above points are particularly relevant when an owner manager decides it is time to retire or their health starts to fail. In fact, many businesses are sold not because of any financial considerations, but principally through some change in the owner's life. On the other hand, many entrepreneurial business owner managers seem to thrive on the activity and mental challenge of running their own business well into their seventies and later.

Boredom
Entrepreneurs and owner managers are human, and they do get bored. Those who are highly entrepreneurial may find that once they have established a business they sooner or later become bored with running the same thing and wish to move on to new projects, while others become bored with living under the continual pressure, and decide they wish to pursue other interests, retire, or occasionally, seek to hand on the administrative and managerial aspects to others in order to concentrate on the particular aspects that they love.

That the owner is a serial entrepreneur looking to move on to the next project may on the face of it appear to be a good sign about the business as it does not necessarily indicate that there is any problem with the business.

However, if the founder is bored you need to consider whether their attention to running the business has lapsed, as if so it may have suffered as a result. Serial entrepreneurs who are always looking for the next big thing tend to be poor ongoing managers and completer finishers so there may therefore be loose ends and risk issues in the business to think about.

By contrast, some serial entrepreneurs who are used to creating new businesses and selling them to move on to their next project become very adept at tidying up their creations for the sale in order to maximise the funding available. In this case be warned, as you will be dealing with a very professional seller who is good at presenting the business in the best light.

Money to grow
The faster a business is growing, the greater will be its demand for working capital to meet its expanding trading, together with investment capital to support it in exploiting new opportunities. For this type of company, achieving a sale of part of the owner's interest to an outside investor can be the route to acquiring the capital needed to take advantage of the opportunities that arise, but this will naturally involve some form of loss of control of the business in return for the external capital introduced. In these circumstances the owner has to decide whether the opportunities offered by this extra money compensate for the restrictions on their independence.

Looming problems
Undoubtedly some business owners sell because they can see trouble coming in that either:

◆ The market is disappearing, which is very bad news. This can be because customers have gone away as tastes have changed; or because new products or services provide them with a better value solution to their needs. In either case the business must follow its customers to meet their new requirements or face extinction.

◆ Or the customers are still there to be supplied with what the business does but other people are supplying them. This can be because new competitors have entered the market taking away the company's market share; or existing competitors have become more effective by better differentiating their products or reducing their costs so as to undercut the company's prices.

It is important to be able to identify any looming problems that the business has and to understand the implications. If you buy a business that is about to get into difficulties you are likely to find that you have overpaid and to end up having to deal with a business turnaround rather than a simple purchase.

Example

An extremely successful company manufactured construction-related products and sold into the independent builders', merchants sector. The owners sold the business to an MBI team from outside the industry backed by venture capitalists' money.

In the years immediately following the sale, there was a major consolidation in the builders' merchants sector with independent outlets being bought up by the larger chains, who then had greater purchasing power to both negotiate discounts and source products more cheaply overseas. The business was squeezed and eventually failed.

> The assumption has to be that the old owners could see the writing on the wall and picked their moment to get out well.

WHY SELLERS DON'T SELL

While on the subject of sellers and their motivation, it is worth looking at what motives will work against a sale. These can be divided into three groups of factors:

◆ those such as a desire to pass the business on to the next generation of the family, which can mean that a business is simply never for sale to a third-party

◆ those which mean that the owner is reluctant to sell the business but which give you an opportunity to persuade them. These may actually work to your advantage in that they reduce the competition to buy the business but they may also recur later in the process and cause the seller to pull out

◆ those that only arise during the process.

It's important to be able to identify as quickly as possible whether the people you are dealing with are going to be serious in going through with selling or not. Once you get into the due diligence phase you will start to rack up real costs and you don't want to then find that the seller ceases to be interested in the deal or gets cold feet, which is a waste of money and time. As far as possible you need to have weeded these out early in your screening.

Therefore from the outset you need to be looking for the things that might cause a deal to fail so as to judge the time, effort and money you put into pursuing any particular target.

Issues that might lead to the owner being reluctant to sell in the first place, and which can also resurface during the deal and cause it to fail, include the following:

Emotional attachment

Whatever their reasons for selling, business owners need to decide that they are serious about selling their business, as it is not a decision that should be taken lightly. After all, once the business is sold, it is sold. In addition, the process will take up an enormous amount of their time and effort and will cause significant amounts of disruption to the business as and when customers, competitors, employees and suppliers find out that it is being sold.

Nevertheless, if they have successfully grown a business, sooner or later they may consider selling it for the reasons already outlined. However, the prospect of a sale for an entrepreneur (who has often founded the business) can create mixed emotions. On the one hand there is the prospect of realising the value of the business that has been built and obtaining both financial freedom and freedom from the demands, risks and worries of running a business. On the other hand, letting go of their 'baby', which they have sweated and worried and slaved to build, can generate a strong sense of loss.

Many owner managers therefore find it harder than you might expect to decide whether or not they ought to be selling the business, even in the face of an attractive financial offer.

Loss of meaning or structure to life

Bear in mind that your business environment gives a high degree of structure to your life. For an owner manager, selling up or moving to a position of retirement will be a major change in lifestyle for which they need to have prepared. They will need to have thought through the implications for their personal life;

how they will feel once they have sold up. What are they planning to do next?

And these issues can be as fundamental and personal as not wanting to face the idea of being at stuck home all day with the spouse; or fear that they will not know what to do with themselves in retirement and will simply fade away from loss of motivation; or a lack of outside interests or friends away from work.

You may think that as a buyer these are not your problems. But if the seller only really starts to consider these issues as you get near to completion and these cause an otherwise good deal to collapse, they will be. So in your process of getting to know the seller it's always worth discreetly trying to get a background on what they're looking to do next and forming a judgement on how well they have thought this through, how prepared they are, and so how likely they are to go through with a sale.

Loyalty to business or staff

Owner managers may feel particularly protective of their business and its good name as it has been so intimately associated with them personally, and can feel very responsible for the prospects and welfare of the managers and staff that work for them. These feelings can be so powerful as to blind an owner to the prospect of selling the business to anyone else.

This can, however, present an opportunity if you are able to get the owner to admit that they cannot be around for ever to look after the business. Your job is then to convince the owner that you are their best chance of securing their legacy. If you can do so, you may have an opportunity of buying a business that is not for sale to anybody else, from a person for whom money is not the principal consideration.

Issues that tend to arise *during* the sale process rather than *before* include the following:

Can't afford to sell

This occurs when the sellers realise that the earnings they will be able to make in investment income from the capital sum that you are proposing to pay them, means that they will take a significant reduction in annual income.

This issue arises relatively frequently in that a business purchase at say five or seven times earnings would mean that the owner of a business generating them a profit of £100,000 a year might expect an offer of £500,000 to £700,000, which initially appears extremely attractive. However, setting aside any reduction of that capital sum required to clear mortgages or other debts, in the current investment market they may then find that it is likely to be difficult to obtain investment return of more than say 5%. This means that this amount of capital is only going to be earning them between £25,000 and £35,000 a year, representing a substantial reduction in income.

The business owner in their sixties or seventies who is seeking a retirement sale may be willing to make such a trade-off as a way of turning the capital value of their business into a secure pension income and clearance of all their liabilities such as mortgages. The younger owner manager in their thirties or forties with perhaps a young family to support and a significant working life ahead of them is likely to be much less willing to undertake this sort of transaction.

Not theirs to sell

It is not unknown for buyers to have been negotiating in the early stages with the apparent owner manager, only to discover subsequently that a key shareholder, or a wide number of small family shareholders, do not wish to sell. The result is that the individual with whom they had been dealing did not in practice have the power to deliver a sale of all shares that they wish to buy. As discussed below, this can be a particular problem in older family businesses.

As soon as you start to look at any business you should undertake a company search (see Chapter 6) and obtain a copy of the company's annual return, which will set out the names and addresses of the shareholders' and directors as well as the shareholders, holdings. This will enable you to establish who owns the controlling shares and whether this is the same people that you are dealing with.

Not serious sellers

Some owners take the attitude that their business 'is always for sale' for the right price. These people are not really interested in a sale but if someone is prepared to make them a silly offer they would consider it. Since, however, they have not seriously thought through the pros and cons of selling and committed themselves to the process, these individuals are amongst the most likely to have second thoughts as the prospect of a sale becomes real and pull out.

The problem for you as a serious buyer with a serious interest is obviously that you will be committing to expending a high degree of cost in time and cash in pursuing an offer through to a sale. Do you want to be committing this in dealing with someone who is not actually seriously interested in selling at the outset?

Dislike of you or of the sale process

A business sale can be a very personal and pressured transaction. There are times therefore when the seller simply takes such a personal dislike to the prospective purchaser – over issues such as the amount of information being required, the buyer's attitude towards negotiating price, or simply personality – that they pull out.

Similarly the pressure of dealing simultaneously with running their business and negotiating a sale of it, a process with which they are unlikely to be familiar, can be intense on the seller and they may even blame you as the buyer for this pressure. And the longer it goes on the more difficult it is for some sellers to cope. This is one of the reasons why, once you have found a likely target and agreed a headline price, you should proceed to undertake your due diligence and move to completion as quickly as possible.

FAMILY BUSINESSES

Family businesses differ significantly from non-family businesses and if you've not worked in a family-owned business it can be difficult to appreciate what is going on.

In any business of any size there will tend to be two groups of stakeholders: those who work in the business, the employees; and those who own the business; the shareholders. This gives rise to three distinct interest groups as in the middle there are the owner managers, who both own shares in the business and work within it.

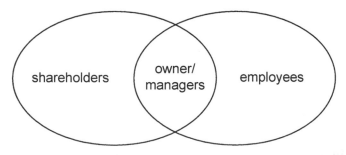

Figure 2. Stakeholders

Looking at the financial interests of these three groups of stakeholders, it is evident that they will have very different concerns in respect of the sale of the business:

◆ **employees** are likely to be focused on security of employment

◆ **external shareholders** (those who don't work in the business) are likely to concentrate on the value to be obtained for their shares

◆ **owner managers** working within the business may well be interested in both aspects and seeking to balance the value obtained for shares against the security of a subsequent employment contract.

In a family-owned company, by contrast, there are three distinct groups of stakeholders: the owners (shareholders), the workers and the family. This gives rise to seven sub-groups of interests which can complicate the position enormously.

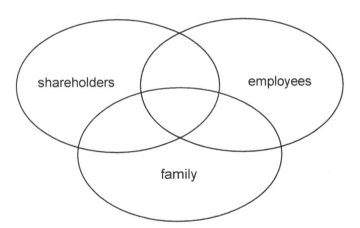

Figure 3. Stakeholders in a family business

For example, family members who are neither shareholders nor employees have on the face of it no financial interest in any sale of the business whatsoever. Does this mean they are without influence? Unfortunately not, in that family considerations in respect of the family name or pride in what the family has achieved through the business may mean that those family members who do own shares come under significant family pressure not to undertake transactions that may undermine this 'family heritage'.

In addition, even if family members do not have a shareholding they may still have a financial interest, either direct such as an ownership of the property, or indirect in that they are supported by the funds generated from the business. This can give them a very strong moral position when putting pressure on the actual shareholders in considering any deal.

Example

The business had been established for 30 years and the father had retired a year ago, leaving three next-generation siblings in charge.

Having retired he now came into the business at 8 a.m. rather than 7 a.m. and left at 6 p.m. rather than 8 p.m. He didn't draw a salary and he had never set up a pension. Instead he owned the site from which the business traded and the business paid him rent.

The father was becoming increasingly concerned, firstly by the strengthening local competition to the business and secondly by the lack of any action by his children to have the business address this.

On investigation it turned out that one of the key reasons that none of the children wanted to make any changes in the business was that they were afraid that if they made a change that damaged the business, they would be held responsible by the family for jeopardising the father's 'pension' arrangements.

Once you appreciate the additional layers of interest that exist within a family business then a number of things follow from it:

In whose interests?
Firstly all family-owned businesses sit somewhere on a continuum as to in whose interests the businesses is managed.

Figure 4. The family/business continuum

In some family-owned businesses, family interests clearly take priority over those of the business, so that for example family members are employed irrespective of their skills or competence. At the other end of the scale, some family businesses are run strictly as a business with very little room left for family sentiment.

When entering into initial discussions with a family-owned business you should try to make a judgement quickly as to where along this continuum this particular business lies, as it will give you significant guidance in how to approach the purchase.

Who actually is the owner?
Secondly you need to establish early on who actually owns the business. You may for example be dealing with a managing director who is quite clearly currently running it from day to day. However, you could quite easily find that the 50-year-old director with whom you are dealing is actually a minority shareholder and that his parents are the key shareholders, with whom you will really have to negotiate any purchase.

Failure to understand quite who has the 'ownership' can lead to a lot of wasted effort. Unfortunately, while this can establish the legal ownership of the shares it is not enough simply to undertake the search of the annual return at Companies House discussed above. This is because in a family situation you also need to establish who is the person who will actually make the decision, irrespective of who in the family nominally owns the shares.

The issue of ownership can be even more problematic in some old established family companies where shareholding is likely to have become extremely fragmented over a number of generations. This can lead to a significant volume of shares being held by relatives with no active involvement in the business whose agenda in terms of preserving grandad's legacy and/or requiring a steady income stream from dividends may be very different from the shareholders involved in managing the business from day to day. This can mean that getting acceptance of your offer from sufficient numbers of shareholders to be able to purchase control may be very difficult.

> **Example**
> The business was established over a hundred years ago by a set of brothers who divided the shares equally amongst themselves. In the Victorian age large families were of course relatively common, so by the time that the shares had been divided amongst the next generation they had already become quite fragmented. As this process was repeated over three to four generations, by the late 1990s there were over 50 small family shareholders, many with no active involvement in the business.
>
> The business got into difficulties and required the appointment of a company 'doctor' to conduct some radical surgery. As the shareholding base was so fragmented the

company doctor was unable to persuade sufficient of the small shareholders to back his plans, so he withdrew. In the absence of a rescue plan the business failed a few months later.

WHO ARE YOU COMPETING WITH?

Finally it is worth considering who your competitors in buying a business might be.

If you are looking at buying a small lifestyle business then the competition is likely to come from other individuals.

As soon as you start to look at buying a commercial or sizeable business you may find that in addition to other individuals, the variety of corporate purchasers that you may be competing with might include:

- **consolidators** looking to buy a number of businesses within one industry with a view to merging their back-office administration and purchasing to obtain the benefits of economies of scale and/or to put together a business of a size that can be floated or sold to an industrial purchaser in the way that the individual businesses cannot

- **slow growth companies** who are looking to 'bolt on' turnover so as to present themselves as having higher growth

- **venture capitalists** looking to back an MBO, MBI or BIMBO team

- **existing buy outs** which have raised money for their business plan from venture capitalists based on an aggressive acquisition policy to grow the business and who therefore have cash with which to make acquisitions

- **focused corporates** that have sold their non-core activities to generate a cash pot with which to refocus on their core area of operations and to grow this if necessary by way of strategic acquisitions

- **changing corporates** looking to move into a new area of business and to avoid the learning curve of starting their own subsidiary by buying their way in.

As discussed in Chapter 8, each of the above may have specific reasons why they may be prepared to pay more for the business than you are based on its existing performance, and obviously some of the above may have deeper pockets than you when it comes to agreeing a price with the seller.

Nevertheless, as we discussed, for some sellers price is not everything and your ability to form a personal relationship with the seller and to relate to their aspirations for the business may give you the edge over some corporate or financial purchasers.

5

Finding a Business to Buy

SEARCH TACTICS

Having decided on your search criteria, covering such matters as industry, location, size, price range and any particular characteristics you are seeking, you now need to find businesses to buy which meet these criteria. And this means planning and conducting a search for these businesses.

I say businesses, as until you have completed the deal you need to be continuing to search the market for prospective targets.

If you're finding very few opportunities to buy, the danger is that you may become desperate and buy something that is not ideal, simply because it is available. The secret to finding a good deal can often be in simply generating a strong 'deal flow' of potential targets to look at so that you have a good choice. In fact some advisers would argue that the biggest problem facing any individual looking to buy a commercial business is uncovering the opportunity, not actually doing the deal.

To generate opportunities on a regular basis you need to have a prospecting machine in action day in, day out, based on the 'sales funnel' principle:

Example

Company A's sales and marketing plan might involve:

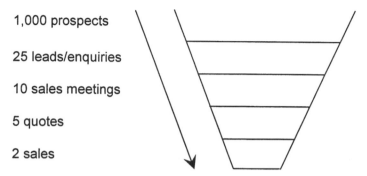

1,000 prospects

25 leads/enquiries

10 sales meetings

5 quotes

2 sales

Figure 5. The sales funnel

On a monthly basis Company A produces:

◆ 1,000 mailshots which produce . . .

◆ 25 enquiries which produce . . .

◆ 10 sales meetings which produce . . .

◆ 5 quotes which produce . . .

◆ 2 sales.

This approach allows Company A not only to have a regular flow of sales, but also to manage the process by either increasing the volume of work or increasing the efficiency of conversion at each stage.

In the same way, you need to have a prospecting programme that generates:

◆ companies to look at

- that pass your desktop screening

- who will talk to you when you approach them

- who will consider an offer

- and agree a price

- where you can complete due diligence; and

- complete a purchase.

Keeping your options open

While you should focus your search around your target criteria, and should pursue discussions with any particular target of interest as vigorously as possible, you should always aim to be in discussion with, or have offers out, with more than one business throughout your search. This means that if your discussions with your current target fall through you can quickly be picking up discussions with the next rather than having to restart your search process from scratch.

While you need to be enthusiastic about any business you're intending to buy (otherwise what's the point?), it's also important not to become emotionally attached to any one particular target (unless and until you have bought the business) as if you do so you may end up overpaying. Having a search programme continually generating alternative targets helps you to keep the business you're looking at in perspective.

Becoming over-committed to the current target also means that you are likely to let your search programme drift and reduce the number of alternatives to be looked at. This will in turn mean that if the deal does fall through you're likely to take some time in getting your search programme back up and running.

In setting up your search approach you have a number of important questions and choices as to how you go about it which will be discussed in the rest of this chapter. These include considering whether you will:

◆ search for businesses for sale, businesses that aren't for sale, or both

◆ conduct your own search or retain advisers to search for you, or both

◆ explore franchising as an alternative.

BUSINESSES FOR SALE AND NOT FOR SALE

It may sound simplistic but the types of business that you want to buy will fall into one of two camps.

Businesses for sale

Some businesses will formally be up for sale. The advantages of dealing with a business where the owners are actually trying to sell it are obvious in that:

◆ they are generally easier for you to identify (although with some exceptions as discussed below) and easier to approach

◆ you can have a reasonable expectation that the owners are serious about selling and are therefore worth talking to.

The disadvantages, however, are also obvious in that if the owners are actively marketing the business for sale either themselves or through brokers or a corporate finance house, then many other prospective purchasers will also be aware that it is on the market. You may therefore face more competition to buy the business which can be expected to drive up the price that you have to pay and increase the uncertainty about whether you will in fact complete the deal.

The business is also likely to have gone through a grooming process with a view to enhancing its apparent value. Again this may increase the price being sought for the business, but it may also work partly in your interests in that the preparation for due diligence should have ensured that as many as possible of the potential snags and risks in the business have been dealt with in preparation for a sale.

Businesses not for sale
Many businesses that you might be interested in are not currently up for sale. Amongst these businesses there will, however, be some where the owners may be willing to consider selling if approached correctly.

The art of successfully buying businesses that are not currently for sale often lies in:

◆ the ability to identify owners whose circumstances mean that they might be minded to sell if they receive the right approach, even if they may not actively have thought about doing so

◆ constructing an approach that is likely to be of interest.

Therefore, ensuring that you understand the potential motivations of different types of owners can be vital to success in this area.

FINDING BUSINESSES THAT ARE FORMALLY FOR SALE
You might expect that a business being sold will be advertised to attract buyers and should therefore be relatively easy to find. However, surprisingly, this may not always be the case.

◆ some advertising of businesses for sale will not be 'public', but will be through private networks

◆ some businesses for sale are not actively advertised at all!

Public advertising

Sellers who want to publicly advertise their business for sale will do so by way of adverts in the relevant press. The definition of what counts as the relevant press will obviously depend upon the nature of the business and its size.

A small business such as a post office or shop is likely to be advertised by either its owners or a brokerage or estate agent in:

◆ the local press

◆ national publications such as *Dalton's Weekly* or *Exchange and Mart*

◆ a property catalogue produced by the agents; as well as possibly

◆ a trade magazine.

The more specialist the trade, the less appropriate is general 'non-business' press and the more the focus will be on trade and specialist press. So a professional business such as an accountancy firm for example is likely to take out an advert in the specialist accountancy press, such as *Accountancy Age*.

Businesses of a reasonable scale which are looking for a significant sale value will tend to advertise the sale in the national financial press, such as the *Financial Times*, which runs a weekly businesses for sale page, or the *Sunday Times* and *Sunday Telegraph*.

Businesses may put the advert in themselves, in which case they will usually give somewhat sketchy details and take advantage of the box number service that most newspapers operate in order to maintain confidentiality. Alternatively brokers or corporate finance sales advisers will place adverts on their behalf and act as the point of contact for purchasers.

Such brokers and the corporate finance departments of accountancy firms may also list businesses they have for sale on their website.

Adverts placed by insolvency practitioners

Insolvency practitioners (IPs) who are appointed to a business where there is some prospect of selling it as a going concern will generally also rapidly place adverts in the specialist trade press and the *Financial Times*' businesses for sale section, giving details of the business that are available.

A quick tip about these adverts from a number of years experience in drafting them is that if they list a 'high-quality and well-trained workforce' as one of the business's key features, this means that the IP's staff could not identify or think of other real attractions or assets to include in the advert and have slipped this in to use up the space!

Also bear in mind that the IP's advertisement may only be appearing less than a week after their appointment and in the interim the IP:

◆ will have actively circulated any parties that the management have identified as potentially interested in the business in the days immediately after the IP's appointment

◆ may also have undertaken a short pre-insolvency sales process in anticipation of being appointed, resulting in the ability to complete a pre-arranged sale almost immediately after their appointment (a 'pre-pack', see below).

The IP may therefore be well advanced in their discussions with potential purchasers by the time you're reading the advert and requesting a sales pack.

Specialist brokers

In addition some specialist types of business broker, such as Fleuretts for the pub trade, who have a regular volume of property-based businesses to sell, produce a regular catalogue which is freely available to potential buyers. This gives a picture of the property and outline details in much the same way as estate agents will sometimes produce a free property paper as well as placing details of houses for sale in the local press.

Private advertising and networks

The market for many businesses is, however, relatively inefficient as there is often a need to keep the fact that a business is for sale confidential. This is because knowledge that it is on the market can have a significant adverse impact upon the business due to the uncertainty that this generates amongst customers about future service and employees about future prospects, not helped by active poaching of customers and staff by competitors looking to take advantage of the situation.

So some sellers will want to find a buyer for their business, without having it publicly advertised.

Business brokers therefore operate what are in effect **private mailing lists**, through which businesses are advertised for sale without all the exposure that a public advertisement will bring. A number of corporate finance houses, specialist brokers and even legal practices offer a business sales service which includes this type of marketing.

Generally brief details giving no more than a headline description of the business sector, a paragraph of description and a reference number for obtaining further information will be included in the listing. This will then be circulated either by post or in a regular email listing or newsletter to potential interested parties, as well as being listed on the broker's website.

By simply identifying brokers from advertisements they place regarding businesses for sale and contacting them to express an interest you may have yourself put on their mailing list. You should then start to receive these private circulations on a regular basis. As with public adverts, however, you will be in competition to buy a business with many other people who are receiving the same newsletter.

Business angels networks

Similarly businesses that are only looking for investors rather than necessarily a complete sale are likely to register their details with a **business angels network**. Again most such networks operate by circulating details of potential opportunities to their investor members.

These sort of investment listings will not normally be from people looking to sell the whole of their business. Instead they will normally be seeking finance from a business angel (a wealthy individual, often a retired businessperson who has already sold one business and who is interested in investing funds personally in smaller or start-up businesses, and who often will want to take an active role in the company's management) with which to develop or grow the business in return for a stake in it.

Many business angel networks cover a particular locality since in practice most business angels tend to want to invest close to where they live so as to be able to keep an eye on, or to facilitate being actively involved with, their investment. There is a national business angels network, www.bestmatch.co.uk, through which you can find a list of local business angels networks as well as details of their joining costs and the investor criteria each requires to be accepted onto their list. The British Venture Capital Association (BVCA) website, www.BVCA.co.uk, also has a downloadable document on business angels with a very comprehensive list of networks which you might wish to join.

Joining can, however, be a problem as a result of the Financial Promotions Order which restricts the ability of intermediaries to forward details of investments to potential investors who meet certain criteria (as discussed in more detail on p111 below). If you're not able to meet these criteria it may be difficult if not impossible to find a business angels network you can join.

Personal networking

You should also **network with intermediaries** such as your personal contacts and professional advisers, including accountants and bankers, since they may become aware of owners who are considering selling. To do so you should:

◆ set up an active marketing programme of regular contacts with these professionals

◆ put together and distribute a description of the type of business you're interested in and your criteria taken from your acquisition plan, as this is where your personal sales pack becomes vital in convincing intermediaries that you are a serious potential buyer who will not be wasting their contact's time

◆ provide some information about your financial backing and capacity to undertake a purchase

◆ say thank you to any intermediary for any lead and actively and quickly follow up any leads generated from such intermediaries to show that you're serious.

You should always contact the intermediary to give them feedback as to how you got on with any lead. Not only is this a matter of simple politeness but:

◆ it's also a way of demonstrating your seriousness

◆ it's another chance to contact them and keep your interest live in their mind

◆ it can allow you to correct or refine their understanding of what it is you're looking for

◆ do not forget a lead that an intermediary has given you is one of their own contacts and the intermediary will be concerned from their own point of view to ensure that this contact has been dealt with appropriately.

Turnaround opportunities

If you are specifically interested in finding turnaround opportunities you should register with the **Turnaround Equity Finder** service at www.turnaroundequity.co.uk. This is a specialist introductory network which is free to investors and is focused on matching investors interested in buying into turnarounds with companies in some form of distress which are seeking equity investors or business sales.

Placed sales

The above types of approach shade off into sources of businesses which are being sold by being actively marketed to parties identified as likely to be interested in buying them ('placed'), rather than being publicly advertised.

In the most basic version of this activity, some brokers and business angels networks do not simply act as passive circulators of all opportunities registered with them to all investors on their database. Instead they will actively seek to match businesses for sale with the interests of those investors registered with them, who have a specific interest in a particular type of business sector or size.

This approach is then taken a stage further in a traditional corporate finance sales process. In this case the corporate finance department of an accountancy firm receives a 'mandate' from a business's owners to sell it. The firm will then typically assist the owners to groom the business for sale before then conducting a specific marketing exercise designed to place the business in front of likely purchasers. This involves them in identifying potential buyers both from within the company's own sector and outside, who are considered to be likely to have an appetite for the deal. The corporate finance firm will then send a speculative sales letter to the identified company or individual to see whether they have an interest in buying the business.

The obvious advantages to you of receiving such a letter are that:

- you are being approached by a business that is serious about selling to the extent that they have instructed accountants to act on their behalf, for which they will normally have had to pay an upfront 'commitment fee' when engaging them to conduct the work

- the business may well not be publicly advertised so the number of potential competing parties may be relatively small.

Against this, however, if the seller's lead adviser is any good at their job you must expect the opportunity to be put in front of people who are seriously interested. The competition to buy the business may therefore be more serious in comparison with the number of 'tyre kickers' generated from public adverts, even if smaller in number.

Pre-packs

This type of placing approach has traditionally been used by corporate finance firms seeking to sell good businesses with good prospects. Increasingly, however, it is also being used to arrange what are known as pre-packs.

A pre-pack is a pre-packaged insolvency, where prior to a receiver or administrator being appointed, arrangements have already been put in place to find a buyer for the business with the finance to conclude the deal, so that the insolvency practitioner (IP) is able to sell the business immediately after appointment. The advantage of this to the IP, their appointer and the business is that it removes much of the uncertainty as to likely outcome.

Under a traditional appointment of an IP as administrative receiver or administrator the IP would have to come in, take control of the business, decide whether it is appropriate to try to trade it on, and arrange to do so; while at the same time attempting to put together a sales pack, advertise the business to generate offers and seek to negotiate a sale on the best terms possible. In the meantime, the value of the business may be suffering significantly as a result of the stigma and adverse impacts of trading during an insolvency, such as the departure of key staff or defection of clients worried about continuity of supply.

In contrast, in a pre-pack:

◆ the advisers may have more time to sell the business, depending on the degree of crisis in the business, than they would have once the business has gone into a formal insolvency; and buyers will have more time to put financing in place, so facilitating the obtaining of a better price. The advisers can also concentrate fully on the attempt to sell the business since they are not having to deal with taking over and attempting to trade or restructure the insolvent business at the same time

◆ the business does not have to trade during a period of formal insolvency, other than say a day or two in order to allow the sale to take place, and therefore the adverse impact of a period of insolvency on the business is minimised

◆ as a result, the appointer knows exactly what the financial outcome of the sale is going to be and therefore has relative certainty as to the deficit they may suffer, whereas without a pre-pack this is always uncertain until the sale is concluded.

Accelerated corporate finance transaction

An accelerated corporate finance transaction is when this type of sale process has been conducted in a short time scale with a view to complete a disposal for the maximum value prior to an insolvency.

Contacting lead advisers

In order to have such leads sent to you, you will need to convince appropriate lead advisers that it is worthwhile sending them to you. This will involve you in undertaking the same sort of marketing programme to lead advisers as outlined in respect of intermediaries above.

Brokers and lead advisers are really two points along a continuum between a high-volume marketing focused exercise offered by most brokers through to a low volume, high value-added bespoke advisory and deal support service provided by lead advisers; and there are obviously brokers and advisers at many points along this line. As a potential buyer you will generally find that it is easy to get on the books of a brokerage firm and to generate a flow of information about the volume of businesses which are on their books, although this is unlikely to be tailored to your requirements. In contrast you may find it is difficult to generate specific placed leads from corporate finance lead advisers for a number of reasons:

- As a bespoke service they tend to be dealing with much smaller numbers of businesses for sale which they try specifically to place with contacts who they know may be interested. The chances that any particular lead adviser will be selling the precise type of business you are interested in is therefore low.

- Lead advisers tend to focus their marketing and contacts upon potential groups of buyers such as large corporates, venture capital houses or business angels networks with whom they may deal many times to sell many businesses. Their appetite for forming a one-off relationship with you as an individual on the off-chance that you might be a buyer for one of their businesses (when you will undoubtedly be talking to many other people) is likely to be limited.

- Many lead adviser firms offer a retained search service for buyers in which they actively seek opportunities. So if they have such retained clients on their books who are paying for this service, why would they give you a good lead for free?

As a result, while it is worth registering your interest with lead advisers, you should be realistic about the chances that they will contact you with an ideal opportunity.

An alternative approach is to network yourself into a venture capital house, as these will be known to all of the relevant lead advisers who will look to place appropriate opportunities with them. If you speak to venture capitalists they will almost without exception say that they don't back the businesses when buying, they back the people. So if you can convince a venture capital house that you're a good person to become involved in an **MBI** in a particular industry, they may find the opportunity for you and of course this will mean that you will already be well-placed to finance the deal.

Essential points

In summary, therefore, to maximise your chances of finding a business that is for sale which may be of interest you have to:

◆ look at the publicly available sources of adverts of businesses for sale

◆ ensure that you get yourself onto the lists and networks whereby you can be circulated with details of companies for sale, which are not being publicly advertised, which is often simply a case of registering your interest with the brokers and business angels networks

◆ actively manage your networking so that intermediaries know of your interest

◆ finally actively market yourself to the corporate finance lead advisers who are managing corporate finance style placings, so that you will be circulated with opportunities that match your requirements, and to venture capitalists who may be looking to put together a team to conduct an MBI.

FINANCIAL PROMOTION

Sending out details of a business that is for sale is an activity that counts as a financial promotion and is regulated by the Financial Services Authority (FSA) under the Financial Services and Markets Act 2000 (FSMA) and the Financial Promotions Order (FPO). The FPO is designed to prevent unsuitable investments being inappropriately sold to unsophisticated investors. All individuals and businesses involved with undertaking financial promotions must be authorised by the FSA and subject to their regulation and oversight.

Many accountants and other professionals prefer not to be regulated by the FSA. Instead, they will seek to be authorised by their own professional body (such as the Institute of Chartered Accountants in England and Wales, ICAEW), which is known as a designated professional body (DPB). Once authorised by a DPB a firm must state on the bottom of its letterhead that it is authorised by its DPB to conduct a range of investment business activities. It is then able to conduct a limited degree of financial promotion, so long as this falls under certain regulations given in the FPO, the most important of which are:

♦ There is no ban on sending out details where a controlling interest (over 50%) or the whole of the business is for sale.

♦ Under Article 55 and 55a, information about investments of under 50% can be sent to people who are already clients of a firm, where this is an 'incidental part' of the overall professional services that they have been engaged to provide. So your own accountant could send you this type of information so long as this is not the main work that they are doing for you.

♦ Under Article 48, communications about this sort of investment to 'high net worth individuals' are exempt. This is designed to allow proposals to be sent to business angels and other sources of informal capital for start-up and small companies. This exemption can only be used where an individual has filed a certificate with the intermediary that has been issued by their accountant or employer to show that they have the appropriate net worth and which states that they are eligible to receive these types of promotions.

◆ To be a high net worth individual under this exemption, the statement must show that you have had an annual income of at least £100,000 in the preceding financial year, or have held net assets of not less than £250,000 throughout it. Since the certificate is based on your prior year's financial position it must therefore be renewed on an annual basis.

◆ Under Article 53, communications to sophisticated investors of this type are also exempt. Again, the investor requires a certificate, although in this case, it is not subject to any minimum solvency requirements. However, only a firm authorised by the FSA can provide an individual with a certificate which states that the person has enough knowledge to be able to understand the risks associated with the investment and shows the types of investment in respect of which the individual can receive information. These certificates are valid for a period of three years.

To register with many of the business angels networks which may involve investors taking minority stakes in businesses, you may need to obtain certification as a high net worth individual or sophisticated investor.

FINDING BUSINESSES THAT ARE NOT FOR SALE

Finding businesses that are not for sale is a matter of conducting a search for businesses that meet your overall criteria that you can then approach with a view to persuading the owner to sell. You can therefore either conduct your own search or retain professional advisers to do it for you, usually as part of their overall remit to act as your advisers throughout the rest of the purchase process.

Do-it-yourself search

To conduct your own search you need to identify sources of information with which to identify businesses.

Online databases

The first port of call is likely to be public websites such as
www.yell.co.uk. This is the *Yellow Pages* website on which you
can search by location and business type based on *Yellow Pages*
classifications. Personally I find these classifications more useful
for searches than the Standard Industry Classification codes (SIC
codes) used by Companies House (www.companieshouse.gov.
uk) as they are more descriptive of what businesses actually do.

If you are looking for a widget manufacturer this will come
under widgets in the *Yellow Pages*, while its SIC code might be
'2924 Manufacture of other general machinery'. That is
assuming that all widget manufacturers classify themselves here
and not as for example '2875 Manufacture of other fabricated
metal products' or any of the other categories. In addition, each
of these categories is likely to include large numbers of
manufacturers of thingamajigs, gizmos and other products that
you are not interested in.

Yell.co.uk used to provide a business service whereby you could
download lists of business classifications by county together with
a limited amount of financial information where this was
available. Unfortunately they have ceased to offer this service
and instead this type of inquiry is referred across to Experian
(see below).

Nevertheless by conducting 'normal' searches on Yell and
consolidating the results onto a spreadsheet you can quickly
build up a list of businesses of the type and location you are
interested in as the starting point for your research, even if you
then have to find the financial information elsewhere.

In addition to Yell there are a number of business data
companies which can be accessed through the internet, such as
Experian (www.experian.com). These generally provide the

facility to conduct searches by SIC code and location and will provide results giving basic details such as the address, telephone number, turnover and number of employees where this information is available.

Another online company, www.192.com, sells a CD-ROM (UK Info Business) covering 2.5 million registered UK companies with financial information on approximately 1 million of them, together with data on 5.5 million directors, while www.cd-rom-directories.co.uk sells a variety of databases on CD-ROM.

Do not expect to be able to rely on turnover information given by any company database, as this is likely to be highly incomplete. Many small to medium-size companies are exempt from the reporting rules which require the inclusion of turnover figures in the accounts filed at Companies House from which these databases are compiled. You will therefore find that many companies listed will apparently have zero turnover. However you will also find that in many cases the databases also contain information on the number of employees which can help you to judge the size of business in the absence of a turnover figure.

Trade associations

The second key source for your search is from identifying trade associations, many of which will have a website which allows you to identify members, or will produce a directory of members that you may be able to obtain.

You should subscribe to the trade press to see which businesses are active and attend trade shows where you can obtain a list of exhibitors and see their products.

Accountants' business databases

Your accountant may well own a business database for their own marketing which could be used to generate you a list of targets.

However you are likely to find that your accountant is reluctant or is simply unable to undertake such a search for you. This is because they will not have compiled the data themselves but will be subscribers to databases provided either direct by the large database companies, or which are provided tailored to specific needs by intermediary companies who themselves will buy the basic data from these large suppliers.

The use that the accountants can make of this data will be strictly controlled by their licence agreement and as the producers of the original data have an interest in selling this information directly to users, the licence will normally prohibit users from providing raw data to a third party.

Once you have your basic list of companies you then need to start to compile more data in order to screen these down to the candidates that meet your criteria.

Retained search

The alternative to undertaking a search yourself is to retain advisers to do it for you as part of their overall engagement. These advisers will often have access to databases with useful company information such as:

◆ directors' ages so that they can target businesses where directors are over 55 and may therefore be interested in retiring

◆ benchmarking and financial health information which can allow you to target the best performing businesses in the industry (or the worst if you're seeking a turnaround opportunity).

Such advisers will normally seek a retainer fee either as a one-off payment or on an ongoing basis throughout the search, which is normally treated as an advance against the overall success fee.

This is not simply to cover costs, although the time taken to find a business can be lengthy and advisers may therefore be keen to structure their fees so as to cover costs as they go rather than having to wait a lengthy period before being paid a significant success fee. As importantly, however, intermediaries will be seeking a sign of commitment from you the purchaser so that they are not wasting their time, as the bulk of their reward will come from some kind of contingent success fee, which of course in some cases may never actually come through.

If you are looking for an adviser to carry out such a search it might be worthwhile attempting to find an industry specialist who will be best placed to uncover opportunities in the sector you are interested in because they will have an extensive network in that industry.

If working with such an adviser, be careful to establish the contractual basis at the outset and make sure that the engagement letter covers:

◆ whether the retainer will be deducted from the success fee in whole or in part

◆ how long the agreement will last for and what happens when it is terminated (so for example, is a success fee still due if you buy a business identified by the adviser, after the expiry of the agreement?)

◆ is the agreement exclusive (so for example, will you have to pay them a success fee if you find a business to buy on your own?).

MBO SPECIFIC ISSUES

If you are contemplating an MBO of your existing business then there is obviously little issue when it comes to finding the business for sale. If you are a director or senior employee of the business there are, however, serious issues concerning the very real conflict of interest that you may be creating in attempting to undertake an MBO that will need to be addressed.

Your first step should be to approach the company's board and notify them of your interest. If you don't you may well be breaching your employment contract and/or your fiduciary duties as a director if you:

◆ disclose confidential company information to potential backers; or

◆ involve other members of staff in your project.

And of course there may be issues concerning how you vote at board meetings on issues that might affect your MBO plans.

The board will have a duty to act in the interests of the company and its shareholders and should not therefore reject any bona fide offer outright without considering it and consulting, if necessary, with the shareholders.

If the board is willing to consider your offer they will generally:

◆ form a board committee of directors not involved in the MBO to consider any offer through to negotiating **heads of terms** and may engage professional advisers to help them

◆ agree with you how you will act during the MBO process including how much information you are able to provide to financial backers, how much time you can spend on the MBO and whether you should relinquish some of your existing duties.

Whilst MBO teams sometimes ask, you should not generally expect that the company will underwrite any of your professional fees in undertaking an MBO, not least because this can throw up issues of potential 'financial assistance'. Additionally the consent of the shareholders is required in respect of any sale of substantial assets to a director (see Chapter 10).

FRANCHISING

As an alternative to buying an existing business or setting up a completely new business from scratch, you could consider buying a franchise. This is really a specialist area and there are a number of books devoted to how to do so successfully.

An initial attraction in comparison with the process described so far in this chapter is that there are many franchise opportunities readily available for purchase which are actively being marketed, as a swift look at publications such as *Dalton's Weekly* will demonstrate.

The advantages of franchising are that it should provide:

◆ a proven business model

◆ often with ongoing business management support to help you run the business

◆ in some cases financing packages which have already been arranged to support buyers.

Points to consider

The issues and disadvantages involved in buying a franchise can be:

◆ Are you really buying a successful business model, or is the model simply successful for the people selling the franchise? The franchisor will usually take a significant upfront payment from you and others for the franchises being sold, so you should ask how committed they are to the future success of your business. It is noticeable that many of the adverts for franchises are of a very 'hard sell' nature, promising reliable good earnings for a limited amount of cash down now. While there are undoubtedly very successful franchise organisations which provide good opportunities for franchise holders to build a successful business, some of these adverts bring to mind that old saying which is very applicable in business: if something looks too good to be true, it probably is.

◆ Is the geographical area for which you are buying your franchise likely to provide a suitable level of business for this product or service? In some cases franchisors may well have already taken the prime territories for themselves and are simply franchising the less attractive ones.

◆ Are you committing to paying a significant level of your turnover to the franchisor into the future, either directly as an ongoing charge or commission, or indirectly as a result of having to buy certain material or supplies from the franchisor (at their markup)?

◆ Will there be any restrictions on your ability to sell your franchise on later should you make success of it? If so this will restrict your ability to create a business with a realisable capital value.

You therefore need to investigate the viability of any franchise opportunity very carefully. Remember that even if the business model you are buying is a very successful one, in your area what you are actually buying is simply the right to launch a start-up business, one of the riskiest things you can do.

In practice you should therefore think of buying a franchise not in terms of buying a business, but simply as a way of attempting to reduce your risks in starting up a new business.

GOLDEN RULES

6. Don't get emotionally attached to any business until you have bought it.
7. Buy something that is not formally for sale and you'll have less competitors.

Phase 3: Approaching and Screening

$$\left(6\right)$$

Before You Approach

DESKTOP REVIEWS AND SCREENING

Your research to this point may have generated you a sizeable list of potential target companies in the right industry and location. Based on some other databases available you should also have an idea of the businesses' size in terms of either turnover or number of employees.

You will then need to reduce this to a manageable number to approach or at least to prioritise them in order of attractiveness so you can concentrate your efforts on those that appear to best suit your needs.

You also need to be as well prepared as possible before you make that initial approach so as to have an idea what questions you want to ask, and be considering your strategy for persuading the owner to sell the business to you.

So the next stage of the process is to:

♦ find out as much as you can about each business, which means identifying both financial and non-financial information

♦ refine your research as you go, moving from desktop reviews to more detailed examination as you focus down on the businesses that are really of interest

◆ undertake a desktop review of the available financial information on the business to obtain a picture of the business's performance.

Since many people lack confidence in their ability to understand or extract useful financial information from accounts, this chapter will set out some basic things to look for that will apply to most sets of accounts. If, however, the business has reached the stage where the accounts contain significant numbers of pages of notes to the accounts you may need to take professional advice.

SOURCES OF NON-FINANCIAL INFORMATION

Many sources of non-financial information have already been touched on, such as the company's website, trade associations and public or government websites about the industry. But don't forget the step of contacting the company.

◆ Ring for a brochure. See how professional both it and the service you receive is. Sometimes it is interesting to see whether you get a subsequent telephone call to follow up your interest as a potential customer who has contacted the business. I am always amazed when this doesn't happen.

◆ Try emailing for a brochure from the company's website or use their contact point to ask a question. Do you get a response? The number of businesses who operate a website that appears to be connected to a black hole for customer inquiries is another constant source of surprise to me.

If you come across either of these situations you may find there are some very easy steps you can take to improve the business' sales performance following your purchase.

As you narrow your search down, there are many practical things that you can do to check out the business before you approach. In fact for individuals looking at buying some of the smaller types of businesses such as shops and restaurants, these activities can form a central part of your due diligence:

Observe the business

By spending some time both during the week and at weekends watching the numbers and types of people that are visiting the business you can get some idea of:

◆ The customer base – is it all old people or is it a good mix of old and young that suggests a long lifetime of customers?

◆ What type of people are they? Do they look wealthy, with money to spend or not?

◆ The variability of trade – is it busy all the time or are there definite highs and lows?

Check the local media

◆ How effectively is the business promoting itself? How does this compare to its competitors' promotional activities?

Check the locality

◆ Are there large numbers of competitors? Dependent upon the nature of the trade, this can be a good thing. A 'cluster' say of antiques businesses or art galleries may bring many more potential customers to an area so that all the businesses benefit. Of course it can also be a disadvantage as an oversupply of, say, care home places, may push down the rates that can be obtained.

◆ Do any of the competing businesses seem to be doing significantly better than the one you're looking at? If so, what appears to be the cause?

◆ Do customers specifically come to the business or does it rely on passing trade? Is one side of the street busier than the other?

◆ Is there a good local transport system to bring customers from the surrounding area?

◆ What are the neighbouring businesses like? Is the business surrounded by complementary ones, residential areas or industrial units?

◆ Are there any particular location issues in respect of the particular type of business you are looking at?

Make inquiries
◆ Talk to the competition. Try using their shop, restaurant or bar as a customer and get into conversation about how business is. Most business owners are happy to talk about their business as part of promoting it to customers so long as you choose the appropriate moment. So ensure you pick a quiet time of day when they're not likely to be busy.

Be a mystery shopper
◆ If possible use the business as a customer, and/or ask your friends and relatives to use it. Try to observe how good the service is, how content the customers appear to be, whether there seems to be a strong regular clientele.

When the property is important
Many of the smaller businesses that an individual might typically be looking to buy (such as shops and sub post offices, pubs,

hotels, guesthouses and holiday cottages, restaurants, nurseries and care homes) are in many ways as much about buying the premises as about buying the business. When looking at these type of businesses you should focus initially on the property:

- From looking at a map or visiting the area, is it in the right location to attract the customers that the business needs? What are the local conditions like in terms of competitors, property trends and trading conditions?

- From walking past, what condition is the building in? Will it need significant refurbishment or alterations to meet future trading or regulatory requirements?

- From undertaking a Land Registry search (www.landregisteronline.gov.uk), what tenure would you expect to be getting? Is the property a freehold or are you buying a lease? (If so you will need to find out the terms early in your discussions with the owner.)

As with any property matter, the old rule – location, location, location – applies. You can always make alterations to the physical structure of the building (obviously with the landlord's consent if it's a leasehold). But you can't move it.

So if the business needs a car park but hasn't got room for one, or if the place is difficult to find, or in a location that is not appropriate for this type of business then you need to think seriously about whether this is right for you.

This whole issue of the property becomes even more important in the case of businesses which include the owner's accommodation, as you are not only buying the business and the property from which it operates, but a home as well.

Only if you're satisfied with the position in respect of these property elements should you be going on to look at the financial aspects of these types of business and their trading performance.

FINANCIAL INFORMATION

If you are looking at a business that is actively for sale you should expect to receive copies of audited and/or management accounts in the sales pack. If not, you will need to rely on what you can obtain from public sources.

Sole traders and partnerships

If the business you are looking at is currently operated either as a sole trader or a partnership you are unlikely to be able to find any significant financial information in the public domain. This is because since sole traders and partnerships are in effect people trading in their own right, they do not have to file public accounts and simply account to the Inland Revenue for the tax on profits as part of the individual's or partners' personal tax returns.

The principal exception to this will be any information that you may be able to obtain on such businesses through various credit referencing agencies.

Limited companies and partnerships

If the business is currently operated through a limited liability partnership or a company it will, however, have to file accounts at Companies House and as a minimum you should undertake a search (www.companieshouse.gov.uk). The principal documents that this can provide you with are the company's:

◆ **memorandum and articles of association** – in effect the company's objectives and its constitution. For the purpose of most business sales these days, these tend to be of little relevance but every so often a situation comes along in which these are vital, as they can, for example, set out that different classes of share exist with different voting and ownership rights

- **annual return** – a form completed every year by the company secretary which sets out details of the directors and shareholders (although since this is always only a snapshot you also need to check the register of shareholders for the current position)

- **register of charges**, which records the security given to third parties such as a mortgage over the company's property or a fixed and floating charge to the bank to secure its overdraft

- copies of any **forms** notifying Companies House of changes in the company's registered office or directors

- **annual accounts** in the standard statutory and UK Generally Accepted Accounting Practice (GAAP) format, which should provide you with information on the business's financial position and performance.

HAVING FAITH IN NUMBERS

If you are not familiar with reading accounts there are some general rules that you should bear in mind throughout this chapter:

- The numbers don't tell you what you need to know. As will hopefully be made clear below, they are guides to help you work out the questions to ask and consider what plans to put in place; and they can help you to test whether information you may be given later is right.

- The numbers are produced as a result of how the business is being run, they are symptoms and evidence of what is happening, not the cause.

◆ The trends in the numbers (over time, such as growth, or in comparison to other similar businesses, known as benchmarking) tend to be more important than any individual absolute figure.

◆ Publicly filed numbers will always be significantly out of date.

◆ Do not be fooled into thinking that the numbers are ever absolutely 'true', as any set of accounts will always be a matter of judgement. For example, a company should provide for bad debts, which means recognising the cost of the bad debts in its profit and loss account and reducing the value of debtors on the balance sheet. But how much it should provide is a matter for the directors' (reasonable) judgement.

◆ The degree of analysis that you will be able to undertake will be completely dependent upon the extent and quality of the data that you are able to obtain. You may need to revisit your financial analysis as more information becomes available during your discussions with a target.

◆ The numbers should be used to plan your actions for the future if you acquire the business by setting quantified and measurable financial targets for the business (e.g. reducing average debtor payment time to 45 days by the end of the first quarter) as part of your plan. You can then use the financial information to monitor your progress.

◆ But the actions you will have to take to make these financial results appear will be real actions in the real world, such as setting tight credit terms for the customers, issuing statements, picking up the telephone to chase in the money when it is due, and putting customers on stop if they don't pay.

UNDERSTANDING ACCOUNTS

Once you have found or been supplied with some accounts, you then have to make sense of them.

The accounts filed at Companies House will be in a standard format and include:

- **Auditor's opinion** – where required in larger companies, which should be a 'clean' opinion that the auditor is satisfied that the accounts represent a true and fair view of the company's position. Any qualification of this opinion should be a matter of extreme concern.

- **Profit and loss account** (or 'P&L' account) – a statement of how the business has traded over the period of the accounts and shows how much profit (or loss) has been generated. Unfortunately, smaller companies do not have to file a P&L account.

- **Balance sheet** – a snapshot at the end of the year of the company's assets and liabilities, although confusingly you cannot rely on this to provide you with an accurate reflection of the market value of all the types of assets at the year-end (for the reasons for this see Chapter 9).

- **Notes to the accounts** – which are vital to be able to understand the P&L and balance sheet, as for example these will include details of the company's accounting policies such as depreciation, which will affect both the profit for the period and the book value of the fixed assets at the period end.

In addition, some companies will attach a detailed P&L to the back of their accounts. Since the standard P&L included in the accounts filed actually shows very little information about the business's costs, I would recommend that even if you are not interested in that particular company, you should keep the example for use in later benchmarking of any targets where you obtain detailed accounts.

HOW ARE ACCOUNTS PREPARED?

The accounts which you will find filed at Companies House are prepared from the company's books and records in accordance with UK GAAP.

If you're not familiar with accounting practice there are two key underlying concepts that you need to be aware of to make sense of any set of accounts. These are the fundamental concepts of:

- ◆ prudence

- ◆ matching (also known as the 'accruals' basis).

Prudence

Accounts should be prepared prudently. This means firstly that they should not anticipate profit before it's been earned, so sales should not be recognised in turnover until the goods or services have been supplied and normally the invoice raised. At the same time losses should be recognised as soon as possible by providing for the costs or writing down any asset whose value has been impaired as soon as appropriate.

Matching

Accounts should also be prepared on the basis that costs should be matched to the relevant sales or periods. So for example if the company has bought three widgets during the year and has sold two of them, then the cost of the two that have been sold will appear in the profit and loss account as the costs of the goods sold, thereby matching the cost to the relevant sales during that period. The cost of the third will be carried forward as part of the stock in the balance sheet to be matched against the sales proceeds when it is sold at some point in the future.

In the same way, overhead costs should be matched to the relevant periods. So, for example, if the company is billed quarterly in arrears, for electricity but the year-end to which the accounts are drawn up comes two months through a quarter, then the company should accrue a cost in profit and loss and a liability in creditors (shown as an accrual) for two-thirds of a normal quarter's electricity bill.

This principle operates in reverse as well in that if, for example, the company has paid an insurance premium in January covering the 12 months of the calendar year, but it draws up accounts to the end of June, then it has actually paid six months of the following accounting year's costs during the current year. This is then dealt with by deducting half of the insurance premium paid from the cost in the profit and loss account, and showing this balance as an asset called a prepayment as part of the business's current assets, under the overall heading of debtors.

WHAT IS IN EACH PART OF THE ACCOUNTS?

Profit and loss account (P&L)

The company's profit and loss account will be made up of:

* **turnover** – the company's total sales that relate to the period (net of VAT)

* **costs of sales** – the costs to the company in buying in materials or producing things, of the goods or services that have been sold which make up the turnover

* **gross margin or gross profit** – the profit that the company has ade by selling the goods or services, before having to pay overheads

* **overheads** – the general costs that the company incurs by being in business (such as audit fee)

◆ **net profit** – the profit that the company has left after covering the overheads out of the gross profit.

You will find that the accounts may look slightly more complicated than this because, for example, interest and other financial charges will be set out separately while profit will be shown before and after tax.

Balance sheet

The company's balance sheet will consist of:

◆ **fixed assets** – such as property, plant and machinery or motor vehicles which the company owns and will use over a number of years

◆ any **investments** – in subsidiary companies

◆ **current assets** – such as debtors (or to use the American term, receivables), stock and cash in hand and at the bank

◆ **current liabilities** – all the creditors (or payables, in American parlance) which are due and payable within the next 12 months. This will include normal trade creditors, balances due to the Crown in respect of VAT or PAYE, the proportion of the capital of long-term loans, HP and leases that are due to be paid during this period, and the total of any bank overdraft as these are always repayable on demand

◆ **long-term liabilities** – all creditor balances due after longer periods than a year.

Net assets

The current assets and current liabilities form the working capital of the business, while the **net assets** is the sum of the fixed and current assets and investments, less the current and long-term liabilities.

The value of the net assets (which should be a positive number) will then match the value of the shareholders' funds, which consist of:

- the **share capital** – the funds introduced to the company by the shareholders

- the **retained profits** (or the P&L account) – which is essentially the sum of money left in the business from profits over the years

- any **other reserves** – such as will have been created by a revaluation of the company's property.

Notes to the accounts

The notes to the accounts will cover a number of areas such as giving more detailed breakdowns of the fixed assets, debtors and creditors. Particular notes to look out for are:

- The **accounting policies**, which set out some information as to how the accounts have been prepared such as the depreciation policy. You should ask yourself whether the policies set out seem reasonable for the business. If not, why not? Also be on the lookout for any changes in accounting policy, as this can be a means of manipulating the apparent profitability of the business. For example, depreciating a piece of machinery costing £100,000 over three years gives a cost of depreciation in the P&L of £33,333 per year. Changing the period to five years reduces this cost to £20,000 per year, and gives an instant profit improvement of £13,333 per year.

- Any note about **contingencies** is a warning that there are some potential liabilities such as outstanding warranty claims or perhaps legal proceedings which haven't been shown in the accounts as they are not considered likely enough in the current directors' judgement to need to be provided for. Your judgement might, however, be different.

◆ Anything about a **'defined benefit' or 'final salary' pension scheme**, which is one where employees' pensions are determined by length of service and their salary at retirement. In the aftermath of the Maxwell affair, the regulations to protect employees' pensions have become more stringent, with strict duties and timescales in respect of the payment across of pension contributions. New pensions legislation is becoming ever more draconian and tending towards making company directors as well as trustees potentially personally liable in the event of any shortfall in the fund for defined benefit schemes. It may be an oversimplification but if the business you are looking at has a defined benefit pension scheme, think very carefully before you consider buying it.

WHAT SHOULD YOU LOOK FOR IN THE ACCOUNTS?

The three key areas that you should measure and understand are:

◆ Profitability – does the business make money?

  – horizontal and vertical analysis

  – types of cost

  – gross profit, contribution and break-even

  – cost drivers

  – profit improvement

  – breaking the business down

◆ Financial stability – how risky are the finances?

– liquidity

– gearing

◆ Financial efficiency – how well is the business managing the cash it needs?

– stock turn and debtor and creditor days

– the working capital cycle

– source and application of funds

– return on investment.

UNDERSTANDING PROFITABILITY

Horizontal and vertical analysis

As a starting point in understanding any set of P&L accounts, 'horizontal' and 'vertical' analysis can be used to spot the trends in turnover and costs over time.

In horizontal analysis you treat year one as your base point of 100% and express the numbers in other years as percentages so that the level of change can be easily seen. This type of approach shows how revenues and costs are changing over time (but you must be careful to adjust for inflation effects over longer periods).

In vertical analysis you express the figures for each element of the P&L as a percentage of that year's sales. This shows how much of the business's sales each category of expenditure is consuming in each year.

Example

Company B

	Year 1 £000	Year 2 £000	Year 3 £000	Horizontal analysis – Year 1 = 100%		
Sales	100	110	120	100%	110%	120%
Cost of sales	50	60	70	100%	120%	140%
Gross profit	50	50	50	100%	100%	100%
Selling overheads	20	25	25	100%	125%	125%
General overheads	10	12	15	100%	120%	150%
Admin overheads	5	5	6	100%	100%	120%
Net profit	15	8	4	100%	53%	27%
Sales	100%	100%	100%			
Cost of sales	50%	55%	58%			
Gross profit	50%	45%	42%			
Selling overheads	20%	23%	21%			
General overheads	10%	11%	13%			
Admin overheads	5%	5%	5%			
Net profit	15%	7%	3%			

In the example above, from horizontal analysis you would want to know why general overheads have grown by 50% in three years.

But from the vertical analysis you can see that even so, general overheads are only 13% of sales. The more immediate issue is the increase of cost of sales to 58% of sales, from 50%.

This process can help you familiarise yourself with the company's performance and start to indicate some areas to investigate, particularly if you have information from other companies in the same sector against which to benchmark performance.

When benchmarking, use vertical analysis, which enables you to compare the relative percentages of different types of cost between businesses of different levels of turnover and see what that might be telling you about their relative levels of efficiency.

Types of costs

To really understand a business's profitability, you must, however, first understand the cost structure. There are essentially three types of costs for any business.

	Variable level of cost varies directly with level of production	**Fixed** do not vary in the short term as production fluctuates
Direct costs relate directly to the cost of producing goods for sale	raw materials piecework wages overtime pay factory energy costs	normal factory wages machinery costs and depreciation factory rent
Indirect costs general costs of being in business, not directly related to particular costs of production	—	auditors' fees sales staff's wages directors' fees

Fixed costs are of course not fixed in the long term (you can move factory or hire and fire factory staff) and will eventually reflect levels of production and activity.

The profit and loss account will, however, divide costs into only two broad areas:

♦ **costs of sales** (CoS) which will include all variable direct costs

♦ **overheads** which will include all fixed indirect costs.

Businesses differ as to how they deal with analysing **direct fixed costs** between costs of sales and overheads.

If they do not include all their direct costs in calculating their cost of sales, they risk underestimating their costs when it comes to setting prices or tendering for contracts. The result for companies of continuously selling at less than their true cost of manufacture (i.e. at a loss) is inevitably failure. It is generally best practice therefore to include direct costs as fully as possible in establishing costs of sales.

If the company's production volumes swing significantly between periods, however, you will need to be careful in using costs of sales to establish a meaningful 'contribution' figure for sales, and you may find it best to treat all fixed costs as overheads for the purpose of calculating break-even levels (see below).

Gross profit and break-even
One of the principal reasons that an understanding of the cost structure is important is the value of the gross profit and gross profit percentage, as these are used to calculate break-even.

> **Example**
>
> | | |
> |---|---|
> | Company C sells each widget for | £150 |
> | The cost of sales per widget are: | |
> | Raw materials | (£50) |
> | Labour and manufacturing costs | (£50) |
> | | ——— |
> | The gross profit per widget is | £50 |
> | | ——— |
>
> The gross profit percentage is 33.3% based on gross profit/sales of £50/£150.
>
> Company C has overheads of £1,000 per month. As its gross profit per widget (or 'contribution' towards covering overheads) is £50 per widget, it has to sell 20 widgets a month (£1,000/£50) before the total contribution is sufficient to cover all the overheads, or 'break-even'.
>
> The break-even turnover is therefore £3,000 per month (£150 × 20).

The above break-even has used 'accounting figures' based on costs taken from the profit and loss accounts. It is often useful to redo this exercise to calculate a 'cash break-even', stripping out the key costs that do not represent cash (e.g. depreciation) and replacing this with the real cash item (e.g. lease payments).

> **Example**
> Company C's overheads include a £100 depreciation charge and a £50 HP interest charge per month. In fact, the HP payment per month is £250 (£50 interest and £200 'capital' payment). So Company C's overheads restated on a cash basis are:

Overheads	£1,000
Less depreciation	(100)
Add capital payment	200
	————
	£1,100
	————

As a result the break-even turnover on a cash basis is 22 widgets or £3,300 per month.

Cost drivers

The relative level of a company's costs compared to its competitors will be due to a number of factors – some of the most common ones are listed below. If your analysis is suggesting that the business's costs are out of line with those of its competitors these are the areas where you might look for opportunities to cut expenditure as part of your consideration of the opportunity. Be alert, however, for the common pitfalls of poorly applied cost reductions, where disruption and other problems outweigh the planned saving.

Cost drivers include:

◆ **economies of scale** – sometimes bigger is better

◆ **capacity utilisation** – the company is paying for that plant and those people, whether they are earning for it or not

◆ **learning curves** – the more it does of something, the better at it the company should become

◆ **location** – relative local costs and transportation costs

◆ **purchasing** – how good at buying is the company?

◆ **operating efficiency**

◆ **investment** – e.g. in automation or training

◆ **waste management**.

Profit improvement

As you start to think about break-even calculations, something becomes very clear. To improve profits, you can do any or all of three things:

◆ increase turnover

◆ increase margin (gross profit percentage)

◆ reduce overheads.

And if you can do all three, the effects multiply.

Example

Company D		10% improvement	
Turnover	£1,000	+£100	£1,100
Gross profit %	50%	+5%	55%
Gross profit	500		605
Overheads	(250)	−25	(225)
Profit	250		380 =52% increase

Even in your initial screening of the businesses to be looked at you need to be thinking how you might be able to improve the profitability of any business once you take it over.

For example, a good management practice for ensuring that overheads are tightly controlled is 'zero based budgeting' where, rather than simply taking last year's costs and adding X% for inflation, you start with a blank sheet of paper and forecast each business cost on a line by line basis. Undertaking this exercise in respect of any business you buy is a good way to ensure that the requirement for all costs are questioned at least once a year!

Breaking the business down

To see what is happening to a business it is often helpful to break performance down by individual area (known as a 'profit centre'), at least at gross profit and contribution level, even if it is impractical to allocate overheads separately.

Example

Company E is an advertising agency designing adverts, booking space for clients and having brochures printed. The monthly management accounts show:

		£000
Sales		
	Media	60
	Printing	50
	Design charges	5
		———
		115
		———
Cost of sales		
	Press charges	51
	Printers	30
	Studio wages	4
	Studio direct costs	4
		———
		89
Gross profit		26
		———
Gross profit %		22.6%

But by breaking this down into different areas of activity ('profit centres'), a clearer picture emerges of where Company E does (and does not) make money:

	Media	Print	Studio
Sales	60	50	5
Cost of sales	(51)	(30)	(8)
Gross profit/(loss)	9	20	(3)
Gross profit %	15%	40%	(60%)

UNDERSTANDING FINANCIAL STABILITY

Liquidity

Liquidity is an indication of the business's likely ability to pay its liabilities. Quite simply it measures: Does it have enough cash?

The basic measure is the **liquidity** or the **current ratio** which divides the current assets by current liabilities:

$$\frac{\text{current assets (debtors, stocks and cash)}}{\text{current liabilities (trade creditors, VAT, PAYE, overdraft)}}$$

Simplistically, one would expect that a ratio of more than one would indicate financial stability, and significantly less than one would indicate problems. Whilst this is generally a safe working hypothesis, you must compare the ratio calculated against that of other businesses in the same industry, as in some sectors an apparent low liquidity is normal. As for all ratios covered in this chapter, what you need to know for any figures calculated is:

◆ whether for the industry, the ratio is relatively good or bad

◆ what the trend is over time (increasing or decreasing liquidity).

In order to generate cash at a known value, stock must first be sold. Stock is therefore less 'liquid' than debtors and cash and is therefore less reliable for meeting existing liabilities than these assets.

◆ The **acid test** measure of liquidity therefore excludes stock to see how readily the business can pay its immediate liabilities:

$$\frac{\text{debtors and cash}}{\text{current liabilities}}$$

Gearing

Gearing measures **how financially exposed the company** is by looking at to what extent the business's long-term finance is based on borrowed money rather than the shareholders' funds or 'equity':

$$\frac{\text{long-term loans}}{\text{total capital employed}}$$

Again, the importance of the figures lies less in the absolute number and more in how it compares to other businesses in the sector and the long-term trends.

As interest charges on long-term loans will need to be paid whatever the profits generated by the business, the higher the gearing (i.e. the greater the proportion of the business's long-term funding that is borrowed money), the higher the 'financial' risk of the business.

Example	Company G £000	Company F £000
Long-term loans	100	200
Shareholders' capital	200	100
	300	300
Gearing	33.3%	66.7%
Interest cost @ 10% pa	10	20

Company F must pay £20,000 per annum or default on its loan whilst the lower geared Company G only has to find £10,000 per annum out of profits.

A related measure is **interest coverage**, which shows the sensitivity of available profit in covering interest payments (e.g. to the bank):

$$\frac{\text{profit before interest}}{\text{interest}}$$

It is of course true to say that your purchase of this business is likely to significantly affect the level of gearing since you may end up completely restructuring the business's finances as part of the transaction.

UNDERSTANDING FINANCIAL EFFICIENCY

Stock, debtor and creditors days

Calculating how efficiently a company's working capital is being managed is a matter of calculating the stock, debtor and creditors days as below and comparing them to the competition. In each case you should take an average value for the assets or liability concerned.

$$\frac{stock \times 365}{purchases}$$ shows how long it is taking to 'turn over' stock

$$\frac{creditors \times 365}{purchases + VAT}$$ shows how long on average you are taking to pay your suppliers

$$\frac{debtors \times 365}{sales + VAT}$$ shows how long customers are taking on average to pay their bills

Monitoring the working capital cycle

A business's 'working capital cycle' should be a virtuous circle:

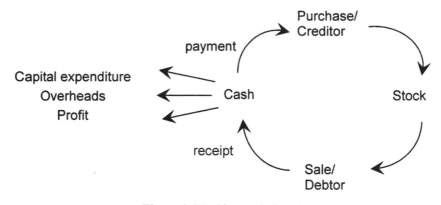

Figure 6. Working capital cycle

The degree to which a business requires financing in order to trade is determined by its actual terms of trade with its suppliers and customers.

Example
Company H only deals with one item at a time, and its current transactions are summarised below:

01/01	Purchases widget at £100 on one month's credit
31/01	Pays supplier for widget
28/02	Sells widget at 200% mark up on one month's credit
31/03	Customer pays £300

Plotting these transactions over time you can see how the borrowing requirement to fund this working capital cycle is £100 over two months:

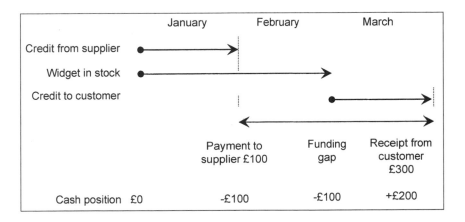

On average therefore it will be another month after the supplier wants paying for the goods before the company sells them, and a further month before, the cash comes in from customers. So company H has to fund two months' worth of working capital from somewhere.

A bank would see this as an appropriate use of an overdraft facility which will swing back into credit as the transaction unwinds into realised profit and cash. However, in practice Company H will need to:

◆ agree the facility in advance with the bank

- offer some other security such as personal guarantees, as the bank will be unlikely to lend against 100% of stock value without it.

Recognising the nature of the business's funding requirement is a critical first step to planning how you will manage its cash requirements by 'working capital management'.

Reducing the requirement to tie up cash in working capital will mean that cash will be available to fund a higher level of trading. In this case, were you to take over this business you might be able to reduce its borrowing requirements to nil by changing its trading:

- **Reduce the investment** in stock and debtors, e.g.:

  - if it only bought in the widget when it had a firm order and could ship it straight out (a 'back to back' deal), then the debtor would pay at exactly the same time as the creditor was due

  - if it only stocked what it could sell in a month for cash.

- **Replace bank lending with supplier credit** by taking three months', credit, which would match the date of receipt and payment.

- **Or a mixture**, e.g. take two months' credit from suppliers and only stock items which turn over in a month.

If you are anticipating expanding the business, you will need to ensure that you put in place the finance required to cover the funding gap as this expands with it. Businesses that expand faster than the financing is able to keep up with, eventually run out of cash and fail for this reason (known as 'overtrading').

Statement of source and application of funds
Profitability is all very well but it is actually cash that pays the
bills and sometimes it can be difficult to see whether the business
is actually generating cash or not.

A statement of source and application of funds (SSAF or 'Source
& Apps' and now more properly known as a cashflow statement)
can be used to demonstrate where the money has come from (the
sources) and gone to (the applications).

These are, however, notoriously difficult to get to balance and you
may find it easiest to ask your accountant to prepare one for you.

The beauty of the SSAF is that it provides a link that shows what
has happened to the profit generated by or introduced into the
business, as shown in the simplified example below.

Example

	Source £000	Application £000
Source of funds		
Profit	100	
Add back depreciation	50	
'Cash' generated from operations	150	
Other sources of cash		
Disposal of subsidiary	50	
Applications of cash		
Investment in plant & equipment		(250)
Net funds used during the period		(50)

Funded by	
Increase in creditors	25
Increase in overdraft	25
	50

Return on investment

The different activities of different parts of the business will generate different levels of profit and require different levels of investment in assets. They will therefore produce different rates of return.

Example

Company I has a manufacturing arm making widgets for sale to third parties, a fitting and servicing arm, and a repair division, each of which makes a net profit of 10%.

	Manu-facturing £000	Fitting & servicing £000	Repair £000
Assets employed			
Land & buildings	100	25	50
Plant & machinery	50	10	25
Stock	100	5	100
Debtors	150	30	20
Total assets employed	400	70	195
Sales	900	360	50
Profit	90	36	5
Return	22.5%	51.4%	2.5%

> On the basis of performance to date, an investment in developing the fitting and servicing business may generate over twice the return of investing in the manufacturing business.

This sort of information can allow you to judge where the available funds for investment should be best applied to the business so as to get the greatest level of return.

Occasionally this type of analysis will suggest that you may benefit from closing some aspects of the business and redeploying resources to areas where you'll get a high return. However, before planning to shut any operation you do need to be careful as you must ensure that you are not simply removing some contribution towards the overall overheads which will then need to be borne by the remaining parts of the business.

SUMMARY

Use this as a basic checklist of financial information to be obtained from the accounts of each business you are looking at:

	Answer	How is this changing over time?	Is this better, the same, or worse than comparable companies?
Company name		—	—
Date of accounts			
Accounts audited or not?			
Auditor name (if applicable)		—	—

	Answer	Changing?	Better/Same/Worse?
Is there a clean audit report?			
Have there been any changes in accounting policy?			
What is the turnover?			
Is the business profitable?			
What is its gross profit as a percentage of sales?			
What are its overheads as a percentage of sales?			
What is its net profit as a percentage of sales?			
What is its break-even point?			
Can you see any potential profit improvements?			

	Answer	Changing?	Better/Same/ Worse?
What is its liquidity ratio?			
What is its acid ratio?			
What are its debtor days?			
What are its stock days?			
What are its creditor days?			
From a statement of source and application of funds (or cash flow statement) is the business generating or absorbing cash?			

GOLDEN RULES

8. Do your research; be as well prepared as possible for your first visit.

Task
Prepare a financial information summary for each business on your current shortlist.

7

Approaching the Business

THE IMPORTANCE OF FIRST CONTACT

Once you have prepared your list of potential targets, which you have screened and prioritised on the basis of the available information, you then need to take the next step of actually approaching businesses to open discussions about a sale.

In doing so, to continue the house buying analogy, you need to be looking to arrange a viewing, on the basis of which, if the target appears to be what you are looking for, you will then want to agree an offer price with the seller.

Your detailed checking work or due diligence will then follow this agreement of an offer in the same way as your survey once you have agreed to buy a house. But be warned, your due diligence work and the preparation and sales contract which will run in parallel will be costly exercises, so before committing to this expense you need to be as certain as possible that:

◆ this is the business that you wish to buy

◆ the seller is really interested in completing a sale.

Until you have the opportunity to conduct your proper due diligence you are likely to have only a limited time to make enquiries and limited information on which to make a judgement, so it is important to be as focused as possible and make the most of any opportunities to understand the business as quickly as possible.

At the same time, if you are dealing with a business that was not formally for sale, you need to be taking every opportunity to sell both the idea of a sale, and yourself as the ideal purchaser to the business owner. Your first impression and approach to the business and its owner during this stage can be critical in deciding whether the owner will commit to a sale or not.

APPROACHING THE BUSINESS

When dealing with a business that is actively for sale the mechanism for an initial approach is relatively simple in that you need to respond to the advertisement or listing direct to the business or to its advisers.

In the first instance you would expect to receive further information about the opportunity in the form of a sales pack, which would typically contain information such as the following.

Business background

- Summary of the current nature of the business and apparent opportunities.

- Summary of the current and projected operating results.

- Summary of the current balance sheet.

- Summary of the ownership structure.

- Summary of the reasons for sale.

- If seeking investment, how much investment is required, what it is to be used for, what return the investor can expect and in what timetable.

◆ Risks facing the business and steps taken to address them by management (say in the form of a strengths, weaknesses, opportunities and threats or 'SWOT', analysis).

Market information
◆ Summary of products.

◆ Summary of markets and trends.

◆ Summary of customers.

◆ Summary of competitors.

◆ Summary of sales trends by product/market.

◆ Key competitive strengths.

◆ Assessment of competitors by product/market segment.

◆ Product/market segment growth and profitability.

◆ Branding.

◆ Sales staff.

Operations
◆ Product lines.

◆ Intellectual property.

◆ Suppliers and products.

◆ Management (including an organisation chart).

◆ Research and development.

◆ Opportunities identified (internally such as improved efficiency, and externally, such as new potential markets and products).

Assets

◆ Description of land and property.

◆ Description of plant and equipment.

◆ Description of data systems.

Appendices

◆ Current balance sheet, profit and loss account, forecasts.

◆ Product information and brochures.

◆ Summary CVs for key management personnel.

◆ Employee details (giving number of employees, length of service, and age, which allows calculation of potential redundancy costs).

◆ List of trademarks and patents.

◆ Detailed lists of land and buildings, and major items of plant and equipment.

Financial information in the body of the pack is normally kept as simple as possible, with the detail available in the appendices (which should tie up clearly and easily to the data in the main pack and be clearly cross-referenced). Look for information about the key assumptions underlying any forecasts or financial information.

Provision of a good comprehensive sales pack should enable you to get a long way down the road of assessing the business with a view to making an offer even before visiting the site.

APPROACHING A BUSINESS THAT IS NOT FOR SALE

Of course if you are looking at a business that is not formally for sale, then there will be no sales pack available. However, you are still going to need similar information in order to make a decision.

It might therefore be tempting to give the above list to the prospective target at an early stage and ask them to provide the information. In many cases this will be counterproductive as the task of preparing the information in a sales pack will usually have taken corporate finance advisers some time and some of the financial information will have been created from scratch.

Many business owners in the early stages of dealing with what is, after all, an unsolicited interest in buying their business are likely to react adversely to what will be seen as an onerous task and will not have been prepared by advisers to expect this as a request.

I would therefore suggest that you use this list as a checklist by all means but keep it private and focus on the specific areas that you believe are significant for you in respect of this particular business. Do not forget that once you have agreed a purchase price with the seller you are likely to move into a period of formal due diligence during which time your professional advisers will be reviewing the business's current and future performance and assets and liabilities in some detail, and any issues arising out of the due diligence process can be reflected in the final sales price negotiated.

Initiating contact

In the absence of any active marketing of the business by its owners, you will need to initiate contact. This is normally done by way of an approach letter to the major shareholder stating that:

◆ you are interested in making an acquisition

◆ you have identified their company as being of potential interest on the basis of publicly available information

- you have funds available with which to make an acquisition

- if this is of interest, you would like to arrange an initial discussion.

Such a letter can either come from you direct, in which case you are obviously giving away immediately your identity, or from your advisers. In any event you should obtain advice from your advisers as to the contents of any letter so as to ensure it complies with the relevant legislation.

Where your adviser is sending out letters they will tend to personalise them to produce a more tightly focused letter to go to a smaller group of target companies. Such a letter might go into much more detail as to why the adviser thinks this purchase might be a good fit and the adviser may even name their client.

THE FIRST MEETING

The initial meeting may take place at the company's premises, its advisers' offices or some neutral location such as a hotel.

Your objectives

Your objectives at this first meeting are broadly to:

- establish a personal rapport with the owner

- gather information about the business

- start to form a judgement on its attractiveness

- persuade the owners to sell (if it is not already being marketed)

- reach some kind of agreement with the owner as to how your interest can be taken forwards.

Obviously the degree to which you can progress each of the above objectives at the first meeting will vary significantly from situation to situation.

Questions to ask

While in every case you should be professional, businesslike and polite, it will be a matter for your judgement as to how to manage the meeting. If the business is obviously for sale then the two parties' agendas and roles are already quite clearly defined and you may wish to move the business agenda along quite quickly and be able to ask questions about the business and their motivation in selling. These might include:

◆ How long has the owner had the business? You want to know whether they have been in it for a long time or whether this is something that is quickly back on the market. If applicable, also ask what the business was like before they bought it and what changes they've made.

◆ What does the owner think are the pros and cons of this particular business, the threats to it to watch and the opportunities that are likely to present themselves?

◆ What has been the owner's approach to the business over the last few years and how would they see it developing after the sale?

◆ What role does the owner need to have in a social sense in interacting with customers or suppliers?

◆ To what extent is the existing owner critical to the operations and sales? How difficult do they think it will be for you to take over?

◆ Why is the business on the market? Many reasons for a business sale have nothing to do with the state of the business but are to do with the owner's circumstances, such as retirement, ill-health, or desire to move on to a new business. Some, however, clearly have implications for you as a

potential purchaser such as problems in the business, or a
desire to escape before major change.

♦ What does the owner want out of the sale personally, and for
their company, employees or management team? You may
need to judge whether for example, it would matter to them if
following a sale you relocated it or restructured its
significantly. Some owners are emotionally attached to their
businesses, seeing them as their life's work, and can be
determined that the company should continue on after them.

♦ Do they have children in the business? Do they want to ensure
they have a continuing role?

♦ Are they looking to stay with the business after the sale, either
permanently, or for a period, or are they looking for a clean
break and an exit? If so, what are they planning to do, retire or
go into another business?

♦ Do they want to retain any particular assets, such as the land
and buildings, or any particular contracts?

♦ If they are selling in order to help their main business develop,
what characteristics are they looking for in the purchaser?

♦ What sort of payment terms would be best suited to them and
their financial situation from a tax and pension planning point
of view?

♦ Will any sale require the consent of any third parties such as
franchisors, licensees or landlords, and does the owner
anticipate any problems with any such parties?

If the business is not for sale
If the business is not for sale then you are likely to have to take
the process more slowly as you will first need to get to know the

owner in order to both establish their confidence in you and to identify the arguments that may help persuade them to sell up. You'll also need to appreciate that they will need time to consider their position and response, and if necessary to take advice.

Important considerations
While you're conducting your initial discussions you need to remember the funnel principle outlined in Chapter 5 and be continually looking at a range of targets.

It's also important to remember that you need to ensure that the target is both really of interest to you and interested in selling, before getting as far as an offer. The real expenditure on professional fees in respect of a purchase starts immediately afterwards in the due diligence process, and you will want to avoid spending time and money on a prospect which then does not complete. It is essential therefore to be able to use these initial meetings to screen out targets that are unsuitable well before negotiating an initial offer.

I would always recommend that you adopt some form of standard approach to your reviews of businesses such as the one outlined in this chapter. Doing so gives a defined structure to your initial review which both helps to ensure that you do not miss anything, and makes it easier for you to compare various businesses.

UNDERSTANDING THE BUSINESS BEYOND THE NUMBERS
Having screened your target list on the basis of financial information before making an approach, there is a natural temptation to see the company simply in terms of what it contains, its balance sheet and profit and loss.

In some ways this is absolutely right as in a share purchase agreement you will be buying the company shell and all that it contains, while in an asset purchase agreement you will be buying specific assets from within it.

But it is also fundamentally wrong. No business exists in isolation and in fact businesses only do exist because they interact with the outside world.

Business as a process

Try to imagine the business as part of a process that brings value to the customers:

Suppliers ⇨	The Business ⇨	Customers
What your material and service suppliers provide from the raw material to the skills of your staff.	What you do with the resources you have to turn this into what the customers want. This is easiest to visualise for a straightforward manufacturing process but is as true for a distribution business turning bulk supplies into local deliveries, or a retail one turning pallet loads of consumables into individual tubes of toothpaste on the local shop's shelf where the customer wants them.	What the customers want.

Figure 7. Business as a process

If you think of the business in this way, you can see how embedded it is in an overall process and how dependent for its success it is on the strength of the overall flow of the transactions and its relationships with the other parties. If either end of this process starts to have problems, where does it leave the business in the middle?

It also vividly illustrates the view of many advisers in that the business's biggest asset is not on its balance sheet but walking around on two legs – its customers.

The other half of this observation, incidentally, is that a business's biggest potential liability is also not on its balance sheet but is also walking around on two legs – its employees.

In order to buy the business, you need to understand how it works, what the business does for its customers that adds value for them, and why customers buy from this business and not its competitors.

You therefore need to undertake what is essentially a basic review of the business's strategy and competitive position, to complement your review of its financial position, since it is this aspect which will drive the business's numbers. Only by doing so can you form a judgement as to whether this is an opportunity worth pursuing. The price you would wish to pay for it is based on the information supplied to you by management at this stage.

REVIEW CHECKLIST

Set out over the next pages is an outline checklist that you may wish to use to review the overall strategic position and strengths and weaknesses of the businesses that you are looking at in a consistent way.

Confidential

Target	
Contact	
First visit date	
Basis of valuation	
Target valuation	
Walk away valuation	
Offer made	
Decision	

1 Business background

What is the business?

Summary of the business's history
Summary of current ownership
Group structure (if applicable)
Products/services & markets (see 4)
Conclusion re business

Attach a copy of:

- the organisation chart
- financial summary from Chapter 6.

2 The owner

Who are you dealing with?

Personal details Age/married/single/children Qualifications Time with business	
Your impression of character	
Reason for selling	
Key requirements from a sale	
Preferred deal structure	
Other key shareholders?	
Third party consents required? Any issues?	
How critical to the business is the owner?	
Are they needed in the business afterwards? If so, how long?	
Advisers in place?	
Is the business privately owned or is it a quoted entity (even if only on OFEX)? Note that additional advice, time and costs will be required when dealing with the regulatory issues around any quoted business	
Estimated likelihood of completing	

3 Summary business healthcheck

Record an overview of the business.

Is the industry, sector or market going through significant change? ◆ See section 5, PEST analysis See section 6, Industry (Porter) analysis	
What is really different about the business, that makes people buy from it rather than its competitors? ◆ See section 7, Competitive advantage	
Does the business have a clear vision/strategy (does it have a map of where it is going?) Is it realistic? Is it a formal plan (can you obtain a copy)?	
Does the business know how it compares to its competitors? Does it use market research? Or benchmarking?	
Is it investing enough for the future (in training its people; upgrading its processes and spending on capital equipment, development of new products and marketing)?	
Does it have a strong enough management team with all the necessary functional skills? Does it work as a team? ◆ See section 8.	

Is the business going through any major change (e.g. high growth, a move of premises or a major acquisition) that is stretching its management and/or financial resources?	
Is it facing up to any necessary changes (e.g. bringing in external management experience where needed)? ◆ See section 9	
Is its financial management strong enough? ◆ Management accounts ◆ Budgets and forecasts ◆ Costings	
Has it got all its eggs in one customer or supplier basket?	
Are there hidden assets? ◆ Distribution channels ◆ People ◆ Intellectual Property Rights (IPR) ◆ Alternative property use or development potential (if so, does the business need to be in this building on this site?)	
Are there hidden liabilities? ◆ Employee costs under the Transfer of Undertakings Protection of Employment legislation (or TUPE) Warranties	

◆ Dilapidations (which might also be crystallised in the lease as a result of a change of control of the tenant company)	
Are there hidden risks not covered elsewhere? ◆ Licences ◆ Landlords ◆ Trademarks ◆ Litigation ◆ Market changes ◆ Environmental issues ◆ A 'big project'	
Is there really a business here to buy?	
How robust are the business's systems?	
How robust is the business's financial performance and stability?	
Is it suffering from some catastrophic event (e.g. a fraud, fire or flood)?	
Is it an attractive business to buy?	

4 Product/market matrix

What products or services does the business supply to what markets?

Market	Product A	Product B	Product C	Product D	Product E
1					
2					
3					

For each product/market, estimate:

◆ market size and rate of growth

◆ the business's percentage share of the market (and rate of growth)

◆ levels of profit generated

◆ value of assets employed.

5 Business environment

Are any changes happening or likely in the future that will significantly affect the industry/business?

Political – legislation	
Economic	
Social	
Technological	
Industry realignment	

6 Industry characterisation

How is the industry structured?

Who has the power in the market? suppliers? ◆ manufacturers? ◆ customers? Why?	
How easy is it for new competitors to enter the market?	
What alternative products exist for consumers?	
How intense is competition within the industry? ◆ growth? ◆ concentration? ◆ exit barriers?	
How rapid is growth in the industry?	
What is the basis of competition? ◆ price? ◆ quality? ◆ service? ◆ terms?	
Who are the key competitors?	
Are there any particular environmental or legislative risks?	

7 Competitive edge

Why do customers buy from the business? What are its strengths that give it an edge over the competition?

Is it better – how do the products differ significantly in the eyes of customers from the competitors?	
Is it cheaper – does the business produce/sell at significantly lower costs than its competitors?	
Is it different – does it meet the needs of any particular group(s) of customers significantly better than its competitors?	
Which if any of the above is the basis of its current strategy?	
Is this sustainable in the future? Why? (Can it be copied?)	
How does the business market and sell its products? What is its strategy on: ◆ price? ◆ promotion? ◆ packaging? ◆ place (how customers can actually buy)?	
What particular strengths/advantages does it have in comparison with its competitors?	

◆ efficient operations? ◆ technology? ◆ special know-how? ◆ market reputation/customer loyalty? ◆ captive markets? ◆ ownership of distribution channels? ◆ control over supplies?	
Has it been investing enough in protecting its position to sustain its advantages into the future?	
In what ways are its competitors stronger (and why)?	
What are the key constraints on the business? ◆ markets? ◆ people? ◆ finances? ◆ operations?	
What is the attitude towards the company of: ◆ key suppliers? ◆ customers? ◆ staff? ◆ the bank?	
Are there any key suppliers/customers that will need to be retained to make the business a success?	

8 Management team

Which members of staff make up the management team? Who is responsible for which aspects?

	Name	Qualification	Responsibility
Chief Executive			
Operations			
Sales			
Finance			
HR			
IT			
Other key			

Obtain an organisation chart. As you review the business, judge how accurately it reflects what actually occurs in the business day to day.

How well do the management team appear to communicate with each other and the staff? Do they operate as a team?

Are there any key staff whose departure would hurt the business? What do you need to do to retain them?

9 Business issues

What are the main issues facing the business?

What are the key issues and challenges facing the business?	What are the critical factors for the business to achieve success?

CONFIDENTIALITY

To make any progress in moving towards a purchase you will need to obtain confidential information about the company's affairs. Before long you should therefore expect that the owner will require you to sign a confidentiality letter or non-disclosure agreement (NDA) in respect of any information that they are going to give you.

This is not an unreasonable request and in practice maintaining confidentiality is actually normally as much in your interests as the prospective purchaser as it is in the seller's. Remember that until there is certainty as to the sale being completed, any knowledge that discussions about a sale are underway will almost invariably have an adverse impact on the business. If, for example, employees find out that a sale is being contemplated, this can only cause them uncertainty about their future and the future of the business. This will be communicated to both the customers and the suppliers, who will also become concerned about the prospects and future of the business, and also to its competitors, who will seek to take advantage of the situation by poaching good staff and customers.

Other than individuals who actually need to be brought into the loop, sellers will only want to inform their staff about the deal once it is agreed, at which point they can announce the name of the buyer and can also provide staff with security as to the timetable for any changes and knowledge about what to expect.

You may therefore find that a certain amount of 'cloak and dagger' tactics will be employed to maintain confidentiality. A meeting and a tour of the plant may be arranged under a variety of pretexts (for example you may have to pretend to be prospective customers who want to meet with the senior management and also tour the premises). Key information that you will need to review in detail can be provided through a data room arranged off-site, say at the office of the seller's advisers, where if necessary follow-up meetings can also be held.

A confidentiality agreement can take the form of either a formal non-disclosure agreement, as in the example, in Appendix A on page 423, or a less formal confidentiality letter (for an example of such see page 115 of *Selling Your Business For All It's Worth*).

GOLDEN RULES

9. Understand why the seller is selling – how serious are they?
10. Only deal with serious sellers.
11. Don't buy on numbers alone, understand what the business is and what it does for its customers. 'Why do people want to buy from this business and not its competitors'? is the most important question of all.

Task

Prepare a checklist in respect of each business you are looking at.

8

What is it Worth?

THE IMPORTANCE OF REALISTIC VALUATIONS AT THE OUTSET

Private sellers will often not have a good idea about what their businesses are likely to be really worth unless they are being formally advised by experts.

Comparisons with listed companies

For example, a seller familiar with the financial press might have looked at the price earnings ratios quoted for listed firms in his industry and used these to multiply his current earnings to estimate a value. However, a moment's thought can show that this exercise is unlikely to give a realistic valuation as:

◆ it's difficult to find any quoted company that would have exactly the same mix of operations as the business being valued

◆ a quoted business has access to both capital and liquidity in the financial markets; the small business does not

◆ investors also have greater liquidity in that they can sell the shares effectively whenever they wish and so are not risking being tied into a specific business long-term

◆ the increasingly onerous corporate governance rules covering listed businesses in theory provide investors with greater safety.

Each of which means that the value of a listed business cannot readily be equated to that of an unquoted owner managed company.

Potential problems

It will come as no surprise to say that many deals fall apart over price. Three typical problems that you may encounter with sellers are set out below:

1 Unrealistic expectations can occur where business owners either have unrealistic expectations as to the multiple of earnings that can be achieved or apply a multiple to an unrealistic level of earnings.

Example

A well-established, stable, cash generative and profitable business was generating a net profit before drawings of £100,000 per annum and the two directors valued the business on the basis of five times multiple to give a value of £500,000. They were then surprised to find the business did not sell.

What they had failed to realise was that any individual purchaser needed to adjust the level of earnings to cover, for example:

◆ a salary to cover the work done by one of the directors who would be going

◆ the likely ongoing interest cost of the finances that needed to be raised.

Thus, while the multiple of five for buying a stable profitable business was not unreasonable, the level of ongoing net earnings to which the multiple should have been applied was probably closer to £50,000 per annum.

---

2 Completely unrealistic expectations can occur when a seller does not realise what a buyer will and will not pay for.

For example, some sellers suffer from the condition known as 'banker's fallacy', that because the business has cost me X to set up (even though it is not actually making any money) it must be worth X to somebody else. Of course as a buyer the amount of sunk costs or sweat and tears put in by the seller are completely irrelevant. All you should be interested in is how much money in future profits you are going to get as a return on your investment in buying this business, and whether this return justifies the risk.

3 In some cases sellers have simply not thought through the implications.

You may find that at some point they realise that they 'cannot afford to sell', as discussed on page 86.

As a buyer you are therefore probably in the longer run better off if the seller has had some professional advice about valuation early in the process. You will not wish to waste time taking your review of the prospective purchase too far only to find that there is no realistic prospect of the seller agreeing a reasonable price for the business.

HOW DOES PRICE RELATE TO RISK FOR EITHER SIDE?

Most sellers' objectives in a sale are a mix of:

◆ maximising the cash received on the sale

◆ minimising the tax suffered

◆ a variety of emotional issues such as the security of their employees' future or the company that they regard as their legacy.

In contrast, the buyer's priorities are usually:

♦ to minimise the cash paid out on the sale

♦ while minimising the risk taken in making a purchase, which usually implies a wish to buy the business and assets rather than the corporate shell.

If the above two paragraphs seem to have made eminent sense, it's probably worth noting that both the buyer's and seller's priorities have been expressed in terms of cash, not price. As will be seen, however, in a business sale terms are clearly as important as price and much of the discussion of terms will focus on the issue of certainty. Remember that:

♦ the seller is looking for maximum certainty, by way of the cash outcome

♦ the buyer is looking for maximum certainty, by way of minimisation of the risks being acquired.

The more certain that the seller can make you feel about the business, such as by giving warranties, the more you ought to be comfortable paying them for the business.

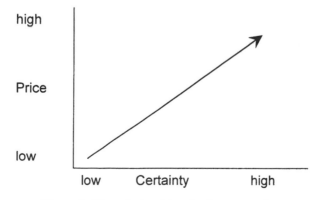

Figure 8. The relationship of price to certainty

And so the buyer and the seller have a mutual interest in establishing as much certainty in the deal as possible – which means as little risk for the purchaser as possible.

VALUATIONS ARE VALUELESS

The fundamental reason for you to buy a business and the one which drives most consideration of valuation is to make money from it.

Business valuation is a mix of art and science and how much you or other prospective buyers will be prepared to pay can depend, not only on the nature and finances of the business to be bought, but also on the nature and finances of the buyers.

You might think for example that all buyers will be taking a fundamentally similar view of the attractiveness of the business and any difference in valuation might therefore simply reflect the differing degrees of confidence that the buyers have in the prospect of the business.

Strategic reasons

This would, however, be to ignore the fact that a particular business may simply be fundamentally more attractive to one buyer than another for strategic reasons. For example, as a buyer looking to purchase a stand-alone business for the first time, you might be in competition with another buyer who is looking to buy the business as a bolt on acquisition to improve their existing business by:

- rapidly entering a new market

- rapidly increasing market share in an existing market

- taking out a competitor

- acquiring a new technology or significant asset.

Any of the above reasons may mean that the other buyer is willing to pay a premium over any normal valuation to acquire this particular business.

In fact in some extreme cases, depending upon their reasons, the amount of money they are prepared to pay for a business bears absolutely no relation to any 'normal' valuation of the business. Three examples of real sales illustrate this point.

Example – The strategically important niche
The business manufactured a basic commodity product, the characteristics of which tended to mean that in any particular geographical area that there would only be one supplier, as a result of both the scale of operation required and the costs of moving finished goods over long distances.

◆ The industry had therefore grown up based on a network of independent producers, each dominant in their own local territory but now consolidating. Essentially there were two big players who were expanding by purchasing the local operators. One consolidator was expanding from south to north, the other was moving from west to east.

◆ This particular business was in the Northeast and was the last independent operator. Acquiring this last niche became firstly a strategically important objective and secondly, and probably more decisively, a matter of pride for the respective CEOs.

Example – The hidden asset

The business manufactured and sold a type of drinks dispenser together with the consumables supplied to go into it. It was a relatively small operation that was essentially a one-man band and the owner ran it as a 'lifestyle' business. The business was sold in a relatively straightforward way and the seller was pleased to obtain a significant premium over the value he was expecting. Effectively, however, the new owners were not actually interested in the business he was running. They supplied a whole range of office products and consumables and simply wanted this business because of its network of contacts and contracts that made it a ready channel to market their other products.

In some cases commercial logic and questions of return on the investment just go out the window.

Example – Pride and prejudice

How much would you pay for a collapsed toilet paper manufacturer in a third world country where the machinery was in such a poor state that it could no longer reliably put the perforations into the rolls? How about three times the value of the next bid?

Why would anyone pay this much? For this buyer it was simply the pleasure of revenge.

Under the country's old regime, the business, in the buyer's view, had effectively been stolen away from him by someone with better political connections. So when it went bust, and was available to be purchased at a price that was (for him) a bargain, it represented a chance to get his revenge by rubbing his rival's nose in the dirt.

The moral of these stories is that different buyers would ascribe different values to a prospective target, depending upon the circumstances and nature of their own business. If you find yourself in competition with a buyer who appears to be willing to pay over the odds for such a reason, do not allow yourself to be forced into overpaying just to beat them. It's better to let this one go – there will be future targets. You should avoid overpaying on the basis of the value the business could have to somebody else, but where you cannot realise that value. Buy in haste, repent at leisure is sadly as true in the world of corporate finance as elsewhere.

Valuing issues

◆ As has already been illustrated, putting a value on a private business is a particularly difficult exercise. Whilst a publicly listed company will be valued every day by the stock markets of the world, no actively traded market exists for the particular business that you are interested in until the day it is put up for sale.

◆ There are, however, a variety of normal financial approaches used to value businesses which will give a range of possible valuations depending on the assumptions used. The detailed bases of these approaches to valuation are given in Chapter 9.

When looking at valuations of target businesses prepared by your advisers, always remember that at best a valuation is an opinion (i.e. a best guess) as to what someone will pay. The only true valuation with any real meaning is the deal that is actually eventually done, when you or someone else puts their hand in their pocket to pay for it, which as shown above may sometimes reflect issues that are completely outside a normal valuation basis.

THE VALUE OF VALUATIONS

Nevertheless you will find that you will need to estimate the value of the target businesses you are looking at, not only for the obvious reason of deciding how much to offer, but also as part of your work in raising finance for the venture and because you must expect that the seller and their advisers will have conducted such an exercise in order to formulate both a target sales price that the seller is looking to achieve, and a drop-dead price below which they will not sell.

Obviously if you can have a realistic view as to these amounts then you will be at an advantage in negotiating price with the seller.

In addition, the process of conducting a valuation may help in:

♦ identifying assets or parts of the business which you might not want and which you can exclude from the sale to reduce either the risk, or the price, or both

♦ understanding the price that competing bidders might be prepared to pay for the business

♦ identifying significant financial risks in the business

♦ helping formulate your plan for financing the purchase

♦ acting as an aid for discussion with the seller's professional advisers.

Valuations should generally all be done on a 'cash now' basis, to enable easy comparison from one basis to another. Of course this may not necessarily reflect the actual cash value of the eventual deal, as the payment terms of the actual deal done may differ significantly from an all-cash offer.

Setting a target price
In the same way that a well advised seller will have both a target price and a drop-dead price, so you too should have a target

price that you are looking to pay for this business and a walk-away price above which you are not prepared to do the deal.

Once you have achieved your target price this gives you the basis on which to decide whether to continue to negotiate in the hope of striking a deal at a price that is significantly better than your target price, or whether it is better to now move to capture the value you have obtained in achieving your target price by seeking to close the deal. Given the difficulties experienced and effort you have to put in to find the right target, it is in general better to seek to close the deal once you have achieved your target price than to continue to negotiate. Don't blow a good deal by being too greedy; or blow the goodwill of the seller, which you may need both to close the sale and to make a success of the business once you have bought it, by attempting to screw every last drop out of the price.

WHAT IF THE SELLER HAS SET A HIGH ASKING PRICE?

In some cases you will be dealing with a business that you have approached, which has no published asking price attached to it. In other cases you will be responding to an advert seeking to sell the business which may state a specific asking price.

If there is a published price of the business and it is significantly in excess of your estimate of the business's valuation, it may be worth asking the seller to explain why such a high price has been put on the business.

You may, however, want to take this as a warning sign that the seller is not serious about selling. There are a surprising number of business owners who take a view that the business is always for sale but only for silly money. You do not want to waste your time dealing with people who are not serious. So if this appears to be the case you should move on to another target.

You shouldn't forget it altogether, however, as setting a ridiculously high price can be a major mistake for the seller. It may well scare away many potential buyers and send out the message that the seller is not serious.

The effect of this is that the business is likely to remain for sale for quite some time. This will tend to further put off potential buyers as the market will start to consider that there must be something wrong with a business which is not selling.

If and when the seller becomes serious about their need to sell, they will therefore have 'spoilt their market' and be unable to get buyers to take them seriously.

It's probably therefore worth going back to contact highly overpriced businesses, where the number of prospective other buyers is likely to be low, say six months later, to see if the owners are starting to get desperate about selling.

IT'S RUDE TO TALK ABOUT MONEY

As a general rule you should always be looking to open negotiations by asking the seller to tell you how much they want for the business.

For example, you might approach a company that you are interested in buying and ask the owners how much they want. A typical owner-manager's first response will generally be to speak to their accountant, who as an adviser to a small to medium-size business will not normally be a corporate finance expert or particularly experienced in business sales.

- ◆ The accountant is likely to give some very generic advice to the client in terms of a multiple, and on that basis the owner will often start to talk to you on the basis that: 'My accountant thinks my business is potentially worth £X.'

◆ The result is that £X becomes the starting point from which you can look to negotiate the price downwards by focusing on both the credibility of the multiple used and the sustainability and quality of the earnings to which it has been applied, hopefully with the result that the business is sold for something significantly less than £X.

In contrast, many professional sellers of businesses such as corporate finance advisers are more likely to take the line: 'My clients are interested in discussing the sale of their business to you, and would like you to make an offer for it.'

◆ The result of this approach is that in order to proceed, you will be forced to give an indication of either how much you're prepared to pay, or the basis on which that sum will be calculated, which may of course be greater than the sum the seller was actually willing to accept.

◆ As with all negotiations, it is usually best to wait for the other party to mention price first so as to avoid under- or over-offering and to get some indication of their possible range of values.

BASES OF VALUATIONS

There are six broad bases of valuations, many of which are interlinked. These are:

◆ **Asset valuation** – the total of the value of all the individual assets, tangible and intangible, in the business.

◆ **Market valuation** – a comparison against the prices achieved for other businesses that have sold recently.

◆ **Discounted cashflow** – takes estimates of cash to be generated by the business in future years and uses accounting techniques to discount these back to a present value (or an implied internal rate of return that investing in the purchase of the business will generate for the acquirer).

◆ **Return on investment** – essentially creates ratios of either the return (the earnings that the purchaser will achieve) divided by the price they pay for the business, or the price/earnings ratio (which is the price they pay for the business divided by the current earnings stream) which shows how long it will take to repay the investment.

◆ **Sector specific** – particular sectors will have their own rules of thumb about how to value a business based on the characteristics of the business (e.g. the number of beds in the hotel, pub barrelage, value of mineral reserves, multiples of fee income).

◆ **Basic multiple** – as a rule of thumb businesses with certain characteristics will be valued at a certain multiple of earnings.

These valuation terms are explained in more detail in Chapter 9.

WHAT IS FOR SALE?

In order to look sensibly at the valuation, however, you first need to consider the fundamental question: 'What is actually for sale?' There are three key considerations that affect this.

What type of sale will it be?

There are two principal methods either by which you can buy an incorporated business (i.e. a limited liability company). These are either to acquire the company by buying its shares, or to buy the business and assets that the company owns from it.

◆ While this raises a number of issues, for the purpose of considering valuation at this stage, it is enough to note that for tax reasons the owner will generally prefer to sell you shares (i.e. the company).

♦ However, you will generally wish to buy the business and assets from the company, rather than the company itself, as this allows you to acquire the individual assets at 'fair value' for incorporation into your new business's balance sheet; and also helps to minimise your risk as it reduces the potential for taking on unknown or **contingent liabilities** as part of the deal.

If you agree to buy the company shares rather than just its business and assets, you are also buying a package of its liabilities. At the same time, the seller is obtaining an important tax advantage. You may therefore wish to seek a corresponding discount on the price you would be prepared to pay to obtain the business and assets without the baggage of the company.

What assets are included?

The second principal consideration affecting value is what actually is for sale. For example, it is not uncommon, particularly in say retirement sales of family owned businesses, for the property from which the business is operated to be retained by the existing owner and to be rented to the new business.

This can be an advantage to the seller as it provides them with an ongoing income, but equally it will obviously reduce the value of the business, as the future earnings will now have to take into account payment of rent.

What liabilities are you buying?

The existing owner/manager may well have had to guarantee some of the company's borrowings, such as an overdraft, or perhaps leases. When they sell the business to you they will not unnaturally wish to ensure that any such guarantee is lifted, either by clearing the debt to which it relates or by the personal guarantee liability being successfully taken over by the new owners. Therefore the impact of a commitment to repay the overdraft, or settle the outstanding leases, is part of the deal, and will need to be factored into the valuation (and into your estimates of the funds you are likely to be able to raise), together with the impact of meeting over time the company's normal business obligations such as payment of existing trade creditors.

IS IT REALLY A BUYABLE BUSINESS?

There are many successful businesses providing their owners with a good income but which are fundamentally unsaleable, as the business is essentially inseparable from the person running it.

An example of this might be a consultancy based on an individual's personal network and reputation as an expert in their field. Such a business probably has no life outside of the individual consultant and their skills and contacts. Therefore there would really be nothing in such a business for you to buy, as on the person's retirement those people who had come to them because of their contacts, specialised knowledge or reputation, will have no real reason to come to you.

Nevertheless such businesses will often have quite a powerful niche presence or name in their particular industry and so the owners often expect to be able to sell them at a good value.

Transferring knowledge, contacts and reputation

◆ If you are interested in buying such a business you will in practice have to work closely with the owner for a considerable period either before or after the sale to 'institutionalise' their knowledge or contacts into the business so that the business has some life outside of the old owner.

◆ So, for example, if the business is based around their personal contact network, you need to take steps to formalise this network into some form of database, setting out which customers and contacts provide which sort of lead or service. This would have to be matched with a contact programme whereby the old owner introduces you to their contacts as their heir apparent and, importantly, actively sells the idea to them that in the seller's absence they should contact you.

♦ Developing this idea further, the seller may then consider engaging sales staff in order to use this contact database and generate more income independent of the seller's personal working of the network. From this they can look to develop the business's brand name such that people who aren't directly known to them or who come across the business through third parties or through reputation will start to use it.

♦ Similarly, if the business is built around some specialist knowledge, again in order to have something which is worth buying, this will need to be institutionalised into a database of information, operating systems, processes, or some other mechanisms whereby the value of what the owner knows can be transferred to you.

♦ In practice the people for whom such businesses have a value are those already in the business and starting to make the contacts or acquire the knowledge as employees or junior partners, who may then buy the owner out over time.

Protecting the company's knowledge base
Of course, for the existing owner there are significant risks in moving from a one-man band to a business with a structure and a greater number of employees in this way. Not least, where they are attempting to transfer the knowledge or some of the contacts which form the basis of their business into a form that can be transferred to others, there is obviously a risk that departing employees may take some of this knowledge or some of the

contacts with them. This obviously also ought to be a concern to you as a buyer, as you do not wish to purchase the business only to find that much of the value can disappear if staff go.

As a result, part of the process of protecting what is being done to make the business transferable is to ensure that all staff have signed proper terms and conditions which include restrictive covenants to prevent them exploiting knowledge if they leave.

Setting up an 'earn-out'
These sorts of cases are ones where there is no real alternative but to structure the sale by way of an **earn-out**, where payments to the old owner are dependent upon the profits generated going forwards. This means they have an incentive to work closely with you for the period of the earn out to make the transfer a success.

DEALING WITH A MIXED BAG
What if there are parts of the business to be acquired which you in fact do not want?

You can of course firstly attempt to exclude them from the sale. Depending upon the business's structure it may or may not be relatively simple to separate out the operations. If, for example, the operations that you do not want are held by a specific subsidiary this could easily in theory be excluded from the sale. I say in theory, however, as in most cases the seller will want to sell the whole business in one transaction and will be very resistant to an attempt to 'cherry pick' particular parts, leaving them with remnants that may be difficult to sell.

Of course this is a generalisation and there may be circumstances where an owner is happy to retain particular parts of the business – for example to give them an ongoing income.

If, therefore, you are involved in a situation where part of the price of acquiring the business that you want to buy is that you acquire operations or assets that you do not wish to keep, do not despair.

In fact in some cases the planned disposal of these unwanted elements of the deal can be used to generate significant amounts of cash. Indeed in some exceptional circumstances, disposals of the unwanted elements have been known to almost refund to the buyer the total cost of the acquisition, leaving them with the business they want to buy for a very small net payment.

It is therefore important, as part of your pre-completion planning, and something which can start at the valuation stage, to identify those parts of the business which are to be disposed of, and put in place a plan to realise them effectively for the maximum value as swiftly as possible.

This can, however, present a very real potential dilemma for your post-acquisition planning. To get maximum value from such disposals you need to have your best people working on them. These businesses will require very effective short-term grooming in order to maximise their value, while your managers handle a very compressed sales process, at the same time ensuring that the business to be disposed of continues to operate at the best achievable level.

This is a distraction, since what you really want your best people to be doing is taking over the parts of the business that you want to keep to ensure that these are quickly and successfully integrated into your own operation (which was, after all, surely the purpose of making the acquisition).

An effective way of dealing with this problem is to engage the services of an experienced business seller specifically to manage this part of the project as a self-contained exercise (such as Resolution Inc's PART service, see page 381), allowing your key managers to focus on the true integration project.

GOLDEN RULES

12. Decide on your target and walk-away price and stick to it.
13. Trade price for certainty; the riskier the business is, the less it is worth to you.
14. First one to mention a price loses.

9

Valuation Techniques

DO YOU NEED TO KNOW ABOUT VALUATIONS?

You may well feel that business valuations are a technical matter which you would like your professional advisers to undertake so that you can rely on what they produce.

While I do not believe that you need to become a master of all the technicalities of valuations, I do think that as it's your money that you will be paying to buy a business based on a valuation generated, you need to understand the basis on which they are put together. Each approach has its own strengths and weaknesses which you need to be aware of; familiarity with the techniques will help you deal with your professional advisers.

For those who would prefer to avoid the detail, however, a summary of the principal methods is set out at the end of this chapter.

RESTATEMENT OF EARNINGS

The first thing to appreciate is that most valuations are based on estimates of future earnings. It may come as a surprise in looking at these that both the sellers and your professional advisers will almost always make significant adjustments to both past and projected earnings information received from the target company. This is a normal part of the process and nothing to be concerned about.

Business owners, particularly in small or family owned companies, are not normally motivated to manage their company's results to demonstrate high profits. Instead, they generally seek to manage their business and earnings in such a way as to minimise the tax payable, and it is fair to say that the degree to which business owners will 'manage' the figures to reduce the amount of tax they have to pay ranges from the completely legitimate, to the marginal, and right through to the completely illegitimate.

Grooming the business

If they have been well advised, the seller will have been working with their professional advisers, over a period of time leading up to putting the business on the market, on what is known as 'grooming' the business for sale.

In some ways the grooming process should help you as a buyer since the activities will include making sure that all the paperwork is in order so that the due diligence process encounters as few problems as possible. At the same time the seller will be looking to manage the business so that it shows as valuable a profile as possible when they come to sell.

In preparing figures for you to look at, they will also therefore be looking to adjust the results to show as high a level as possible of underlying sustainable profit, and hence to persuade you that you should pay a high price for the business.

The normal sorts of profit management that might be adjusted for include:

◆ salary for the owner set at a high level so as to soak up all available profits and avoid double taxation, or for family members working in the business (e.g. spouses)

- high levels of fringe benefits for family members, such as expensive cars

- above market rents charged to the company for use of property owned by the owner or their family personally.

In addition to the above, business owners may well also have been undertaking practices such as:

- paying salaries to family members who have absolutely nothing to do with working in the business

- charging personal expenditure such as pleasure trips to the business

- putting assets bought for personal use (such as a home computer) through the company, etc.

To obtain a realistic picture of the sustainable level of earnings of the business, the sellers' advisers will therefore be looking to strip out all such elements and where appropriate, replace them with reasonable open market estimates of, for example, a director's salary, as someone has to run the business, and market rent for the building.

Similarly, your advisers will be looking to ensure that all costs are taken into account on a realistic basis going forwards. So, for example, if the owners have not been charging the business for certain costs then these will need to be provided for in assessing likely profitability going forwards, as well as any financing costs that the business will need to bear as a result of the sale.

IN THE BLACK
And finally, in thinking about the quality of earnings when considering the business's value, you should only pay for what

you can see. Your valuation must therefore only include easily recognisable and traceable streams of income.

So what happens if the owner tells you that the business has significant earnings that are not going through the books? My view is that the discovery of this sort of issue should cause you to seriously think about walking away from the sale completely, because the obvious questions are:

- How can you audit and rely on these claimed receipts? After all, you certainly won't be able to sue the seller later if it turns out not to be true.

- How do you know there aren't matching liabilities that aren't on the books?

- What else is not on the books?

- Do you really want to buy a business which might be subject to a significant tax investigation at some future point?

- What happens when you take over? If you keep income off the books you are laying yourself open to all sorts of tax problems. If you put it all through the books, sooner or later the tax authorities are going to notice the significant change, which may cause them to ask questions.

You should also remember that under current legislation, if your professional advisers become aware of any grounds for suspicion of any activity that comprises tax avoidance, they are now under a duty to report this to the National Criminal Intelligence Service or face criminal proceedings that can land them in jail. So if you know, the chances are your advisers will know, and if your advisers know, the police and tax authorities will do so very shortly afterwards.

Overriding all of this must of course be the thought what you really want in a business you are buying is certainty about what you are getting. And if you can't trust the existing owner, then you shouldn't be buying the business.

ASSET VALUATION

Since you are acquiring the assets of the business, the value of these is a logical place to start in valuing a business.

Indeed, for businesses that are loss making or that have failed, this is normally the fundamental basis on which a liquidator's valuations are based, because if the company is loss making, it has no stream of profits to multiply or project in order to generate any of the other forms of valuation.

There are essentially three bases of valuation of assets that you may see referred to. These are **book value**, **going concern** and **forced sale value**.

Book value

Book value represents the total value of all the assets (net of the relevant liabilities) as stated in the company's accounts. It is also referred to as **net asset value** or **net worth**.

However, you should never confuse these accounting 'values' with real values. Accounts are based on a convention of historical cost, which means that an asset is booked into the company's accounts when it was bought. It will then have been subject to depreciation to write the cost of the asset off over its useful life. The net book value of that asset in the accounts is therefore its original cost less the depreciation charged against it over the years since it was bought. The resulting 'book value' may be accurate from an accounting point of view, but you cannot rely on it bearing any resemblance to the open market value of the asset involved.

The Royal Institute of Chartered Surveyors (RICS) publishes guidelines on preparation of valuations known as the 'Red Book'.

MARKET VALUATION

Going back to the house buying analogy in the introduction, this approach is somewhat akin to valuing a house for sale. To find a reasonable estimate for a property's value, all you normally have to do is look in the property pages of local newspapers and find houses in a similar area of the same size to work out the average price for a house with the same number of bedrooms. It is then a matter of making any adjustments needed for the decorative state, potential, land, or any other special features of the particular property in question.

Similarly, with many businesses, by looking at the trade press or by contacting professional valuers specialising in the industry, you should be able to identify a number of businesses that have sold and the prices achieved in the recent past to form a view on values.

Using price/earnings ratios

As discussed in the last chapter, you might also consider the value of publicly traded businesses in the industry as a guide, based on the ratio of their price (business value) to earnings (profits), or **P/E ratio**, as published in the *Financial Times* and other financial press. As already shown, however, there are many weaknesses with this approach. If you do wish to use it, additional points to be careful of include:

♦ The earnings figure on which any calculation should be based should be the **sustainable earnings figure**, that is to say one that has been adjusted to remove some of the items described, but also needs to reflect the realistic prospects of the business.

◆ Ensure that you are **comparing like with like** as you will find that most P/E multiples published will be based on earnings after tax. Applying an after tax P/E ratio to a pre-tax earnings figure will obviously give you an inflated valuation.

◆ Most publicly quoted companies will be of a scale significantly different to a private company and again the **scale of operation** and perceived reduction in risk means that an investor is likely to accept a higher P/E ratio in a publicly quoted company than in a private one.

◆ As has already been discussed, public companies are under pressure to manage their figures so as to show good earnings for their shareholders, whilst private companies are not motivated to maximise earnings on paper, as this tends to result in tax that owners would rather not pay. Therefore the underlying approach to accounting policies, gearing and tax management may differ significantly between a private company and a public company in an equivalent industry, leading to significantly different earnings figures.

There has been some research done into the relative P/E ratios achieved from the sale of public and private companies. This tends to show that private companies obtain a P/E ratio roughly 50%–60% of the equivalent public company P/E ratio.

High P/E ratios

When reviewing P/E ratios published in the financial press, you may well come across some that appear to be extremely high. You may, for example, wonder why anyone would buy a share with a P/E ratio of 75 or 100, when this indicates that they would have to hold the share, in effect, for 75 or 100 years to generate sufficient earnings to pay back the price of the share. The answer is that P/E ratios tend to be determined by the perceptions of a company's growth prospects. Therefore, a publicly quoted company with a high P/E ratio is one which the market believes has high growth prospects, and investors are prepared to pay a high amount for shares now in the belief that the earnings will grow significantly in the near future so as to give a good return on their investment.

Given the numbers of assumptions that will have to be made in terms of determining an appropriate P/E multiple to use in coming up with a valuation, for the reasons given above, a P/E ratio approach to valuation is usually considered too subjective, particularly when compared with the discounted cashflow approach.

DISCOUNTED CASHFLOW

Discounted cashflow, also known as **net present value**, works on the following basis. Which would you prefer, £1 now or £1 in a year's time?

If you are rational, you would prefer £1 now, because:

◆ not only is £1 in a year's time by definition more uncertain than £1 now (I might not be around to offer it or have changed my mind), but

◆ £1 in a year's time is actually worth less than £1 now because you could place the pound I give you now in a bank account and earn interest on it for a year. In fact, if you could obtain a 10% net rate of interest, then in theory £1 now is equivalent to a minimum of £1.10 in a year's time. Similarly you can see that £1.10 in a year's time, given that rate of available interest, is the equivalent discounted back to a present value of £1.

Discounted future cashflows are therefore used as a way of estimating what you would be prepared to pay now, for the future stream of cash that is going to be generated by having bought a particular asset, business or project. This discounting of anticipated future cashflows is the method used in most large corporate transactions for business valuations for the purposes of mergers, acquisitions and disposals. For the purpose of valuing businesses, a theory called the capital asset pricing model generates a discount rate based on:

◆ the 'risk free' rate of interest that you require for investing your money rather than spending it (which is equivalent to the rate of return you can earn by putting your money into, say, government stocks)

◆ multiplied by a risk factor for investing in a particular sector, known as **beta**, which is generated by looking at returns generated by quoted companies.

For smaller businesses it is more appropriate to use the weighted average cost of capital or WACC. A simple example of how this is calculated is shown below for a company that is funded by £50,000 worth of long-term loans and £100,000 worth of share capital, where loans have an interest rate of 10% per annum and the equity is rewarded by a dividend rate of 20% per annum.

	Capital £000	**Cost as %** %	**Cost of capital** £
Equity (share capital)	100	20	20
Debt (long term loans)	50	10	5
	——		
	150		25 = 16.66% weighted average cost of capital

Under the discounted cashflow approach to valuation, the value of the target business to you is the total of the future discounted net cashflows after tax. A simplistic example of a discounted cashflow covering three years is set out below.

	Year 1	Year 2	Year 3
Operating profit	100	120	140
Add back depreciation	10	20	20
'Cash profit' generated from trading	110	140	160
Movement in working capital	10	(5)	15
Capital expenditure	–	(100)	–
Tax payment	(33)	(40)	(40)
Net post-tax cashflow	87	(5)	135
Discount rate compound 10% pa	1.1%	1.21%	1.33%
Cashflow discounted to present values	79.1	(4.1)	101.5
Total present value	176.5		
Price paid	(150)		
Net present value	26.5		

Notes:
No residual value after year 3
Discount from year 1

Thus the net cashflows generated by the prospect of £227 (£87 + £135 − £5) are equivalent to £176.5 now when discounted back to present values. Deducting the £150 that you have to pay to acquire these cashflows therefore gives a net present value of £26.5.

Disadvantages
The disadvantages of the discounted cashflow technique are:

◆ The appropriate discount rate for the valuation is either your weighted average cost of capital, or the rate you wish to apply to a business with your risk profile. Obviously this figure will vary from purchaser to purchaser and therefore competing buyers may have a different discount rate to you, which will affect the value they place on the business.

◆ For how many years going forward should you calculate a discounted value before inserting a residual value that represents the entire future value of the business from that point to infinity?

◆ To what extent are you prepared to pay for the benefits in increased operational efficiencies, synergies, etc., that will come about from your purchase of the business? How far should these be stripped out of any projections?

Advantages

Nevertheless there are many advantages to using a discounted cashflow approach in that it forces a rigorous and quantified examination of a variety of issues that will be relevant to the performance of the business going forwards, such as:

◆ Any expected movement in profitability (up or down), whether for reasons already inherent in the business or from factors that come into play as a result of your purchase.

◆ The profitability of individual areas of the business, which may vary significantly from business unit to business unit.

◆ Capital expenditure required to develop the business or the scope to realise capital repayments by way of future disposal of parts of the business.

♦ Any increases required in working capital to cope with growth and turnover, or any reduction of working capital that might be achieved by way of better financial management following completion.

♦ Any other synergies or changes arising from the acquisition such as changes in the accounting date which impact upon the due date for taxation payments.

Whilst they may appear complex, discounted cashflow forecasting approaches lend themselves to spreadsheet applications, and once these are set up, the key assumptions can be varied, and revised forecasts run off with ease.

It is, however, easy to become confused as to which forecast was based on which set of assumptions, so ensuring strict rules about 'version control' and fully annotating the assumptions that lie behind each alternative forecast are vital so as to minimise confusion.

Such models can also easily be flexed to reflect changes in assumptions (what if sales are 10% better than forecast, or 10% worse than forecast?) to see how these affect the outcome. This process is known as 'sensitivity analysis' as you are looking to see how sensitive the outcome is to changes in key assumptions. It is a vital tool in planning your financing and trading after completion.

Discounted cashflows are also used to calculate the **internal rate of return** (IRR) of the project. The IRR is the percentage discount rate at which the net present value of the interest is zero. For the case above it is 18.88%. This means that the project overall gives a return of 18.88% as shown below.

	Year 1	**Year 2**	**Year 3**
Net post-tax cashflow	87	(5.0)	135.0
Discount rate compound 25.15%	1.1888	1.4132	1.6800
Cashflow discounted to present value	73.2	(3.5)	80.4
Total present value	150		
Price paid	(150)		
Net present value	0		

From your point of view, the decision whether you should buy or not in practice comes down to which is higher, the WACC or the IRR, as:

♦ if your weighted average cost of capital is 10%

♦ and the return on the investment (i.e. the IRR) of this purchase is 20%

♦ then it makes sense to employ your capital/borrow funds and pay out WACC of 10%, to invest and make 20%.

RETURN ON INVESTMENT

You are presumably looking to buy the business on the assumption that it will make profits which will provide you with a return on your investment. In addition to IRR above, this return can be expressed as a simple percentage. So if you pay £1 million and expect it to generate earnings (i.e. profits) of say £200,000 a year, then your anticipated return on your investment is £200,000 ÷ £1 million = 20%.

Reversing the formula (£1 million ÷ £200,000) also gives the P/E ratio referred to above.

These values can also be used to express an indication of risk by way of the payback period. Assuming that earnings will continue to run at £200,000 per year, the payback period in this case (i.e. the period it will take until the original investment has been paid back) is £1 million ÷ £200,000 or five years. Obviously the shorter the payback period, the quicker the purchaser will be 'seeing his money back'.

Of course none of the above take into account the cash implications of the deal (such as capital expenditure, movement in working capital, etc.), in the way that discounted cashflows and therefore IRR does. They are therefore more crude measures, but as they are easy to express and easy to compare against returns on another investment, such as simply leaving your money in the bank, they are widely used by purchasers.

SECTOR SPECIFIC

Many trades, particularly those where there are a relatively large number of small businesses with therefore many sales during any business year, tend to develop their own specific basis of valuation and normal deal structure.

For example, you will often see a professional firm such as solicitors or accountants sold on the basis of a multiple of gross recurring fees, while valuation of a hotel will be a function of room rate, occupancy rate, and number of rooms; restaurant valuations will be driven by numbers of covers; and pubs by barrelage.

Brokers in these areas of business will often express a valuation in terms of these key metrics. So, for example, brokers dealing with residential care homes will often express a value in terms of £X per bed for comparison purposes.

Standard bases for valuation and deal structure

As a result, fairly standard bases for sales valuation may grow up, such as: 'For business type X, the sale value is likely to be twice annual gross sales plus the stock, furniture and fittings at cost.'

In addition, there may also be fairly standard approaches to structuring a deal. This is particularly applicable to small service or professional businesses where as discussed at the end of the last chapter, the value of the business often lies in the personal contacts and network of the existing owner of the business. If you are interested in buying such a business you firstly have to make an assessment as to whether there will really be a business once the principal has gone. Assuming that you believe you can manage the business after the old owner has gone, you then have to consider how far the business's earnings will be reduced by their departure and how you can best manage this to minimise the damage.

In these circumstances, a payment spread out over a period of years based on expected earnings is not unreasonable. It is also usual for the old owner to stay on as either an employee or a consultant for a period of say, one, two, or even three years, in order to ensure a smooth handover of the business and the contact base to the new owner, with a payment being structured as some form of an earn out.

EARNINGS MULTIPLES

The most commonly used basis of valuation in dealing with small owner-managed businesses is the multiple of earnings approach.

This is calculated simply on the basis of:

◆ earnings/profits (before interest and tax, known as **EBIT** or **PBIT**)

◆ times the appropriate multiple.

The level of multiple to be applied is then obviously a matter of judgement, given the strength of the business and the current economic circumstances. If, for example, you were looking at an established manufacturing business with a good market position and established management team you might expect the seller to be seeking a multiple of say five to seven times current earnings.

Obviously, the worse the competitive position or reliance on strong management, the lower the multiple that should be expected. The clearer the competitive advantage and steadiness of the earnings stream, the higher the multiple that would be sought.

WHAT YOU SHOULD NOT PAY FOR

It is evident from the above that earnings, both current and future, are crucial to almost every business valuation whether in terms of profit or cash. So earnings, current and future, are the starting point for both you and the seller to consider valuation. This reinforces the point that the seller needs to be able to demonstrate to you the business's real earnings potential, by pointing to demonstrable profits and earnings in the business, and that these should all be clearly and demonstrably flowing through the business's books.

Do not fall into the trap of in effect paying for the benefits you are going to bring to the business. It may be that you are confident that you can grow the business's turnover from £1 million to £3 million and earnings from £100,000 to £500,000. But if this value will only arise as a result of the work that you have to do on the business once you have bought it, why should you pay the existing owner for it?

Remember also that turnover, as such, does not have a value. Turnover is only a tool to generate profit and it is the profit that the business generates as a return on your investment that has a value for you.

SUMMARY

The business's value is only what somebody in the market is prepared to pay for it, it is not some real value set in stone. And what buyers in the market are prepared to pay for is a return on their investment in the form of future streams of profits and cash. The only question therefore is how much money you and other buyers are prepared to pay for that future income given its apparent degree of risk or reliability.

In summary, the basic methods of valuation and their pros and cons are as follows:

	Pro	Con
Asset value: The value of all the assets, less the value of liabilities on either a 'book' or a professionally valued basis	Going concern and forced sale values provide 'cover' against worst case	Book values are 'meaningless' and asset valuations do not reflect value of the trading business being bought
Market value: The going rates for this type of business	Easily understood comparison	Difficulty of getting the relevant reliable comparable information
Discounted cashflow: The value of the future annual	Makes everything explicit and qualified	Finding the correct discount rate and the underlying

	Pro	**Con**
cashflows, discounted back to the present value in terms of cash today		uncertainty of future cashflows
Return on investment: The profit earned in future years expressed as a percentage of the investment required	Easy comparison between investment opportunities	Not cash based and dependent on projection of future earnings
Sector specific: Standard basis used for the particular trade	Common basis for comparison	Does not reflect the individual circumstances of the business and its properties
Multiple of earnings: Profits times a 'multiple'	Subjective but readily understood	Not cash based and relies on a projection of future earnings

(10)

Financing the Deal

WHAT DOES THE MONEY NEED TO COVER?

It is important to remember that you are going to need to raise finance to cover significantly more than just the purchase price. To make a success of the deal, the funding you have available will additionally need to cover:

◆ Clearance of any debt to be satisfied as part of the deal.

◆ The working capital required to trade the business afterwards. It is no good buying the business only to find that you do not have the cash with which to run it. You will therefore need to work closely with your advisers to ensure that your financial projections are robust and that you raise sufficient funding to see the business through.

◆ Any restructuring costs that you will incur to make the changes you want to put through such as redundancy costs.

◆ Any investment required in the business following the sale. These might range from some simple expenditure on relaunching the business under new management through to significant expenditure on updating the products, introducing new lines or replacing machinery.

Don't forget that the old owner may have been considering the sale of the business for a number of years, and it is not unknown for such owners to run the business on a harvesting strategy, whereby rather than reinvesting in the business to keep it up to date in the years leading up to the sale, instead they draw out as much of the free cash as possible for their own use. The result can be that a business requires significant refurbishment in order to ensure its competitiveness.

It's also true to say that you will always need more cash than you thought you did, as demonstrated by two examples.

Example

Management bought out a specialist manufacturer that was turning over approximately £13m. Within a year turnover had increased significantly with prospects of hitting £20m after the failure of one of its main competitors. As a result of the nature of the working capital cycle as discussed in Chapter 6, within a year the business was seriously overtrading and came very close to collapse, only being saved by a sale and lease back of the property which raised approximately £1m cash.

Example

At the same time (and only 20 miles down the road) the managers of an electronics business had bought their plant out of a receivership. Unfortunately in this case, rather than turnover recovering from the receivership level of £30m to the expected £40m, things got worse, falling to closer to £20m. Given the business's cost structure this translated into severe losses which there was insufficient cash to cover. As a result the business failed again within 18 months.

Since neither you nor your advisers will have a 100% reliable crystal ball, always ensure that you have a significant contingency reserve built into your cash to cover the inevitable ups and downs.

This point is especially true if you're buying a business that is in difficulty, as it is likely to have stretched its creditors and you may find that the deal precipitates a rush for payment by existing creditors. This means your planning of your working capital must take into account provision for payments to bring overdue creditors up to date, or a plan for how these are otherwise to be dealt with.

Finally, do not forget to build into your valuation of the business and the financing requirement shown by your cashflows the level of interest and capital repayment in respect of the borrowing you undertake.

WHERE DO YOU GET THE MONEY?

Funding a business purchase is a large subject but in essence there are four main sources of money to consider at the outset:

Equity

This will come from a mixture of:

- your own equity (which in many cases essentially means borrowing against equity in your house)

- friends and family

- your business

- a venture capitalist (VC) who is backing the purchasing team

- a business angel

◆ joint or co-venture partners

◆ the seller if you can persuade them to take paper (shares in your
company) as payment in whole or in part, rather than cash.

Grants and soft loans
This is of particular relevance in development areas.

Debt by way of borrowing against the assets being purchased
Most forms of borrowing money to finance a business (including
mortgages, leasing and hire purchase, factoring and invoice
discounting, and most overdraft arrangements) require the
business to provide some form of security by way of charges over
business or personal assets. The level of borrowing obtainable is
therefore determined by the level of security you or the business
have to offer.

In some sales, the seller's advisors will have already put together
a package of financing 'in principle' that will be available to a
buyer. This is known as 'stapled finance'.

The only usual sources of significant unsecured lending to your
business will come from credit given to you by suppliers and any
unsecured loans you or friends or family decide to put into the
business.

The seller
Funding might come by way of vendor finance (a form of debt)
such as deferred consideration or an earn-out.

Bootstrapping
In addition, once in control of the business you may look to run
its finances in such a way as to maximise the cash retained in the
business, a process known as bootstrapping. This usually
involves:

- reducing or eliminating non essential expenditure ('what you don't spend you get to keep')

- agreeing terms with suppliers that allow you longer to pay

- keeping the level of stock held (and hence cash tied up) to a minimum

- ensuring that customers pay you as quickly as possible so that you do not have excess money tied up in debtors.

You then need to build up the business's financial reserves by retaining profit within the company to grow the shareholder's funds.

The degree to which you believe you'll be able to reduce the business' requirement for working capital by use of bootstrapping techniques obviously reduces the overall amount of cash that you need to seek to raise.

Over reliance on bootstrapping can, however, be dangerous.

Example
An MBI team bought out a £20m turnover manufacturing business. Critical to their assumptions was an expectation that they would be able to reduce costs significantly by better purchasing and therefore reduce the working capital requirements. In practice they found that the old owner had already beaten prices down to rock bottom and there was little further saving therefore available to be made. The MBI ran out of cash and failed within a year.

WHAT FORM OF EXTERNAL FINANCE IS RIGHT?

The way you finance the business will effect how financially stable it is. A business with high levels of borrowings (**'high**

gearing') will have a high level of interest and capital payments that it has to make irrespective of its trading results. A similar business which you have funded from equity can decide not to pay a dividend if times get tough (although if you have generated this equity by borrowing against your house the problem of covering your personal gearing will remain).

Generally it is also good practice to match the type of finance used, to what you are going to use the cash for. So to buy an asset with a long useful life such as a property, it is better to borrow over a long period by using a mortgage so that the cost of the finance is spread over the useful life of the asset. Short-term working capital needs are better met with short-term flexible facilities such as an overdraft or debtor finance.

Another useful tip is wherever possible to borrow long and pay short. If you think that the business can pay off a mortgage in 10 years, borrow over 15 instead (making sure that there are no hidden penalties for early repayment). Then, if times get tougher than you had expected, the repayments you are committed to are less than they would have been, while if everything goes well, you can still pay off in the 10 years you had originally planned.

Preparing a business plan and forecasts

As with any exercise in raising external finance, doing so for a business purchase will require at the minimum the preparation of a business plan and full set of forecasts, including cash flows. These act as the main tool for communicating to the finance provider:

◆ what you are going to do with the money

◆ how much you need

◆ how long you need it for

◆ how you are going to repay the debts; or what return the investor will get on their equity

◆ what risks the lender/investor is taking and how these are to be managed.

As this is a vital 'sales' document, you may well find it helpful to obtain professional advice and assistance in preparing it in a suitable form. At the same time, you should also take advice on the most appropriate financing structure for what you are proposing.

CAMPARI checklist

While doing so, bear in mind the banker's CAMPARI checklist, as you will need to satisfy this for almost any external lender or investor.

◆ Character – will the investor or lender see you as honest, do they trust your integrity and reliability or have you made exaggerated claims in the past?

◆ Ability – do you and your management team clearly have the necessary skills and ability to run the business?

◆ Means – how much are you worth (both as a guide to your past money-making performance and your ability to provide cash to cover any short-term problems)?

◆ Purpose – what are you intending to do with the money? Is it a feasible idea, that matches funding against the need appropriately? Are you also looking to do something that the investor or lender finds acceptable given its own policies (e.g. the bank may not be interested in lending to businesses in your sector due to its internal policies).

- **A**mount – how much are you putting in compared to the risk you are asking the lender or other investors to take; and are you asking for enough to properly see the project through to completion?

- **R**epayment/return – how long do you need the money for and how is it to be repaid (or what return is an investor going to make on their money?

- **I**nsurance – what sort of security is available to cover the loan? This might include:

  – the business assets

  – a personal guarantee (PG) which may also be backed up by a charge over your personal assets (supported PG)

  – the **Small Firms Loan Guarantee Scheme**.

Additionally many lenders will need you to take out insurance cover (e.g. keyman life cover) as part of their insurance that their money is safe.

EQUITY

The money that can be raised as debt will generally be limited by the assets available to give as security. Any money that the business needs to trade, which cannot be raised as debt or grants, has to be supplied by the shareholders, either by introducing external money by investing (in shares in a company) or later by leaving profits in the business.

An equity provider is taking a risk. They are putting money into a business in return for a share in its hoped for future success. As a result, if you seek other equity investors (such as backing from a VC firm), you will be selling part ownership of your business to others, diluting your own holding and ultimately perhaps, your control over the business.

Potential sources of equity for your business are:

Personal
Investing your own cash or cash that you have raised by borrowing against your other assets (e.g. mortgaging your house). The advantage of this approach is that you retain control of your business. The disadvantages can be that you do not have sufficient resources to fund the deal and business properly and your personal assets are now mortgaged to the success of the business.

Your family, friends or others known to you
Here you have direct access to people who may be able to provide cash without incurring costs and you have some idea as to whether they are actually likely to invest or not. However, think very carefully about the implications of using such money and how these relationships will be affected by this arrangement (e.g. what happens to your relationships if there is a business problem?).

Business angels
These are usually successful business people who have made sufficient money to have retired or sold their own business and are now interested in investing in small businesses both as a way of making money and as a way of continuing to be involved in business.

For most businesses looking to raise less than say £250,000 (e.g. for a start-up or seed development money), business angels usually offer the only realistic option (other than some smaller specialist regional venture capitalists). They bring not only cash but usually significant business experience and often a good network of business contacts. The downside for the entrepreneur can be that they may seek to be actively involved in the direction of the business which can lead to conflict, so it is important to see how hands on they want to be and how you feel about this.

As they are investing their own hard earned money, however, business angels tend to be very choosy about which businesses they invest in and potential business angel investments have a reputation amongst some business advisers of falling away at the last moment.

They tend to invest locally and a good business adviser will have working relationships with local active business angels and/or can put you in contact with some regional and national networks of business angels.

If you are looking to buy a business in difficulty you should already have registered with www.turnaroundequity.biz as an investor as part of your search. However it might also be worth using this service as a way of contacting potential backers.

Venture capitalists
Other than some smaller regional funds that specialise in smaller amounts, most venture capitalists are looking for large investments to justify their time in undertaking the transaction. They will be looking for businesses with high growth potential and ambitious experienced management; where they can expect to be able to sell their investment on within say three to seven years by way of a sale of the shares back to the company, sale of the company or a flotation; and obtain a return on their investment of over 30% a year.

If you are looking to raise venture capital you will undoubtedly need a business adviser both to sell the proposal to the venture capitalist and to help you in structuring the deal.

Trade partners

You should think about whether there are any potential trade partners who might be interested in a stake in your business or in helping to fund a project in some kind of joint venture.

You need to be careful about how this arrangement may affect your business, however. If you have a joint venture with a supplier, are you then tied to them for supplies or are you free to shop around? If you have a joint venture with a customer does this give you problems with other customers who might be their competitors?

Points to remember

In all cases where you are bringing in outside investors you need to consider:

◆ how much control you are handing over

◆ the need for a business adviser to help you in the process

◆ how long it will take to raise the money

◆ how certain you are of getting it

◆ the costs involved in attempting to raise cash (and to what degree your advisers will require an upfront payment or will work on success only fees).

BORROWING AGAINST PERSONAL PROPERTY

Most individuals' major store of personal capital is within the equity held in their personal property. When you are looking to buy a business and need to put in equity, borrowing against this capital is therefore many people's only option.

It's also true that cash raised against the security of residential property can be amongst the cheapest sources of financing available, as it is raised at domestic mortgage rates.

Personal borrowing through mortgages is, however, an area that is becoming increasingly regulated and if you are seeking to raise finance against your property you must take professional advice from an independent financial adviser (IFA) or deal with an appropriately regulated mortgage broker. In any event, you must always remember that as it says in the small print, your home is at risk if you do not keep up the payments on a mortgage or other loan secured on it.

There are obviously an enormous number of mortgage products on the market which change all the time. However, it is worth noting three types of product in particular which may be of assistance in buying a business.

Fleximortgage – flexibility

This is a residential mortgage that provides a revolving loan against your property that can be drawn down and repaid up to a specified number of times a year without penalty. It can therefore provide a ready source of flexible funding at domestic mortgage rates, which gives you the ability to draw down your domestic equity over short periods at short notice without the high costs of bridging.

Loans of up to 85% of **open market value** (OMV) are generally available up to an upper capital limit of £250k (but higher loans may sometimes be available by discretion). A satisfactory prior lender reference is required but a small amount of adverse credit history is generally acceptable. Loans are normally for up to a 25-year term and rates are similar to high street rates.

15-day mortgage – speed

Some lenders have stripped down the search and credit referencing procedure to provide a residential mortgage which can deliver a draw down of funds within 10 to 15 working days from application, providing that all aspects of the transaction are completed exactly on timetable.

Again the advances available are normally up to 85% of the property's value can be on a self-certified basis with no requirement for an accountant's confirmation or lender reference in most cases. These loans are available to individuals with a significant adverse credit history and are for terms of up to 25 years. Rates tend to be slightly higher than normal highstreet levels and there will be redemption penalties.

Domestic bridging – speed and short-term exposure

If you only require the cash on a very short-term basis, as for example you believe that you will be able to take sufficient cash out the business to repay this equity within three to six months, you might consider taking out a bridging loan rather than completely remortgaging the whole of your property.

Loans of up to £500k at up to 70% of OMV with rates from 1.1% per month are normally available from a range of lenders and can be swiftly put in place.

These are, however, very short-term and costly funds and if you have any doubt about your ability to repay the bridging at the end of the arrangement you should not go into it.

GRANTS

Obtaining grants can be a long and frustrating process that involves:

◆ Finding out what grants are available for your business. This can be difficult as there are a wide variety of grants available across the country funded by local authorities, central government, european and non-government organisations such as the Prince's Trust. To find out what is available in your area contact a business adviser or your local Business Link or log on to www.j4b.co.uk which has a facility to search for grants by postcode.

◆ Finding out if you have to apply before you incur the expenditure. Many grants are not retrospective.

◆ Finding out if you can obtain cash prior to the expenditure. Many grants provide repayment to you of part of an expense or investment that you have to make and cannot be retrospective.

◆ Completing the application process which you will generally find includes attempting to estimate how many jobs will be created, or staff helped to obtain NVQs, etc., as a significant part of the selection criteria.

◆ Awaiting approval of your application and payment of the funds required, which may take some time.

All of the above tend to suggest that grants will have little relevance to most business purchases, although they may well be important for funding investment required downstream.

Nevertheless there are some occasions, particularly in relation to buying out businesses from insolvency, where grants can play an important role, particularly **Selective Finance For Investment** in England, the new name for regional selective assistance grants. These grants are made towards capital expenditure, where all other sources of funds have been exhausted, and are available in what is known as Tier 2 and Tier 3 development areas (see www.dti.gov.uk/regionalinvestment for details).

Be careful if you take up such a grant, however. The terms will normally make specific reference to the number of people employed, which can cause a problem in the future.

Example
An electronics business MBO had obtained a significant grant which specified the number of jobs to be secured. When the industry had a downturn and its competitors laid off staff, the company was unable to do so as this would trigger repayment of the grant. The company staggered on without reducing its cost base until eventually it failed.

There are, however, two sources of government funding via the DTI that you should be aware of:

◆ A department called the **Redundancy Fund** steps in to pay employees for statutory redundancy in the event of insolvencies. What is less well-known is that if persuaded that by making some staff redundant, other jobs can be preserved, the Redundancy Fund will sometimes lend companies the money to make statutory redundancy payments, with repayments typically over a three-year period. If you anticipate needing to make redundancies as part of a restructuring this may therefore assist in meeting part of the cost (use www.dti.gov.uk/er/redundancy/forms to identify the appropriate office).

◆ The **Small Firms Loan Guarantee** scheme (SFLG) under which a business which has a viable business plan but which is unable to get bank lending due to lack of available security, can have this borrowing underwritten by the DTI. Again this is not really of relevance to raising the finance for the immediate purchase of the business, but may be of great assistance in helping to fund the ongoing working capital or future investment in the business (www.dti.gov.uk/sflg).

DEBT

The finance you can raise by way of loans against the company's assets will comprise a 'structured finance' package of borrowings against its:

◆ property, by way of commercial mortgage or sale and leaseback

◆ plant and machinery, by way of sale and leaseback

◆ debtors (and sometimes stock), by way of a factoring or invoice discounting facility.

Providers of this type of funding include:

◆ **Banks** who will have a range of financing subsidiaries (and don't forget that you will also need a trading bank account anyway). Banks are, however, unlikely to want to fund such deals by way of overdraft facilities.

◆ **Package lenders** who are normally invoice discounters; they are also able to offer financing against property and/or plant and machinery, as well as in some cases stock. While such funders are key to many successful MBO/MBIs, some limit their overall exposure to a certain percentage of debtors (e.g. 150% of the debtor book value).

◆ **Stand-alone independent specialist funders** who will finance against any one particular class of asset (such as a factor to cover debtors, a building society to lend on the property, and an asset financier to cover the plant and machinery). Use of such funders in whole or in part in combination with a package lender can provide greater financing (**headroom**) than use of a package funder alone. This can be critical in ensuring you raise the maximum funds available.

The types of borrowing available are discussed in more detail below but the levels of advance available are generally:

- **Property** – 70% of the open market value (OMV) by way of a commercial mortgage, or 100% by way of a sale and leaseback which therefore removes the requirement to 'fund the deposit' out of equity. In fact in some cases the actual sales price achieved can be well in excess of the surveyor's OMV for borrowing purposes, resulting in an injection of working capital into the business at the outset.

- **Plant and machinery**, from 70% to 100% of the machinery's valuation dependent on the lender on a three to five year sale and leaseback basis.

- **Debtors**, up to 85% of available debt, which is to say of the right type, under 90 days old and subject to credit limits, etc.

- **Stock**, by way of an increased ability to draw down against debtors (say up to 100% or more of the debtor book) but such borrowings will only be against finished goods stock.

A series of two-page 'frequently asked questions' guides to financing issues can be downloaded from the asset finance brokers Creative Finance's website on www.creativefinance.co.uk. Their checklist of the basic information that a broker will need to establish how much debt funding can be raised for purchase is set out below:

MANAGEMENT BUY-OUT FINANCING INFORMATION CHECKLIST
Tick box when information collated

The deal
Type of sale (share purchase or business and assets) ☐

Purchase price ☐

Expected working capital requirements following sale ☐

Equity, grants, vendor financing (by way of deferred consideration
or earn out) or other funding being put in (including details of
MBO teams' investments in the deal) ☐

The business
Industry and nature of trade ☐

Trading history covering three years (with last audited and current
management accounts) ☐

The business forecasts (with underlying assumptions) ☐

If in difficulty, details of the turnaround plan ☐

The management team
CVs for all key team members ☐

Personal wealth statements (house values less mortgages, other
assets) ☐

The assets and liabilities
Property: freehold or leasehold, valuation and description, details of
any environmental/contamination issues, existing mortgages ☐

Plant and machinery: valuation (or if not, asset listing with
sufficient information re machinery make, model, age and condition
to allow 'desktop' valuation), outstanding HP/lease liabilities ☐

Debtors: aged debtors, aged creditors, sample invoice, contract
and delivery note ☐

Stock and confirmed orders: list of finished goods stock and
confirmed order list ☐

Reproduced with permission from Creative Finance

Using an experienced broker to put together a funding package can make a real difference to the amount of cash you are able to raise.

Example
The buyout included the company's property which was worth £1.6m. However for a variety of reasons the price apportioned to the property in the sales contract was only £1m.

When the buyer sought to raise finance he found that for a purchase, mainstream lenders would only lend 70% of the lower of purchase price (£1m) or value (1.6m) restricting the borrowing to £700,000.

His finance brokers arranged a short-term bridging loan based on the valuation which they were then able to replace with a second normal term loan as a refinancing exercise after the sale had gone through that allowed borrowing of £1.1m.

Borrowings divide into short- or long-term funding. For accounting purposes, anything due for repayment on demand (such as an overdraft) or due within the next 12 months (e.g. trade creditors or the next year's worth of lease instalments) will count as current liabilities on the company's balance sheet, whilst money not due until over a year's time will count as long-term liabilities.

Short-term borrowing
Short-term sources include:

Trade creditors
When suppliers provide goods and allow the company time to pay, this is in effect an interest free loan (although the supplier

should have costed in the credit they will allow the company in pricing the job!). The more that the company is able to borrow from suppliers with their agreement in this way, the less they have to borrow elsewhere.

Overdraft

Much UK business funding has traditionally been by way of overdrafts as they tend to be the most flexible banking facility offered. An overdraft is a short-term facility intended by banks as a 'revolving credit' to cover temporary timing differences between payments you have to make to suppliers and receipts from customers. Banks will therefore expect to see the account swing back into credit on a regular basis and do not expect to see it used for purchasing long-term assets. As a short-term facility, an overdraft is usually repayable on demand.

The bank will also generally look to take some form of security for an overdraft by way of charges over a parcel of assets. Because of this approach to taking security over a range of assets (some of which, such as stock and debtors, will vary in value significantly from day to day), banks will take a relatively cautious view in assessing the real value of their security, while specialists in lending against specific types of asset may be able to lend more.

Overdrafts are also time-consuming for banks to manage so expect to see banks moving more and more customers across to factoring facilities as an alternative to overdrafts.

Factoring/invoice discounting

This allows the company to raise money against its outstanding debtors by assigning the outstanding invoices to the lender, who will advance you say 80% of the approved invoices immediately.

As the lender takes over the debtors as security, these are then not available for a bank to secure its overdraft. So completion of a factoring deal usually involves paying off the overdraft out of the proceeds of factoring the ledger being taken over.

In factoring, the lender takes over management of the sales ledger and actively chases payment, which can in itself be an advantage if the company's credit control has been poor. In some cases factors will allow a **CHOC**s arrangement for key accounts (**client handles own customers**) whereby the company retains control of the contact with the customer.

Invoice discounting is usually only available to businesses with turnovers of greater than £1m and differs from factoring in that the company continues to run its own sales ledger and collect in the debtors. As the company is continuing to do the work, it is therefore possible to have **confidential invoice discounting** (**CID**) which means that the customers will not be aware of the arrangement.

Some invoice discounters will take stock into account and are then able to offer higher levels of advance against invoices (sometimes exceeding 100% of the debtor book).

The issues you need to consider are:

- With factoring you will lose control of how your customers are chased for payment.

- Your facility will be based on a percentage advance against approved invoices. The actual advance you receive as a percentage of your total debtors can be significantly less than this 'headline' percentage as the factor may disallow debts over three months old and overseas debts, or may set 'concentration limits' where individual customers' debts cannot be more than a set percentage of your sales ledger. You need to look at the nature of your debts and ensure that you will not run into such problems with your factor.

◆ Some debts are difficult to factor. There are only a limited number of factors who will deal with 'contractual' debt involving stage payments (such as construction contracts).

◆ As the advance is tied directly to invoicing, factoring is well suited to fast growing companies – the financing automatically expands as the business grows, reducing the danger of overtrading.

◆ However, as the facility is tied to sales volume, if sales fall, so does the funding available (which may be just the moment that you need finance the most!).

◆ Once you have this type of facility in place, it can be extremely difficult to get to a position where you can exit the arrangement.

◆ There is still a stigma attached to factoring in some circles as it has been seen as financing of last resort. However, as banks have moved more customers to this form of financing, this stigma is disappearing (and of course is avoided with confidential invoice discounting).

◆ Factoring and invoice discounting are often perceived as expensive, although when comparing costs against bank facilities it is important to compare against the total cost of equivalent bank facilities including interest, management charges, etc. to get a fair comparison.

Block discounting
Where you have a long-term stream of income such as a rental income from property or machinery that is rented out, then you may be able to borrow what is in effect an advance against this

future income through block discounting. This is a specialist market where each deal is very much a one-off so you are likely to need to use an independent broker to explore this if it is appropriate.

Bridging loans

These are normally short-term loans that typically allow you to spend money that is anticipated (usually from the sale of an asset such as a property), before the cash has been received.

There are some specialist funders who will offer 'bridging' loans against property essentially as 'emergency' funding. However, while this can raise say 70% of the security value of a property within two weeks, this type of funding is extremely expensive and interest rates can often run at 2% a month together with substantial arrangement fees.

Long-term borrowing

Long-term sources include:

Bank loans (term loans)

If you are looking to invest in long-term assets such as plant and machinery or property you should borrow over a period that matches the expected useful life of the asset being bought so that it repays the borrowing over its useful life.

Fixed rate loans offer you certainty over the payments you will make (but can therefore be inflexible and have repayment penalties built in).

Variable rate loans tend to be more flexible but leave you exposed to uncertainty as interest rates change over time. If you are borrowing significant sums (say over £250,000) you may be able to buy what is in effect an insurance policy against interest rates going up in the form of a rate cap.

Mortgages

A mortgage is essentially simply an example of a long-term loan secured against a property and all the points above apply.

Where a business has a property that is not fully lent against, remortgaging it is usually the cheapest and easiest way to obtain finance.

Hire purchase

Hire purchase involves you in agreeing to purchase an asset by making payments in instalments over a set period.

Hire purchase agreements vary widely in their terms, offering fixed or variable interest rates, and you need to check the rates carefully (particularly where there is an interest free period as rates for the balance of the term are likely to be high).

Some hire purchase agreements are structured with low ongoing payments and a large (balloon) final payment in settlement at the end. In general, while you will be responsible for maintaining and insuring the asset from day 1, legal ownership will remain with the finance company until the last instalment is paid.

Leasing

With leases, the finance company always retains ownership of the asset and there are two basic types of lease:

- **Finance leases** are usually used for major items of plant and equipment where the finance company buys the asset and the business pays a long-term rental that covers the capital cost, interest and charges and is responsible for insurance and maintenance. Once the capital is repaid there may be an option to purchase the equipment outright or to continue to rent it indefinitely for a small fee (peppercorn rent).

◆ **Operating leases** are typically used for smaller items such as photocopiers where the equipment is rented for a specified period and the finance company is responsible for servicing and maintaining the equipment. **Contract hire** is a type of operating lease where the renter is responsible for day-to-day maintenance and servicing (e.g. often used for motor cars).

You may need to pay an initial deposit in setting up a lease and from a tax point of view, while the rental can usually be treated as a cost, as you do not own the asset you cannot usually claim capital allowances on it (nor can you generally use the asset as security for other borrowings).

Sale and leaseback

As an alternative to borrowing against an asset, it is sometimes possible to arrange to sell the asset (plant and machinery or property) to a finance company to release cash and then to rent it back. The amount of cash you can obtain will depend on the value of the asset being sold. This is a specialist area (particularly in relation to property where this is only normally applicable to properties worth over £500,000) where you will need to engage a good finance broker.

Directors loans

Finally, there is nothing to stop you as a director putting money into the business by way of a loan rather than equity if you have the funds available. This should be considered when discussing the appropriate financial structure of the business with your advisers.

PG tips

Don't, if you can avoid them. The taking of **personal guarantees** (**PGs**) from company directors by lenders is becoming increasingly common. By giving a personal guarantee, you are promising that if your company cannot repay whatever has been guaranteed, then you will do so personally.

If you have to give a personal guarantee then try to:

◆ have the guarantee limited to a specific amount (e.g. up to £25,000 of the company's overdraft) rather than unlimited, which would mean that you are liable for the whole of the company's borrowings

◆ avoid giving a supported guarantee (where the guarantee is backed up by charges over specific assets such as a charge on your home) and instead give an unsupported guarantee, not tied to any particular asset that can be seized

◆ ensure that you understand the circumstances under which the guarantee can be called; in practice you (and your spouse if there is to be a charge on your matrimonial home) will be advised by the lender to obtain separate legal advice.

HOW MUCH CAN YOU BORROW?

To allow you to estimate how much you may be able to borrow against the target business's assets from these different sources, Creative Finance's 'ready reckoner' is given below. By completing this with estimates as to the value of the business's assets, you can calculate how much you are likely to be able to borrow either from a mainstream bank or from a mix of asset based lenders.

Business borrowing ability ready reckoner

To calculate a business's indicative borrowing ability, complete the form below using:

◆ the basis of valuation noted to calculate the 'security value' of the assets

◆ the percentages shown to calculate the likely borrowings available.

Actual borrowing ability will be determined by a number of factors and the table below can act as a general guide only.

In particular this form only takes into account the security value available from the business's assets. It does not therefore make any allowance for other security that you may be able to provide by way of personal guarantees against personal assets or that may be available through schemes such as the Small Firms Loan Guarantee Scheme.

Asset	Typical bank lending	Typically available from asset based lenders
Property value with a restricted period to sell (say 3 or 6 months)	60% commercial mortgage	70% commercial mortgage 100% open market value by sale & leaseback (if worth >£500k)
Plant and machinery value on the second-hand market with 3 months to sell		70%+ by sale and leaseback over 3 years
Normal debtors invoices for services (e.g. temporary labour on timesheets) or goods (e.g. parts supplied), less than 3 months old	50%	70%+

Asset	Typical bank lending	Typically available from asset based lenders
Contract debtors applications for stage payments on long term contracts (e.g. construction contracts)		50% from limited number of funders
Stock		Variable, contact Creative Finance for details
Total borrowing available		

Reproduced with the permission of Creative Finance

VENDOR FINANCE

A business for sale will typically have been valued at a multiple of its annual earnings. This can easily mean that even a relatively small business may come with a target purchase price of many hundreds of thousands of pounds.

This is likely to be a problem for both you as a buyer and the seller, as you or any other buyer will only able to afford to pay the amount of cash that you are able to raise. Not many people actually have hundreds of thousands in cash available with which to buy a business, even having taken into account the amount you may be able to raise from remortgaging your domestic property; while the funds that can be raised against the business's assets may be limited as shown by the percentages given above.

This means that the only realistic source of payment to the seller for much of the business's goodwill is likely to be from the future profits generated by the business under your new ownership. But because this does not provide any realisable form of security, you are unlikely to be able to borrow against this from banks or other lenders apart from the seller.

So sellers who are not prepared to allow you some degree of credit ('vendor finance') are in effect reducing the amount of money they can be paid for the business.

But in allowing credit they are taking a risk that they will not be paid this deferred consideration, and so will want to look to cover themselves by charging interest and taking security.

Bonding insurance

There is a solution to this problem for business sales with a value in excess of £2m as there is now a service available backed by a major institution which will guarantee payment of up to 100% of the deferred consideration to the seller by way of an insurance policy. This bonding approach therefore eliminates the seller's risk in offering such credit, covering up to 100% of vendor consideration of £2m–£50m in transactions of £2m–£250m with deferred consideration periods of up to five years.

The policy is non-cancellable and 100% underwritten by an investment grade backer with very limited exclusions covering vendor fraud or deliberate misrepresentation. It can also be combined with raising asset based finance against the business's assets to fund payment of the premium.

This approach has benefits that can be shared by both you and the seller:

◆ the seller can have confidence that they will receive their payment whether or not the business is a success

◆ the seller does not have to take further security and the phasing of payments can give tax planning advantages

◆ agreement by you on the seller's headline price is easier to achieve

◆ you can reduce the level of gearing needed to buy the business, reducing the financial burden on the business and the risk of failure.

FINANCIAL ASSISTANCE RULES

In many business purchases you'll be acquiring significant business assets such as land and buildings or plant and machinery against which as discussed above you would expect to be able to borrow. And indeed if the value of these assets forms a significant part of the value of the business this would appear to be one of the most logical routes to raising the money with which to buy them.

However, this is to reckon without the **Financial Assistance Rules** of the Companies Act. These prohibit you from pledging the assets of the company to be brought as security to a lender for money to be raised to buy the company's shares. They were designed to prevent 'asset stripping' where a company with significant assets could in the past be bought by someone with money raised from financial institutions on the basis that the business would be broken up and the assets sold off as soon as the deal had been completed, with the proceeds used to repay the borrowed money.

In practice the Act provides a mechanism whereby so long as certain procedures are met, you can borrow against the value of the assets being acquired in order to fund the deal. You will, however, need to instruct professional advisers to prepare what is known as a '**whitewash report**' to allow the borrowing to take place.

For a whitewash report the target company's directors have to swear a statutory declaration that the company will be able to meet its debts in the year following the sale and this declaration has to be confirmed by the company's auditors.

The Companies Act also imposes restrictions on the sale of substantial business assets from the business to the directors (designed to prevent directors looting a company's assets without the knowledge of the shareholders). The effect of this is that if you are a director and you wish to buy either substantial assets (in effect anything with a value of over £100,000 or 10% of the balance sheet) then under Section 320 of the Companies Act, the transaction requires the approval in advance of the shareholders. This has obvious implications if, for example, you are looking to undertake a management buyout of part of your existing business.

GOLDEN RULES

15. You'll always need more cash than you thought you did.
16. Remember you need cash for not only the deal, but working capital and investment; don't leave yourself short.
17. Use a good asset finance broker to maximise your borrowing potential.
18. Work out what you can afford and sort out your financing early.
19. The seller is a source of cash.

Phase 4: Negotiating the Purchase

(11)

Negotiating the Price

THE NEGOTIATION PROCESS

As a business is an extremely complex thing to buy, with a whole range of issues to consider in addition to dealing with the seller's interests which are not necessarily exclusively financial, the negotiations to buy one are often complex and prolonged. You must therefore expect negotiations to have significant ups and downs. Even if negotiations appear to break down altogether, it is best not to burn your bridges as you may be able to restart them at a later date. Your objective during the period leading up to the agreement of a sales price is to manage the negotiations as positively as possible by paying attention to the project management of the process and also by actively attempting to build consensus between yourself and the seller as to what has been agreed, so that the remaining items for discussion can be gradually overcome.

The keys to successfully managing the negotiation process are as follows:

Listen to the seller

It is important to understand the seller's needs and wants and therefore their reasons for selling the business as well as the concerns that they need to address (such as security of employment for employees, for example) in order to feel comfortable in doing so. In particular, do not assume that a seller's concerns have gone away just because they have not mentioned them for some time. However, once you have agreed with them that a concern has been addressed, you should avoid unnecessarily reopening this as an area for them to consider.

Whilst listening, attempt to identify any particular issues of how the seller wants to structure the deal that may present you with a serious problem, given your objectives in the deal (for example, they want to retire immediately, whilst you are going to want them to stay on for a number of years in order to smooth the transition).

The key to achieving this is to let the seller talk so that they can disclose their attitude towards the items under discussion.

Keep focused on your objective

Your objective is to reach an agreement to buy the business for an acceptable price. It is not to dominate the conversation. You should try to avoid becoming emotionally involved (which is one reason for leaving much of the basic price negotiation to professionals working on your behalf).

Consider the degree to which you are going to require the seller's active co-operation following the sale to make a success of the business when negotiating the price. Also remember that the seller is likely to be extremely emotionally attached to the business and that as a result, rather than being a valuable negotiating tactic, an excessively low opening bid may simply end up with the seller feeling insulted and in some cases breaking off negotiation completely.

Remember that price negotiation is a process, not an immediate event. It requires that you interact with the seller to attempt to seek a deal which is acceptable to both sides. You should therefore:

- Retain a clear focus on your priorities and both your target and walkaway prices.

- Avoid becoming bogged down in unnecessary details (although appreciate that all the details will need to be covered by way of the final agreement).

- Remember it is a process with a purpose. What is important is buying the business on the right terms and not, in retrospect, the process that led you there. Therefore remain flexible so as to be able to work round any objections or problems arising, and consider and make alternative proposals as part of the negotiation process.

- In a negotiation you should not expect to win every single battle and therefore it is important to prioritise your objectives. You can then trade concessions on items of lesser importance to you in order to obtain concessions from the seller on items of critical importance to you.

Be flexible
Whilst being flexible, remember that any business sale is not simply about the headline price for the business, but is also about the terms on which the deal is done. So be prepared to trade items to do with price against the nature of payment.

Be positive
Be positive and co-operative in your approach to the negotiations as at all times you are looking to increase the seller's level of comfort and confidence in you and this deal, particularly if you're going to need them afterwards, if you're in competition with other buyers or if you're expecting to pay part of the price on a deferred basis.

Be open and honest

You'll be looking to buy this business in order to achieve your objectives and you will also be working within your constraints in terms of, for example, the finance available, or your own experience in this industry. Communicating these openly and honestly to the seller can help in the process of arriving at a mutually acceptable solution.

Know when to stop

Once you have achieved your objectives, stop. Bear in mind that just as you will have your walkaway price above which you're not prepared to pay, the seller will have their drop-dead price below which they are not prepared to sell. If you have achieved your objectives, do not be tempted to over-negotiate, as while you might obtain extra funds, on the other hand you might drive away a perfectly acceptable deal.

WHAT IF NEGOTIATIONS RUN INTO DIFFICULTIES?

It is a fact of life that not all negotiations go smoothly.

Becoming involved in an auction

You may find that in an advertised business sale, the seller may be dealing at this stage with more than one prospective purchaser. It is not unreasonable for you to ask what the position is so that you know where you stand.

In line with the principles of being open and honest, it is generally appropriate that seller should advise you of this, put in place a sensible timetable during which to obtain offers from all interested parties and make clear to all parties how they are going to deal with considering such offers. This could be by way of soliciting best and final offers by a specified date or by running some form of auction between the parties.

If you find yourself placed in an auction situation, think carefully whether you wish to continue to spend time and effort in negotiation with this target or whether you should exit the process in search of an alternative.

If you discover, however, that the seller has invented a fictitious offer in order to try to drive up prices, this tells you quite a lot about the business ethics of the seller. Given that certainty about what you're buying is of paramount importance in underpinning the value that you're prepared to pay, such tactics by the seller should give you significant pause for thought as to whether you wish to complete this purchase at all, and if so at what price.

Don't walk unless you mean it

Whilst you must have your walkaway price and must not be afraid to exit any negotiation if it does not seem to offer the prospect of achieving this, you should only threaten to do so if you really mean it and if you have explored every other opportunity, and every other option to try to negotiate around the problem. You should never 'grandstand' on points of pride or ego in this process.

Leave doors open

If you reach the stage where you need to withdraw from discussions because it appears a deal cannot be reached, you should always attempt to end on a positive note, express your regret for the fact that you do not appear to be able to be in a position to conclude a deal with the seller at the present time, emphasise the points on which you have managed to reach agreement and leave a channel open for them to come back to you should they be willing to reopen negotiations over the points which at the moment cannot be resolved.

STRUCTURING THE DEAL

Whilst much of the detail of structuring the deal will be negotiated during the period of due diligence and drawing up of the final sales contract, some of the overall elements will need to be thrashed out in order to agree the basic price and shape of the sale. These will be incorporated into a formal offer letter from you to the seller that sets out the main terms of the proposed deal (known as **heads of terms**, or **heads of agreement**).

Negotiations at this point are therefore not simply about price, but will also be about the overall shape of the deal.

Some of the principal issues that will need to be dealt with at this stage are detailed below.

How is the sale to be structured?

Broadly speaking, if the business is operated through a limited liability company there are two alternatives. Either:

◆ the owner of the shares in the company can sell these to you (or a company that you form to hold them, which is usually referred to during negotiations as 'Newco') so that you then own the legal entity that is the target company, together with all its assets, business and liabilities; *or*

◆ the target company can sell its business and assets to you or Newco in return for cash or other consideration which then belongs to the company under the seller's control (sometimes referred to as a 'cash shell').

For tax reasons (see Chapter 16), the business's owner is likely to want to sell you their shares. However, for accounting reasons, you are more likely to want to buy the business and assets, as you then have choices as to how you account for these in bringing them into Newco's books, which will affect the amount of goodwill you have to account for and therefore your tax liability.

Additionally and perhaps more importantly, if you only buy the business and assets you will have limited your risk in the transaction, as you will not be picking up the company's liabilities, other than some specific ones which may carry across, such as:

◆ employees' accrued employment rights which will be carried across and become rights against the new owner of the business as the new employer under the Transfer of Undertakings, Protection of Employee Regulations (**TUPE**)

◆ any liabilities arising that relate directly to specific assets (such as the new owner taking over liability of the property or plant and equipment leases).

If, however, you buy the shares, the company now under your ownership continues to have all its own old liabilities. The worry for you here is that there may be claims of which you are not aware that may arise subsequently and give you problems. For example, the company might have had some form of legal dispute which the owners quite reasonably feel can be defended or is unlikely to be pursued further by the other side. There is always the risk for you as the purchaser, however, that the complainant may decide to take it further and may be successful. Alternatively the company may have supplied goods which have a warranty attached to them and with which at the time of the sale there appeared to be no problems; however, at some point after the sale it transpires that problems have arisen that are covered by the warranty for which the company is now liable.

So if you are considering buying the business's shares you must expect to undertake a greater level of due diligence work in respect of potential liabilities to ensure that you avoid any of the above problems as far as possible. Alternatively, if you are looking to only buy the business and assets, you may expect the seller to seek a higher price than in a share sale because of the potential adverse tax consequences they may suffer in comparison.

HOW CERTAIN IS PAYMENT GOING TO BE?

Many buyers and sellers involved in a deal become so focused on the headline price of the sale that they fail to take into account how this interacts with the terms of payment.

Leaving aside for a moment any payments made in respect of future profits above certain targets, consultancy after the sale, or interest on finance for the sale provided by the seller; the core of the deal will be a payment made by you to the seller for the business and assets or the shares in their company. This payment can either be made by way of:

◆ **cash** or **cash equivalent** (within which I would include shares in your company if your shares are listed and readily tradeable on a stock exchange, so that the seller can immediately convert some or all of the shares received into cash); *or*

◆ **paper**, by which I am referring to payment using instruments that are not immediately realisable by way of cash. Such paper instruments can include such things as:

  – loan notes, whereby the purchasing company agrees to pay consideration over some period into the future

  – options over the purchasing company's shares which are not immediately exercisable

– shares where there is no immediate market through which the seller can turn them into cash (for example where the company is private and therefore not listed on any stock exchange).

Some deals will be a mixture of the two. As illustrated in the chart below, the greater the element of cash or near cash in a deal, the greater the seller's certainty of payment. The more paper there is in the deal, the less certainty the seller will have as to the eventual cash outcome, and they will therefore generally seek a higher price to compensate them for this extra risk.

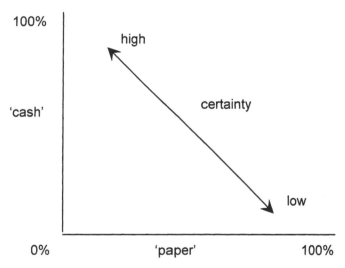

Figure 9. Composition of purchase price

Example
An Internet start-up sold a percentage of its equity to new investors (also in e-business) in return for listed shares in those investors valued at £8m. By the time the company decided to sell these shares in order to raise cash, the technology market had gone into decline and the shares were eventually sold for £4m.

HOW MUCH IS THE SELLER FINANCING?

Aligned to the above, what degree of the financing is the seller going to have to provide?

In many business sales, such as for example, to a management team conducting an MBO, the buyers will not have sufficient cash to pay the full purchase consideration upfront as well as to run the business following sale. In these cases, as discussed in Chapter 10, the sellers have little option but to assist by financing part of the purchase price if they want to complete a sale.

Where sellers are helping to finance the sale by allowing you a period of credit they will look to take precautions to reduce their risks by:

◆ Treating this the way they would any other credit sale and obtaining credit references and undertaking credit searches on you and your businesses.

◆ Insisting on having at least some of the consideration in cash so that you have had to produce a significant down payment and have a significant investment tied up in the new business that you will not wish to see at risk by defaulting on the liability of the old owner. At its most extreme, there is a view among some sellers that they should insist on the maximum possible cash upfront and treat receipt of any deferred income as 'a bonus' if it comes in. However, refusing to finance does in effect to reduce the amount of money that prospective purchasers will be able to pay them for the business.

◆ Taking a personal guarantee from you for the outstanding payment (if you are buying for a company), which they may seek to be supported by a charge on your house. If assets such as a property are included in the sale, the old owner may also seek to take security by way of a charge over these so that if you default, they can appoint a receiver to sell them and get their money back. This may, however, give rise to problems with your ability to raise finance against their assets as commercial lenders will also want to take these as security.

◆ As their payment is coming from the business's future profits, insisting on being provided with regular sets of accounts. They will also want the right to inspect the company's books and records at any time.

◆ Seeking a bond, as discussed in Chapter 10.

Sellers will try to keep the period over which they are to be paid as short as possible. However, equally importantly, they will need to appreciate that they have to make the period long enough to be practical for you as a buyer. The payments must be set at a level that allows you to retain sufficient working capital out of the profits generated to trade; and enough profit to live on. Having the business fail following the sale because payments to the seller makes it run out of cash, or you call it a day because you are not making any money out of it, are both self-defeating in the long term for the seller.

And finally, if they are providing finance, you should of course expect that they will charge an appropriate rate of interest both to cover their risks and to incentivise you to pay the debt off as quickly as possible.

You should also appreciate that in some circumstances obtaining payment over a period may actually help the seller in dealing with their tax position.

HOW CERTAIN IS THE PRICE?

The price that you will be prepared to pay for any business will be largely determined by your confidence in the likely level of sustainable profits going forwards. Where there is any concern or dispute over the likely level of those profits, use of an 'earn-out' can be a way of bridging the gap between the price you are willing to offer and the upfront price the seller is demanding.

In an earn-out the future payment due is generally not fixed but is to be determined on the basis of future trading performance such as a percentage of profits over the next two years in excess of specific target. This can make sense if there is some real uncertainty about future performance, or you want to incentivise the old owner while they stay on for a period to hand the business over.

But be very careful about any such arrangement. However tightly the agreement is drafted it will never cater for all the changes that may happen in the business over this time and this is an area where there is always significant potential for disputes. You should only consider an earn-out if you are very confident of your relationship with the seller following the sale.

If you do decide on such a scheme there are some key points to cover in order to minimise disputes. You should agree:

◆ how items which will affect the level of profit, such as changes in accounting policies, new interest costs or group cross-charges, will be dealt with

◆ what level of control over the business the seller will have to make certain that it delivers the profits required

◆ how any major changes that are planned after the sale and which will affect profit levels, are to be taken into account when comparing performance against targets.

An earn-out will usually last either one or two years, and sellers will often want to include within the contract a clause stating that in the event that you are able to sell the business on during this period at a significant profit, then the seller will share in this (a **non-embarrassment clause**).

OTHER KEY TERMS

Price and payment are not the only issues. Other factors to consider in agreeing the deal structure are:

How much support will you need after completion?

Will you need the seller to stay on for a month or two to train you in running the business? Maybe you need them to stay on for one or two years in order to ensure a smooth handover of contacts, relationships and clients.

What restrictions will you place on the seller?

If you are buying a business you are actually buying a flow of transactions where a group of people (the customers) come to your business to buy goods or services that you in turn purchase from another group of people (your suppliers). You are therefore really buying a network of relationships. Once you've paid for this, the last thing that you generally want to happen is for the old owner to set up in business again immediately or in the locality, as the chances are that customers and suppliers will simply want to deal with the person they have been used to dealing with. The value of the relationships that you thought you had bought would be very quickly compromised.

Almost every sales contract is therefore likely to include some form of non-competition covenant whereby the seller undertakes not to set up a new business in competition with the one you have just sold within a specified time or area.

Obviously the seller's circumstances and objectives in achieving the sale will have a significant impact on how strong or far-reaching a covenant they are going to want to sign. If they are simply looking to retire, for example, then the effect of such a covenant may be completely irrelevant to them. If, however, they are looking to cease trading this particular business but may be interested in doing, say, consultancy in the area in the future, then the detailed wording of the covenant may become a significant issue which you will have to factor into the price you are prepared to pay.

HEADS OF TERMS

By the end of this process you should reach the point where you have agreed the basic price and terms of the sale with the seller, and you will be in position to agree **heads of terms** or **heads of agreement**.

This usually takes the form of a formal letter from you to them confirming the general outline of your offer, which they have agreed to accept, subject to contract.

As such your letter should set out broadly:

◆ The **price**, either by way of a specific number (£Xm), or by way of some kind of formula (X% of profit over the next three years paid annually three months after the end of the year).

◆ The **deal structure**, either a sale of shares or a sale of business and assets (in which case if there are any assets which are to be specifically excluded, such as land, property or debtors, these should be noted).

◆ **Specific description of your requirements of the seller**, such as their staying on for a specified period as an employee or under a consultancy agreement, and details of any proposed non-competition covenant.

◆ **Conditions** attached to the offer such as the need for audit and due diligence, together with an indication as to the scope of work required and how the process is to be managed, particularly in respect of access to staff, papers and maintenance of confidentiality.

◆ **Exclusivity**. Having reached this point you can now expect to start to incur significant professional costs as you will need to instruct your professional advisers to undertake formal due diligence and the detailed negotiations of the sales contract. If you are going to commit to spending this cash it is not unreasonable to seek to ensure that you are not wasting your time in doing so. You should therefore demand that the seller agree to deal exclusively with you for a reasonable period of time in order to give you a fair chance of completing the transaction.

Whilst unless there are particular circumstances, sellers will usually agree to such a condition, they will want to ensure that this period is limited to a specific period sufficient to allow you to undertake your due diligence and a contract to be agreed (say 45 to 90 days).

The offer may also specify specific conditions that have to be met in order for the deal to proceed (such as the net worth remaining over a specified sum) or set out events that will cause the deal to fail (such as the loss of specified key customers).

It is important to stress that the heads of terms letter is essentially a letter of intent to complete a deal and is not the contract for sale itself. It is important, however, for a number of reasons, as:

◆ It marks the stage at which you have an offer that you have negotiated and agreed with the seller.

◆ It does have legal implications (and therefore you should take legal advice about drawing it up) in, for example, the terms surrounding any period of exclusivity.

◆ It provides a degree of moral commitment on the part of both you and the seller to move towards completing a deal.

◆ The granted period of exclusivity clears the decks for you to commit to what is the most expensive part of the process leading up to a sale.

◆ It provides written evidence of the structure of the deal and terms you have agreed with the seller for future reference in moving towards the sale contract.

However, it is important to remember that you have made this offer before carrying out your detailed due diligence. It is therefore an offer made based on the information you have received from the seller and on which you are relying at this stage. Once your advisers gain access to the business's books and records to conduct their proper due diligence, if significant issues arise these will obviously have a serious impact on the price that is finally agreed for the sale.

GOLDEN RULES

20. Don't blow it by being too greedy once you've achieved your target price.
21. Understand what is important to the seller; it's often more than cash.
22. Terms are as important as price – sometimes more so.

Due Diligence

WHAT IS DUE DILIGENCE?

Due diligence is the term used to describe the detailed investigation and audit that you should undertake prior to exchanging contracts. Going back to the analogy in the introduction, it is akin to the survey you would carry out on a house prior to exchanging contracts, to ensure there is nothing untoward that might affect your decision to complete the purchase.

Having achieved agreement on the heads of terms, due diligence and the negotiation of the detailed sales contract will then tend to run in parallel, as the treatment of issues arising out of the due diligence process will need to be negotiated for inclusion in the contract.

Traditional due diligence has always focused on legal and financial matters, and generally is undertaken by your solicitors and accountants respectively. Over the last few years, however, a broader 'commercial' due diligence has increased in importance, normally covered by the work of your accountant.

There is significant crossover between these three broad areas, as indicated below.

The areas to be considered under each of these broad headings of due diligence headings are set out in this and the following

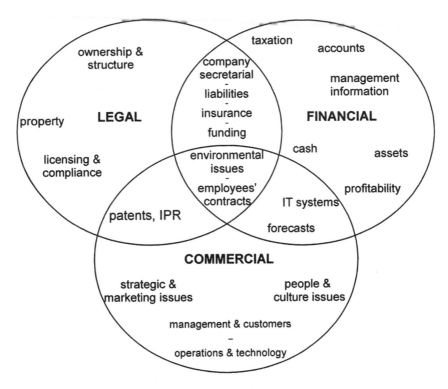

Figure 10. Interlocking fields of due diligence

chapters, where you will see for example that both legal and financial due diligence will look to cover areas such as insurance. Since the topics that due diligence will cover are well known, these are obviously areas that a well advised and prepared seller should have addressed during their grooming of the business prior to putting it on the market, so that due diligence goes as smoothly as possible.

Attempting to undertake 'DIY due diligence' on any meaningful acquisition in order to save costs may be very dangerous in the long term, as you may not have the experience or the full range of skills required to assess the issues and you will have no recourse if it goes wrong.

> **Example**
> A company bought a mineral extraction business to gain access to a new site, undertaking its own survey to estimate the reserves, to save under £50,000 in costs. Having begun work and therefore committed to the site's eventual restitution costs, they subsequently found that they had over-estimated the reserves by over 50%, which equated to some tens of £ millions.

LEGAL DUE DILIGENCE

Legal due diligence is broadly about:

- establishing the basic information surrounding the company and the legal status of its relationships with other parties so that problems can be spotted and adequate warranties taken

- ensuring the company's compliance with the regulatory framework within which it needs to operate

- establishing the legal position in respect of a number of specific areas of assets and liabilities.

The main areas to be covered are set out below.

Ownership and structure

To prepare a sales contract you will firstly need to establish who the parties to the contract will be. Legal due diligence will look at the business's formal legal structure – a partnership with a partnership deed, or a company with authorised share capital. If it is a company it will investigate the authorised issued share capital, who the shareholders are, whether there are any agreements between shareholders, whether there are any restrictions on the shareholders' ability to sell shares, or restrictions in the company's memorandum and articles of association that will impact on the ability to do the proposed deal.

You will also want to:

◆ know whether any of the shares, or the company's assets, have been offered as security to any third party (for example, a debenture given to secure loans from a bank)

◆ check to ascertain whether the business is solvent and whether there are any insolvency or other legal proceedings pending and if so, the detailed status of each item

◆ ensure that there are no other bars to completing a sale, such as: Do any contracts, licences or agreements entered into by the company require the consent of any third party to the sale and change of ownership of the business?

Statutory compliance

Your solicitors will need to check that the statutory books and records are up to date, reflecting all the currently issued shares, meetings of directors, debentures and other charges, and whether the business has filed all necessary tax and/or company secretarial returns (such as filing of annual returns and sets of accounts at Companies House).

Funding facilities

Any or all loan and related security or guarantee documentation will need to be reviewed to consider:

◆ Are the business's banking facilities in place with up-to-date mandates? Have the directors and/or owners personally guaranteed any such facilities? If so, how is it proposed that such facilities will be dealt with?

◆ Will the potential sale make any grants received liable to be repaid?

◆ Has the business given any guarantees or indemnities in respect of any third party's obligations and do any third parties have any options over the company's shares or any of its assets?

Liabilities

The solicitors will need to investigate whether there are any potential claims against the business not provided for in the normal accounts.

◆ A complete list of all disputes, claims, and any known legal proceedings will be required, together with full details of progress of the case and the company's position.

◆ A full list of all contingent liabilities wil be needed, including employee claims, guarantees, warranties, produce returns, maintenance and support obligations, and any claims from suppliers for payment that are being disputed.

Contractual relationships

Your team will want to review all material agreements with suppliers or customers, such as any joint ventures or partnerships, any agents, licences, distribution agreements, franchising, or outsourcing arrangements, and any material supply contracts with customers or suppliers.

They will also need to review:

◆ any standard contracts for sale of goods or supply of services as well as standard purchasing documentation

◆ reservation of title clauses built into your terms of sale and the details and potential exposure under all warranties that you

offer with your goods and services to see how effective they are
likely to be

◆ a list of all material contacts to establish whether any of the
business's contracts are directly with either the individual
vendors or related parties, and if so, whether any of these are
undertaken on the basis of arm's length transactions or on
non-commercial terms.

Licensing and compliance

Your solicitors will need to check that the business meets all the
necessary regulations and licensing requirements for carrying out
its trade, and whether it is in default of any regulatory matters.

Where appropriate, a detailed health and safety review should be
undertaken (which may involve the employment of a specialist),
which will require the full disclosure of all health and safety
meetings, recent reviews and inspections (including fire safety
issues), and any disputes.

Similarly, you will need to take a view as to the extent to which
any environmental due diligence is required. Given the strictness
of current environmental legislation and the way that directors
can increasingly be held personally liable for environmental
issues, this is almost becoming inevitable in a business sale of any
size. Again, a specialist consultant is likely to be required to
consider the potential environmental risks of the company's
activities, review the necessary licensing and consents and review
compliance with rules and regulations concerning waste
discharges, spillages and so on.

And don't forget to check to ensure the company is properly
registered under the Data Protection Act and is complying with
the requirements of the Act.

Intellectual property

A key part of the business's value to you will be its ownership of any licences or **intellectual property (IPR)**, such as trademarks, brand names, patents or designs. These need to be checked to ensure that all such intellectual property has been registered where applicable:

* with the relevant authorities, such as the trademark registry or the patent office, and

* that this has been done in the company's name (and not the name of the business owner personally).

It is also worth considering if there is any intellectual property of significant value which has not been registered.

* Does the company trade under its own corporate name or under other trading names?

* If so have these been properly protected by registering as trademarks and possibly by registering dormant limited liability companies under these names at Companies House?

* If so, who owns these dormant companies, the business owner or the company?

* Have domain names been registered so as to protect its trading names in e-commerce? If so, who owns these?

* Is the business party to any confidentiality agreements?

Employees

Employees can be a major source of claims against a company. You will need a detailed list of all current employees, together with copies of their standard terms and conditions of employment.

◆ Do any employees have materially different terms and conditions of employment? If so, you will need to see copies.

◆ What are the procedures for dealing with complaints and disciplinary matters? Ask for full details and the records of such activities.

◆ Request details of all employees who have been dismissed over the last, say, three years. Are there any cases pending for unfair or constructive dismissal? Have any employees been dismissed within the last six months (which are still within the time limits for a claim to be lodged at an employment tribunal)? Are there any cases currently at an employment tribunal?

◆ Has the company engaged the services of a professional firm of employment advisers in order to ensure its procedures and practices match the requirements of current employment law?

◆ Are there are any profit sharing, bonus or option schemes for directors or employees? If so, what are the details?

◆ What pension arrangements are offered by the company to employees? If there are more than five employees, has the company instituted at minimum, a stakeholder pension scheme? Ask for full details of all existing pension schemes. If the company operates any form of final salary scheme (also known as a 'defined benefits' scheme) ensure you obtain details of the trustees as well as a copy of the most recent actuarial valuation. This is so that you can establish the degree to which the scheme is adequately funded, as if the scheme is underfunded this will need to be made up out of future profits – and increasingly legislation is making directors potentially personally responsible for protection of the pension fund. If you discover that a final salary scheme is significantly underfunded you should seriously consider pulling out of the purchase.

◆ Look particularly at all contracts of employment for directors (often known as service agreements). In addition to basic information about salary and notice periods, do such contracts include provisions for restrictive covenants preventing them from entering into competition with the company, specific bonus, profit sharing or option schemes and/or provisions specifically regarding the sale of the business (for example, a 'golden parachute')?

◆ Finally it is always worthwhile for your planning purposes to calculate the notice pay and redundancy that would be due to each employee if required. This quantifies the liability that you will be taking on under TUPE and allows you to plan any cost reductions required in your restructuring of the business.

Property
You will need a list giving the details (address, whether freehold or leasehold, and if leasehold, length of the lease and name of the landlord) of all properties used by the business (including details of any premises it has leased in the past), together with all the documentation needed to be able to establish that the business has good title to its current properties in order to be able to hand them over to you.

Your solicitors will need to investigate a range of commercial issues as regards all such properties, including the terms of leases; details of any specific rights or restrictions on your rights to deal with the property arising out of any transactions such as mortgages; and charges, easements, sub-tenancies or options that have been granted, either to or from the business. Often a surveyor's report will be requested to provide a valuation of the property, together with a costing of any dilapidations that may exist and for which the business is liable under the lease.

Key issues will include:

◆ Are there any disputes with the landlord or owners of adjoining premises?

◆ What planning exists in respect of the properties, and have all the necessary planning permissions and building regulations necessary for the business's required use been obtained?

◆ Is there any planning consent for use other than as currently that might have an affect on the property's value?

◆ Who is responsible for insuring the property, the business or the landlord? If it is the company, obtain details of the insurance.

◆ Does any change of ownership of the company require the landlord's consent?

◆ How long do any leases have left to run?

◆ What are the current rentals and when, and on what basis, are rent reviews conducted?

◆ Has the company previously rented property where it has then signed the lease to a third party? If so, does the company still have a contingent liability in respect of that lease?

◆ Are there any specific environmental risks associated with any of the properties such as a history of contamination or subsidence?

Insurance

Does the business have adequate insurance to cover its assets, as well as its trading activities (such as business interruption cover, and product liability insurance)? Obtain copies of all the insurance documentation together with details of any outstanding claims in progress.

See Appendix B, page 431, for a sample legal due diligence information checklist that illustrates the depth to which legal due diligence will look to go.

GOLDEN RULES

23. Don't stint on due diligence – you'll pay for it later.

(13)

Financial Due Diligence

WHY FINANCIAL DUE DILIGENCE IS IMPORTANT

Since your decision to buy the business and the price to be paid for it are highly dependent upon the forecast levels of sustainable profit, financial due diligence has long been used to underpin the purchaser's confidence in the figures being talked about. Purely 'financial' due diligence tends to be historic in focus and is looking at checking the underlying performance in the past as a basis for drawing conclusions about the likely achievability of the forecast future performance, together with the current position as regards assets and liabilities.

Accounts, policies, systems, and management information

The basic areas that will be reviewed are the company's procedures, systems and policies. Since a company's results are materially affected by the accounting policies adopted, the starting point for most reviews will be the policies to ensure that they meet current **generally accepted accounting practice (GAAP)**. Your accountants will be looking to see whether the policies adopted appear reasonable in respect of the business. For example, has the company been:

◆ depreciating assets such as computers over a sensible lifetime of say three years

◆ calculating the value of stock in an appropriate way

◆ providing for bad and doubtful debts and slow moving stock at appropriate levels given the company's experience

◆ not booking anticipated profits before they are actually earned (revenue recognition policies).

In doing so, they will be looking to compare the business's accounting policies with those generally used in its industry.

The accountants will review the general basis on which the accounts are prepared and how the systems operate in much the same way as would be done during a normal audit to prepare a set of audited financial accounts.

They will also consider the adequacy of the financial information produced and used by the company and its management. They will therefore want to look at management accounts, stock reports, aged debtor reports and so on, and to discuss how these are used in the business.

They will be interested in establishing:

◆ Is the accounting information adequate to control the business and can the management, for example, demonstrate that it knows the gross margin on a product by product basis or the profitability and cash profile of particular contracts?

◆ Do management demonstrate that they use financial information when making decisions such as investment in plant and equipment or in managing the business?

◆ How widespread is 'financial literacy' within the business?

◆ How integrated is the finance team with operations and sales or does finance appear to operate in isolation?

Profit and loss

Having looked at the systems which produce the financial information, they will want to look at detailed trading results on a business unit by business unit basis to show trends in terms of:

- sales
- growth
- margin
- overheads.

They will be looking to see the degree to which these vary, are seasonal, or differ from the industry average, and will discuss the details of this historical performance as an aid to understanding the basis on which future performance is being forecast and how reasonable this therefore is. A forecast that is broadly in line with past trading trends is going to appear much more reasonable than a forecast that suddenly shows a 50% increase in sales and a 50% increase in gross margin for the same or less level of overhead.

At the same time they will be looking to see:

- Are there any exceptional items or significant changes or events over the last say three years, which have had an impact on the financial performance of the company? If so what are they? Could these repeat themselves?

- Has all the income and expenditure been correctly allocated to the right year, or do the accounts give signs of having been manipulated to show a particular position or trend?

- Do the company's contractual relationships seem to make commercial sense in that they are designed to make the company profits based on the costs of its services or products and the risks associated with the contract? Or do some appear to be set up in order to divert profits to other entities or to the owner's family?

♦ Does the company undertake regular cash flow forecasting exercises and does it actively manage its liquidity and effectively chase in debtors?

Overall review of forecasts

Following this detailed review, your accontants will be asking themselves:

♦ Are the forecast results 'reasonable' based on past performance?

♦ Do the forecast cash flow, profit and loss, balance sheet and ratios all appear to flow smoothly on from existing trading results, or are there significant changes which require explanation and substantiation?

Assets and liabilities

The current level of assets will be reviewed in detail, including:

♦ **Land and buildings** – Are these incorporated at cost or at some later valuation? If so, was this a professional valuation or that of the directors?

♦ **Plant and machinery** and other fixed assets – How old is plant and machinery? What outstanding hire purchase, finance or operating leases exist? What period are assets being depreciated over (and is this appropriate)? Is the plant and machinery in good condition? How does the estimated value of plant and machinery match up to the book value? There may need to be an independent valuation of all plant and machinery and property as part of the process.

- **Investments** – Does the company have any interest in other businesses? If so, what are the nature of the investments and their current values?

- **Debtors** – What is the current pattern of aged debtors? What is the history of provision for bad and doubtful debt? Does the company have a significant level of old or disputed debts? Does the company collect in its own debts, or are they collected by a finance house under a factoring arrangement? Does the company appear to have adequate backup in terms of customer orders, copy invoices and proofs of delivery in order to be able to collect old debts?

- **Stock and work in progress** – What level of stock is the company holding? How does it divide between raw material stock, work in progress and finished goods stock? How many days/weeks/months of turnover does the stockholding represent? Does any of the stock appear to be significantly slow moving or obsolete? If so, has it been provided for? On what basis has the stock been valued and does this appear reasonable in relation to the information in the company's accounting system?

- **Cash** – How many bank accounts are held by the company? Where are they? What are the balances on each? Do these match up with the company's cash books? Looking at the cashbooks and bank statements for each account over a period, is there any evidence of other bank accounts or any unusually large transactions that need to be investigated?

- Who are the **signatories** on each account? Is there a copy of the facility letter and mandate for each account? Are there details of all security given in respect of borrowings? Have any balances been personally guaranteed by the directors or owners?

◆ Are there any significant **cash balances** held within the company?

Liabilities will be subject to equally searching, if not greater scrutiny:

◆ Having obtained an aged credit listing your accountants will look to identify the **key suppliers**, to check that supplier statements have been reconciled, and investigate any unreconciled or disputed items.

◆ They will review the process for **accruing for costs** where invoices have not been received (Goods Received but Not Invoiced or GRNI), and will check the adequacy of the accrual against recent goods received notes and stock records, as well as the level of accruals being carried in respect of utilities and other such overheads.

◆ They will need to obtain a schedule setting out all **leases and hire purchase agreements** held by the company and showing the balance due and payment schedules to ensure that the outstanding amount and future commitments to payments are clearly understood.

◆ They will also need a list of all **potential contingent liabilities** from both the company and its solicitors, which will need to include a list of all outstanding claims and litigation, and they will need to discuss the results with the company in some detail.

Obviously in many areas the financial due diligence team will liaise with the legal team, such as in the areas of pensions and insurance.

IT systems

The business's IT systems (both financial and operational) should be reviewed to consider a variety of legal, financial and operational issues, such as:

◆ Is there a disaster recovery plan in place?

◆ Does the company have adequate backup security and antivirus protection, and is it licensed to use all its software?

◆ Is all of the company's data under its own control or does it use third party supplies or outsourcing agreements?

◆ Does the company's IT infrastructure adequately support the business now and into the future with information and controls or will further investment be required?

Taxation

Past tax computations will be reviewed in detail (together with correspondence with the Inland Revenue) to ensure that all tax due has been properly accounted for and dealt with. Treatment of deferred tax will be reviewed and the status of the company as a group or close company will be checked.

If the company has tax losses, the effect of the proposed sale and any changes in the business's ownership and nature of trade will need to be considered to see whether these losses can be carried forward and used or will be lost. As part of this review of taxation, the financial due diligence team will be looking to see whether there are any potential tax liabilities which were not otherwise apparent in the accounts.

In addition, compliance with PAYE and VAT regulations and liabilities will be reviewed in detail, checking for any disputes or correspondence with the relevant authorities, filing of returns by the required due dates and absence of any penalties, surcharges or interest.

See Appendix C on page 451 for a standard financial due diligence checklist showing the extent of information and documentation that your advisers will typically be requesting from the target at the outset of a due diligence process.

MORE THAN JUST TICKS IN BOXES

You may think that having engaged highly paid professionals to conduct a thorough due diligence regarding all the areas above, that you have covered everything you need to do in relation to due diligence. This would be a mistake for two reasons.

Firstly, the due diligence process provides you with one of the most important opportunities to help make your purchase a success because it allows you to conduct the detailed planning of your post-acquisition strategy before the deal is actually completed.

Whilst allowing the professionals to get on with their areas of audit in order to reduce risk, you should therefore be proactively making the most of this opportunity to assess what steps you need to take immediately after your purchase and beyond. This way you can hit the ground running as soon as you take control and can present yourself to the staff, customers and suppliers as an owner with a clear strategy and sense of direction and with a plan to take you there which you are already implementing, thus dealing at a stroke with any potential uncertainty that these people might otherwise face.

Secondly, you need to look for yourself at the commercial implications of any matters thrown up as part of the due diligence. The professionals you would hope will find the issues, and you would further hope will give you an indication of the implications of anything they have found.

But remember, once you have completed the deal it will be up to you to manage the business and deal with these implications. So it is absolutely vital that you understand the real impact of anything that comes out of the due diligence.

Example

Experienced executives bought out an underperforming subsidiary with a view to turning it around. However, the old owner had agreed excessively generous severance terms with the employees. As a result the business was unable to afford the cost of cutting staff in order to reduce overheads and the business eventually went into administration as a direct result.

CONTENTS OF DUE DILIGENCE REPORT

The following is an outline, provided by Baker Tilly, of the typical contents of a due diligence report.

Key findings and executive summary

This will contain a brief summary of the contents of the report and details of principal matters arising from the report.

History and business

◆ Key events in recent history.

◆ Brief description of business activities and milestones in the company's development.

◆ Company structure, including capital structure, details of ownership and recent changes therein, minority interests in subsidiaries, investments and joint ventures.

◆ Company strategy and objectives.

◆ A brief summary of:

   – company profit and loss for the . . . years and . . . months ended 200 . . .

   – company net assets as at 200 . . .

   – company future prospects for the year ending 200 . . .

◆ Contracts and transactions involving directors; details of any other legal agreements influencing the nature of the business or structure of the company.

◆ Markets, and competition (particular in the light of recent and planned changes), including market growth and changes in market share.

◆ Marketing strategy.

◆ Sales (including strategy, sales organisation and control, dependence on individual customers, contracts and pricing).

◆ Services provided (including range, description, development, revenue and contribution).

◆ Customer service and quality policy.

◆ Purchasing and supplies (including strategy, purchasing organisation, relationships and principal suppliers and associated purchases).

◆ Description of all premises, including location, locality, site area, current usage, date of acquisition, subsequent expenditure, and analysis between freehold and leasehold. In the case of leased properties, details of terms of lease, rental income payments, any onerous covenants, any planning restrictions or planned development and comment on availability of spare space.

◆ Any recent independent or internal valuations or insurance reports.

◆ The suitability and adequacy of plant and premises.

Organisational structure, management and personnel
◆ Management structure, reporting lines and division of responsibility.

◆ Outline of directors' and senior executives' biographies (including their qualifications, experience, length of service, responsibilities during the period under review, service contracts, benefits and remuneration and the role of non-executives).

◆ List of any former directors and senior executives who have left during the . . . years ended 200 . . . with brief details.

◆ Management style, succession and gaps or weaknesses.

◆ Analysis of employees (including total number of staff at the date of the report, to be analysed by full-time and part-time employment and by function, movement in numbers over the recent past) and basis of remuneration (including salary/wages structure, compliance with industry average rates and dates of salary reviews).

◆ Current state of labour relations and details of trade union membership, if any.

◆ Pensions (including current status of the fund, existence of unfunded liabilities, level of contributions and security of assets) and other employment and post-employment benefits.

◆ Details of share incentive, share option and profit sharing schemes.

◆ Ability of staff to meet development plans, recruitment policy and training.

Financial control environment

◆ Description and assessment of the key financial systems and internal controls, including financial information supplied to management, estimating and forecasting procedures, cash management and the debtors and creditors control systems, including systems and controls currently in operation.

◆ Details of key financial (and other) information used to manage the business, including accuracy, timeliness and sufficiency.

◆ Details of key computer systems (including IT strategy, systems developments to date and proposed prior to flotation, security and disaster recovery plans, extent and effectiveness of use).

◆ Cash controls and treasury management.

◆ Description and assessment of management accounts.

◆ Organisation and effectiveness of finance function.

◆ Weaknesses identified by the auditors and significant matters arising from the audit work in respect of the . . . years and . . . months ended 200 . . .

- Summaries of budgets should be included and compared with actual results for each of . . . years and . . . months ended 200 . . ., together with comments on the main reasons for deviations from budgets.

Accounting policies

- Details of accounting policies applied over the . . . years and . . . months ended 200 . . . (including detailed practices and procedures adopted).

- Impact of any restatements for consistency.

- Comparison with industry and 'best practice'.

- Impact of any proposed changes.

- The compatibility of the target company's accounting policies with those of the purchaser.

Trading results

- Summary of the profit and loss accounts for the . . . years and . . . months ended 200 . . . including analysis of sales and profit margins for each of the business segments and reasons for significant fluctuations.

- Analysis of revenues, costs and gross margins by business segment (including key operational statistics, comparison with competitors, seasonality), commentary thereon and explanation of trends.

- Assessment of the company's dependence upon any individual customer by reviewing top five customers by revenues.

- Details of overheads together with commentary on significant fluctuations therein.

◆ Analysis of and commentary on 'exceptional' and 'extraordinary' items.

◆ Analysis of interest and taxation charges (historical and prospective).

◆ Details of any prior period adjustments considered by the investigating accountant to be necessary.

Net assets

◆ Summary of balance sheets at each year end for the last . . . financial years and at . . . 200 . . . and an explanation of significant trends.

◆ Detailed analysis of each balance sheet heading at . . . 200 . . ., including:

– details of fixed assets and normal depreciation (including leased assets), asset lives, proposed capital expenditure programme and current commitments

– analysis of debtors, including bad debt history and provisions, and creditors including accruals and basis of provisioning

– details of banking arrangements and loan facilities (including terms, covenants and details of security granted to third parties) and of contingent liabilities and capital commitments as disclosed by directors

– summary and implication of any off balance sheet financing arrangements; and

– details of any material long-term and/or onerous contracts.

Cash flow

◆ Summary of cash flow for the . . . years and . . . months ended 200 . . . and commentary thereon.

- Details of seasonality in working capital requirements.

Taxation

- Summary of the company's current corporation tax position with regard to the agreement of taxation computations, highlighting material outstanding issues.

- Summary of the taxation charge within the accounts, the basis of provisioning and deferred tax.

- Summary of the availability of corporation tax losses.

- Impact of the flotation on the taxation position.

- Compliance with PAYE/NI regulations and VAT regulations. In respect of these matters, work will be restricted to enquiry as to compliance with submission of returns and normal procedures and the status of any outstanding queries or issues.

Current trading and future prospects

- Review and commentary on the profit and loss, balance sheet and cash flow forecasts for ... months ending ... 200 ..., including a review of any management accounts produced for the year to date, a comparison with previous years' trading, recent experience and budget and commentary on the assumptions underlying the forecasts. Consideration will be given to:

  – sales and the order book

  – cost of sales

  – overhead expenditure

  – interest charges

  – exceptional items

- credit taken by customers and granted by suppliers

- capital expenditure and disposals

- the proposed treatment of any arrears of trade creditors

- the potential impact of volume changes, overtrading and seasonality

- the availability of new external capital, loans and the continuance of existing loan and overdraft facilities; and

- any restrictions imposed by lenders.

◆ Areas of vulnerability.

◆ Any sensitivities in the trading position and downside risks.

◆ Any other factors in the areas covered that might significantly affect the company's future prospects and that appear material in the context of the flotation.

Other matters
◆ Summary of insurances.

◆ Summarise any current, pending or threatened litigation by or against any member of the company or its directors and the adequacy of contingencies associated therewith.

◆ Contingent liabilities.

Document provided by Baker Tilly ©

$$14$$

Commercial Due Diligence

WHY COMMERCIAL DUE DILIGENCE IS IMPORTANT

The most important thing to realise about the due diligence process is that it is not simply an exercise in checking to make sure you are not buying a 'pup'. Properly used, it is actually a vital part of the process for making sure that the entire purchase is a success.

Traditionally, financial due diligence involving a review of the target's recent trading performance was used as the basis for judging the reasonableness of its forecasts and likely levels of sustained profitability. As in all investment decisions, however, past performance is not necessarily any guide to future performance.

Therefore over recent years, in addition to financial and legal due diligence, buyers are undertaking a far more commercially orientated due diligence designed to look at the strategic picture and the business's competitive position within its sector and industry. As discussed in Chapter 7, this is because it is the position of the business in real life and its relationships with customers and suppliers which will drive future business results.

Strategic position

So commercial due diligence is designed to establish whether the business 'makes sense' and is essentially a more in-depth look where possible at the commercial and strategic issues covered in

Chapter 7. It looks at trends within the economy, within the industry, and within the particular market which the company operates, assessing the company's mix of products and markets, its relationships with important customers and suppliers, its degree of competitive advantage or weakness, and the basis for its existing or potential competitive strategy. There should also be a detailed review of the key terms of any important contracts so as to give you comfort as to the commercial position in the short-term.

Internal review

Alongside this review of the business's strategic position you will also be conducting an internal review as to how efficiently the business operates, the quality of its decision making, and its management style and culture. This leads on to the second reason why commercial due diligence is increasingly seen to be of importance.

Research into corporate acquisitions consistently suggests that the majority of purchases fail to deliver to the buyer the value they were expecting to obtain and can therefore be regarded as failures. Further, the research goes on to suggest that in the majority of cases the reason for the 'failure' of the acquisition has nothing to do with the nature of the business being transacted by the target company or any problems that crawl out of the numbers after the sale has gone through having been missed in due diligence.

They are first and foremost to do with people issues, culture clashes, and failure properly to bring the two businesses together so as to achieve the envisaged greater whole.

Post-acquisition integration

The internal aspects of commercial due diligence are therefore becoming increasingly important for corporate purchasers, as it is increasingly being recognised by such buyers that the success or failure of acquisitions usually depends on how well or poorly they are able to manage the merging of the acquired company's culture and management into that of their existing organisation (known as post-acquisition integration).

By spending some time during the due diligence process looking at the business's existing structures, culture and management style, you can get a much better feel for how you are going to approach dealing with the existing staff and management once the sale has gone through, what changes you may want to make, and how you wish to make them.

As a result, you can hope to get a much better result going forwards from the deal than otherwise.

ASSESSMENT OF THE MANAGEMENT TEAM

Having identified the key individuals in the business's management, you will need to assess how strong the team is and how to ensure that those members of the team that are critical to the business's future success are tied into the business.

You should therefore adopt some structured way of assessing the skills and competencies of the managers in the business to the extent that you are able to obtain the relevant information.

Ideally you would want the chance to interview the key members of staff and conduct a formal assessment of their capabilities. Increasingly, psychometric tests form a key part of such management assessments, and some useful tests can be ordered online at www.turnaroundhelp.co.uk and at www.belbin.com.

This may be a problem as it may conflict with the need to keep the process confidential, since some of the key members of staff may not be in the know concerning the sales negotiations. As a minimum you should have the seller provide you with detailed

CVs for each of the key team members and if possible you should arrange to meet them during one of your site visits on whatever pretext seems appropriate.

If you have not been able to meet all the key members of staff, a vital part of your post-acquisition planning must be to arrange to hold detailed meetings with each of the key members of staff as soon as possible once the deal has been announced.

An example of the areas such an assessment of management might want to cover is set out below.

Management assessment checklist

Person	Fred	George
Role	Production Manager	Accountant
Qualification	Engineering degree	'By experience'
Experience and industry knowledge	7 years with Widget Inc as line manager	Company bookkeeper since 1956
Ability to think strategically	Limited, very much a 'nuts and bolts' man, internally focused	A bookkeeper's bookkeeper
Financial awareness	Focused on cost management. Can read a P&L	None, a number cruncher, not a manager
Team type	Driver, comes up with a plan, ensures it is seen through. Good evaluator and completer-finisher	Solitary worker

Person	Fred	George
Personality type	Goal orientated, practical. Reserved with people, works in a structured way	Jobsworth. Poor communicator. No imagination
Record of delivery	Strong within own sphere	Produces numbers, does not manage finances
Willingness to change	Will change having understood that change is needed	Dislikes change
Commitment to company	Appears loyal and strongly committed	Retiring in 2 years
Critical to business?	Yes	No
Attitude to sale	Positive	Negative
Your strategy	Retain	Replace

Retaining key staff

If you decide that you need to retain a key member of staff you then need to assess the likelihood that they may wish to leave as a result of the sale. If so you then need to put together a strategy which ensures they are locked into the business, which might involve incentivising them with bonuses or other forms of recognition. Again, being able to understand specifically what motivates the individual from the use of psychometric testing can be of great assistance in designing a tailored package designed to stand the best possible chance of retaining them.

Redundancies

Where you have decided that you may need to let staff go you will need to conduct any such redundancies for compliance with the legal requirements (as discussed in Chapter 17).

Finance directors

Where your review of the management structure has identified that there is a gap you will need to plan to fill this as swiftly as possible following the purchase. In particular if you are buying an owner-managed business you may well find that you will need to appoint a finance director, as the absence of such a person is often a weakness of this type of business (even if initially on an interim basis, contact Bob Snell at bs@resolutioninc.biz or James Wheeler on j.wheeler@ashtonpenny.com, or as an outsourced function, contact Garry Mumford of Insight Associates on gmumford@insightassociates.co.uk).

When appointing a finance director bear in mind that they may be asked to fulfil two very different roles and you will need to be clear in your own mind as to what job description you are looking to fill.

Some finance directors act essentially as glorified bookkeepers or financial controllers and are very focused on the technical aspects of the work and the business's finance function, systems and reports. There can be a tendency to become too involved in a hands-on way in the minutiae of the company's accounting function.

There obviously needs to be a strong **finance function**, for which the finance director takes responsibility, that:

♦ produces reliable financial information in the shape of management accounts and costings

- prepares regular cashflow forecasts and budgets, including profit and loss accounts and balance sheets

- assists in the preparation of feasibility studies on major development projects

- integrates accounting systems as required and installs adequate internal controls

- plans your tax strategy to minimise tax costs

- oversees the company secretarial functions.

The role of the finance director should, however, be to delegate the detail of these tasks to appropriately qualified staff, freeing them up to have a more **strategic viewpoint and role** in:

- providing the board with strong guidance and advice in respect of its strategy

- providing financial advice on major decisions

- focusing on managing the financial performance and financial structure of the business

- driving communication of the business's financial performance with its stakeholders such as employees, shareholders and bankers.

WHAT ABOUT THE OLD OWNER?

The old owner can present a particular problem to be managed following the purchase.

Obviously the sales contract will specify a number of ways of dealing with them, such as:

- any earn-out under which they will remain with the business for a handover period, during which time the sum to be paid to them is determined by the business's trading profits

- any consultancy agreement whereby payments may be made to them for specific services that they are rendering; *or*

- any non-compete agreement whereby they are prevented from setting up or taking part in a business that directly competes with the sold one.

However, outside these contractual matters, there may be a variety of relationships and ways in which the old owner interacts with the business which may need to be considered.

Example

The owner and managing director was having an affair with a member of staff. This continued after the sale of the business, which initially was of no real concern to the buyer. Subsequently, however, relations between the buyer and the old owner deteriorated, at which point the position of the member of staff in the relationship became extremely difficult.

Example

The old owner remained 'drinking buddies' with some of the key members of staff. A little while after the sale, the business got in to difficulties and there was a prospect of the old owner buying it back again.

This gave the current owners two problems in managing a sale, since not only did the old owner have a direct line into the key employees and so access to a wide variety of information to help him with his bid; but he was able to spread the message through the business that he would be buying it back, reducing the sellers' ability to have staff co-operate fully in discussions with other interested parties.

The above examples illustrate how sensitive and difficult to handle some of these situations can be.

The general principle, so far as possible given any need for ongoing consultancy or a handover period, should always be to try to ensure there is a clean break between the business and its staff and the old owner. By doing so you minimise the degree to which they may be able to interfere with the business or that there is any confusion in anybody's mind inside or outside of the business as to who is now in charge.

As illustrated above this can be a problem particularly if the old owner is a dominant person in the local economy and social life, or if the transaction is simply a handover between generations in a family firm.

PROBLEM DUE DILIGENCE

The impact on the success of a purchase of missing commercial and cultural issues out of the due diligence process as well as financial and legal ones is illustrated in the example below. In this case the due diligence was done in-house in order to save money, leaving no outside adviser with professional indemnity insurance (PII) to look to in the case of problems.

Example

The buyer was a highly valued quoted company with a high P/E ratio on the basis of a strong growth record. To maintain its high valuation it therefore required all parts of its business to continue to grow strongly in turnover and profit year-on-year.

The target was a professional services firm, which had a high level of long-term cost in retaining appropriately qualified professionals while its market went in five year cycles. During each cycle there were generally a number of years where the business only broke even or made a small loss, before being in a position to make significant profits during the remaining periods.

Clearly the first commercial issue was that the likely earnings profile of the acquired business was a poor fit to the buyer's earning pattern requirements. The buyer's approach to any business making losses was to reduce costs until a profit could be achieved.

Attempting to cut staff numbers as the business was in the low part of its cycle was, however, a problem, both commercially because of the difficulty that would occur later in gearing up again to take advantage of the upswing in the cycle, and culturally because of the significant conflict with the established culture within the business.

Attempting to reduce the extensive network of small local offices also presented a problem in that as part of its grooming, the seller had negotiated new long-term contracts for many of the sites.

Furthermore, following acquisition it became clear that the pension scheme had a significant deficit which would have to be covered.

The net result was therefore a business which was commercially a poor fit with the group's financial requirements; with a strong professional culture which would be very difficult to integrate into the rest of the business; which had some significant potential liabilities associated with it; and which it would be very difficult for the parent to restructure. Arguably, many of these issues would have been flushed out in an external financial and legal due diligence exercise.

GOLDEN RULES

24. Ensure you get a non-competition covenant.

The Sales Contract and Completion

THE TWIN TRACK PROCESS

Negotiation of the sales contract will be taking place at the same time as you carry out your due diligence. Detailed negotiations with the seller will therefore proceed side by side with information that you are obtaining as part your detailed reviews, which will be feeding into your view of the business's value and the price, terms of the deal, and specific representations, warranties, indemnities and covenants that you will therefore wish to have incorporated into the contract.

Having agreed heads of terms, it is important from both your and the seller's point of view to ensure that the due diligence and negotiation of the final sales contract are completed as quickly as possible. The longer a deal goes before closure, the more likely it is to fall apart as a result of a wide variety of events ranging from the seller getting either cold feet or a better offer, through to the person pushing the deal at their end changes jobs, leaves, is made redundant, or news leaks out of the deal which adversely affects the business.

Having reached this stage, do not let a deal slip away from you by simply letting the process run out of steam. You and your advisers will need to keep pressure on the seller to complete the deal within the time frame discussed. Remember, the clock will be ticking on any specified exclusivity period in the heads of terms so that if you do not do the deal within the term specified, you will again be open to competition.

THE SALES CONTRACT

The sales contract is the legally binding document which, once signed, sets out the contract for sale, specifying:

◆ the assets that are sold

◆ the price

◆ the terms of payment

◆ the effective date

◆ the conditions under which the sale will actually be concluded.

To protect you from agreeing to buy something that is apparently worth the price agreed, then subsequently completing the sale only to find that the business is now worth less, almost all sale agreements will specify conditions that have to be met for the sale contract to be valid at the time of completion. This might cover items such as no loss of a specified list of key customers, turnover continuing to run at a specified level, or net assets not having fallen below a specified level.

Representations, warranties, covenants and indemnities

In addition, and probably more crucially, the sales contract sets out the representations, warranties, covenants and indemnities that will define where and how risk lies in the deal between you and the seller (and those in respect of tax may be codified into a separate tax indemnity agreement). It is over the nature and wording of these areas that much of the discussion in drawing the deal to a conclusion will take place and where you need a sharp, experienced legal adviser acting on your behalf to ensure that you achieve the deal you want.

The sales contract is usually initially drafted by your solicitor, which gives you the advantage in that they will be acting to protect you, their client, as they do so. The first draft presented to the seller is therefore likely to contain quite onerous representations, warranties and covenants for them to agree to, together with potentially ruinous indemnities, and possibly contractual points and arrangements which weren't actually what they may have thought they had agreed with you.

However, this is of course only the starting point and the object of the exercise is to negotiate to a mutually acceptable set of terms for the sale.

Conflict of interest

You must appreciate when it comes to the sales contract that there is a fundamental conflict of interest between you and the seller, which is:

♦ You want to be certain that what you've bought is really worth what you've paid for it, and if you come across anything subsequently that reduces its apparent value you would like to be able to get some of your money back.

♦ You would therefore like a sales contract that says: 'I [the purchaser] will buy the business from you [the seller] for £X, less any amounts by which the value of the business once we are in charge of it falls short of the expectations we had before we took it over.'

♦ The seller on the other hand wants to be certain about how much they have got for their business. They would ideally like a sales contract that says: 'I [the purchaser] will pay you [the seller] £X for the business, full stop.'

The difference between these two positions – of a sales price which is completely contingent on future satisfaction and one which is completely certain – is dealt with by way of the sharing of risk through the representations, warranties, and indemnities (and to a certain extent, covenants).

SO WHAT ARE REPRESENTATIONS, WARRANTIES AND INDEMNITIES?

Representations

A representation is any statement made to you about the business. This may be in initial discussions, by way of answers to due diligence questions, or in connection with a formal **disclosure letter**. A disclosure letter is a document prepared as part of the answers to due diligence questions in connection with the negotiation of the sales contract that sets out specific facts about the business. In some cases the disclosure letter is specifically incorporated into the sales contract as a schedule; in other cases it may simply be referenced.

A disclosure letter should give all the relevant facts in respect of any particular item covered, the emphasis being upon *all*. Whilst it is up to you as the purchaser to draw the relevant conclusions from any particular set of facts, the full facts around any circumstance known to the seller should be disclosed by them.

Since the sales process will last for a prolonged period and you will deal with a large range of individuals within the seller's organisation and advisers, in practice the seller will have very little control over the full range of representations that have been made to you during the pre-sale process, or due diligence.

Both sides therefore run a real risk that at some point during discussions some employee may, innocently or otherwise, have said something to you or your advisers which may subsequently give rise to a problem. Therefore, to protect the seller against this, they will normally seek to include an 'entire agreement' clause setting out that the purchaser has not relied upon any representations (written or oral) except for those that are specifically stated as being incorporated into the agreement, which in practice will be those given in the disclosure letter.

Warranties

A warranty is a guarantee that the particular facts are as they are stated to be. During the process of precontractual negotiations and then due diligence, you will have gathered a huge number of representations, either written or oral, about the nature of the company's business, its trading and its assets and liabilities.

Obviously these will all feed into your understanding of what the business is worth to you. What you will seek to do by use of the disclosure letter and by warranties, is to get comfort as to those specific matters that are most important to you as the basis on which to value the business.

Therefore, you will be looking for the key points on which you have made the decision to buy the business to be confirmed to you by way of warranties. This gives you protection that if these facts turn out not to be right, then you have some comeback against the seller to seek what is in practice a discount on the price you have paid.

The use of warranties also forces the seller to ensure that they have been accurate and thorough in providing you with information, as only if they provide you with accurate information in the disclosure letter will they be protected from any action concerning misrepresentation.

A warranty is therefore a contractual term, and should the term of that warranty be breached, then the seller is in breach of the contract and you can claim against them for damages. In order to do so, however, you are going to need to be able to demonstrate that:

◆ the warranty was actually specifically breached

◆ this breach was not excluded by way of specific disclosure in the disclosure letter; and

◆ the breach results in a specific and quantifiable reduction of the value of the business against what has been paid.

In the event of a breach of a general warranty, you may have a general claim against the seller, the value of which may vary. You will therefore need to quantify any claim in respect of the circumstances giving rise to the breach of warranty.

Indemnities

In contrast, an indemnity is a guarantee of specific recompense to you for a particular breach or claim. An example might be in respect of outstanding tax liabilities where the disclosure letter might say that the estimated liabilities are £X. The contract or a separate tax deed might then include a pound for pound remedy for specific loss that in the event that the liabilities are more than £X, this amount can be clawed back from the seller.

Therefore whilst in general if the seller breaches a warranty, you have to prove that the breach has damaged the value of the business in order to chase for money, if the seller breaches an indemnity, you have a specific remedy against them even if the value of the business remains unchanged.

As indemnities have to be very tightly specified, they are usually much more narrowly drawn than general warranties and limited in nature.

Example of how the terms interact

A set of disclosures, representations, warranties and indemnities might operate as follows:

Warranty	There are no claims against the company in respect of defective widgets except as disclosed in the disclosure letter.
Disclosure letter	As at the date of the sales contract, the company has two claims against it in respect of malfunctioning widgets: Mr Smith, who is claiming £10 and Mr Bloggs, who is claiming £20.
Indemnity	In the event of any claims being received by the company following the date of sale in respect of malfunctioning widgets sold prior to the date of sale, the seller will reimburse the purchaser the full amount of any settlement made to the complaining customer.

Therefore:

♦ The warranty sets out the issue being addressed and the comfort being given by the seller.

♦ The disclosure letter sets out the detail of any exceptions to the general comfort being given.

♦ The indemnity sets out a specific basis upon which the purchaser can claim against the seller in the event that the warranty turns out not to be true and the company receives a claim from Mr Jones for £30 in respect of malfunctioning widgets.

How they affect you

Whilst the best sales contract is without doubt one that once signed is filed and is never seen or used by either you or the seller ever again, you can see that warranties are a vital part of your strategy to confirm as far as possible the certainty as to what you are buying.

At the same time, you can appreciate that the more warranties and potential indemnities that the seller agrees to, the more recourse that you may have against them after the sale, and the less certain the final sales value will be to them.

The degree of warranties and indemnities to be provided by the seller is therefore a critical item in negotiations and may well impact on the final price paid and terms of payment. Whilst you must expect the seller to seek to negotiate the minimum warranties applicable, look out for any unusual reluctance or refusal to give a specific warranty as this may be an indication of a problem area that you ought to investigate further.

At a minimum you will be looking to establish:

- what warranties you need to have in place to confirm the facts upon which you have decided to buy the business

- what indemnities you need to have in place in order to ensure you are covered against foreseeable problems or liabilities

- under what circumstances might a breach of the warranties be so serious that you might want to write to rescind the contract

- as to practical issues how you establish the breach; what your procedure is for claiming damages; whether money be set aside in an escrow account for a period, to provide you with money to claim against for warranties or breaches; how long the period is within which you can claim; and whether there are any limitations on the value you can claim.

At the same time, the seller will generally be looking to ensure that:

◆ the warranties and indemnities given are as limited as possible

◆ the disclosure letter fully sets out items which could otherwise give rise to some claim for breach of warranties

◆ there are restrictions as to the maximum overall level of any claims, a limit on individual claims, a limit on the time under which claims can be made, and a limit on the type of claims, so that items other than those specifically included in the sales contract cannot be claimed for.

Basic warranties

However, a professionally advised seller will normally appreciate that there are a number of basic warranties that they need to provide about the state of the business and its affairs such as (subject to any exceptions disclosed in the disclosure letter):

◆ tax returns have been filed and payments are up to date

◆ financial statements fairly and accurately represent the company's position and current performance

◆ there is no pending or existing litigation against the company

◆ the company's assets belong to it, it has full title to all its assets and properties, and there are no encumbrances or security granted over the company or its assets

- there are no undisclosed liabilities

- the company is meeting relevant health and safety, and employment regulations

- the company has all the licences necessary to operate within its business, and is not in breach of any regulations

- there are no notices served to terminate any leases or contracts

- all the company's intellectual property is the property of the company and not individuals within the company.

Sales by liquidators or receivers

The only real exceptions to this are in sales of businesses by liquidators or receivers. Insolvency practitioners always sell on an 'as seen' basis (or the only two words of Latin most accountants know, *caveat emptor* – buyer beware) and will therefore insert into any sales contract a clause stating that the purchaser has relied solely upon their own enquiries in forming a view as to whether to buy.

This is an important *caveat*, as the sales contract will also say that the insolvency practitioner only sells whatever right and title the company may have to the assets involved in the sale. In other words if you buy a business from a liquidator and it subsequently turns out that the assets you've bought actually belong to other people (because the plant and machinery was on lease, or all the stock was covered by effective retention of title clauses), then that is your lookout.

How sellers minimise their exposure

Taking it as read that the sales contract will include indemnities and warranties, sellers will look to manage their exposure to these by building protection into the contract. Typically they will seek to:

◆ Limit the duration of the period under which any claim can be brought to a specific period, say one or two years. The argument here is that you are likely to have discovered if there is anything untoward within that time.

◆ Match this period to the length of time any money is held back in an escrow account. This makes sense, as the purpose of holding money in an escrow account is to allow you to have some certainty that should you need to make a claim there is money to meet it. Sellers will therefore want to have this money released from the escrow account as soon as the period under which any claims can be made is reached, or even on a sliding scale basis in the period leading up to the end of the claim period.

◆ Ensure that the whole of the sales proceeds are not at risk by limiting the total amount of any claim to a percentage of the sales value (from say 20% to 50%) on the argument that in completing the sale you will have done all your due diligence.

◆ Avoid being bothered by lots of small claims as it is likely that in any sales contract, there may well be a myriad of small technical breaches of warranties or indemnities, depending upon how widely these are drawn. Sellers do not want to have to deal with lots of small claims from you and one technique for managing this is to have a minimum threshold which either individual claims have to reach or a basket of claims have to reach before they will be dealt with, on the basis that a number of small claims are not worth bothering about.

◆ Avoid having too much of their money tied up in the escrow account by ensuring that only a percentage is there and that the account is interest bearing.

Obviously if part of the sales price is being paid by way of an earn-out, the need for some form of escrow account can be discounted, since in effect the deferred payment will act as the escrow account.

COVENANTS

There are two types of covenants involved in a sale, which can loosely be described as pre-completion and non-competition.

Pre-completion covenants

Pre-completion covenants relate to the seller's promises as to how they will manage the business in the period between exchange of contracts and completion. They should generally be required to sign a covenant that they will manage the business in such a way that there are no major changes in its legal structure, financial arrangements or basic trading patterns, and that they will not make major changes to the company, take on major new debt or sell assets.

Non-competition covenants

In almost all sales, you will require the seller to sign a non-competition agreement. This may either be part of the main sales contract or may occasionally be a separate contract with them as an individual for which there will then be separate payment. A non-competition covenant will be used to prevent them competing with the company once it has been sold. This is vital for you in order to protect your investment in the intangibles of the business you have bought, including the know-how, the contacts with customers, the relationships with key suppliers, and so on.

While courts will enforce properly drawn up non-competition covenants, particularly where the seller has clearly accepted specific consideration for giving this covenant, there is also a general principle that people have a right to earn a living. Therefore the courts will look at any non-competition covenant and only allow it to be enforced where it is fairly specific in terms of a geographical area, a period and an activity in which the seller agrees not to compete.

So if you try to obtain a very widely drawn non-competition covenant, this may in fact be counterproductive as it is likely to be unenforceable in practice.

While the strength of the non-competition covenant is always a negotiating point, as with warranties, be on the lookout for any surprising reluctance to agree to reasonable terms in this area as this may be indication that the seller has some intention of trading in the future. If so, what impact is this likely to have on the value of the business you are buying?

CLOSURE

Once the sales contract has been signed and exchanged, there may then be a period between exchange and completion. This gap may for example be required to allow you to complete your financing arrangements where final release of the funds from lenders may be dependent upon the bank or finance company having sight of the contract. There may therefore be a period of, say, two or four weeks between exchange and the proposed date of completion.

If you have bought the business with others you need to ensure that key person insurance is put in place in the event that something happens to any of the main players, as well as your shareholders' agreement which clearly sets out what happens in the event of any future disagreement and specifies how shares are to be valued if any member of the team decides that they wish to exit.

The way in which the seller manages the business in the period between exchange and completion will be covered by way of covenants, as discussed above. The sales contract should also specify the conditions that must be met for the contract to be completed, again as discussed above, in order to protect you from buying a business that has suffered severe deterioration between the date of exchange and the date of completion.

Date of completion

The date of completion will be the day on which all documents are completed and funds are formally transferred. In practice completion day is often hectic, involving a large amount of work for advisers for both sides. Legal teams will be involved in ensuring that all the documents of title to assets or share transfers are passed across and that funds have been received into the right bank accounts, in the right amounts, at the correct times. At the same time, valuers may well be on site undertaking an inventory of fixed plant and equipment and a stock count, while accountants may be involved in doing cut-off tests on debtors and creditors so as to be able to quickly draw up completion accounts showing the trading performance in the last set of accounts to the date of transfer.

Since there is so much to be finalised, particularly in terms of transferring legal documents, you are relying on the seller and their advisers to have ensured that all the legal documentation (including such paperwork as intellectual property rights, trademarks and patents) is reviewed and readied for transfer. Completion day will be a very busy, long and stressful affair. You should therefore ensure that your advisers liaise closely with the sellers to ensure that there are no unnecessary hitches with documentation.

Looking beyond the accountants, valuers and surveyors who will be running all over the business, and the immediate tasks of ensuring that all the details are caught, such as taking over utility supplies and confirming insurance is in place, there are other vital matters to attend to.

In addition to completing the deal, completion day is also the first day of the real task – which is making the deal work – when you announce the deal to your workforce, your customers, suppliers, the press and any other interested parties. And you have to hit the ground running, with your communication strategy in place and your detailed post-acquisition plan ready to roll.

But meanwhile, eventually the day will all be over. You will have heard from the solicitor that the wire transfers have been made and that all the documentation has been dealt with.

Congratulations! The business is now yours and it is time to open that bottle of champagne and start the post deal party.

TYPICAL SHARE PURCHASE AGREEMENT

Appendix C on page 451 is an example of a share purchase agreement that you might expect your solicitors to reach through negotiations between parties of relatively equal bargaining power.

As you will have seen from this chapter, the key issue to look out for is how risk is to be dealt with in the sale, both by the warranties that are suggested, but also by the degree of protection for the seller of their sales proceeds. This is the time when having an experienced corporate finance lawyer fighting your corner during the negotiations that are to come is invaluable.

In a contract for a purchase of business and assets, the terms will define what particular assets are to be purchased and which liabilities are to be acquired, together with specific matters such as whether the sale is on the basis of a sale as a going concern and how VAT is to be dealt with.

(16)

Trouble with the Taxman

THE IMPORTANCE OF TAX

The taxation implications of a business sale are usually very high up on the seller's list of priorities. Almost invariably the seller will look to take tax advice from their accountant and as this advice can have a significant impact upon the terms that sellers are likely to want, it is worthwhile briefly reviewing the issues involved.

Tax is a complex area and also one where any information given may become out of date very quickly as the relevant rules, regulations and rates of tax will vary from budget to budget, albeit that the basic principles tend to remain the same.

This chapter therefore sets out the four principle taxes that may have an impact on the seller's planning of their sale. It outlines how the treatment of each tax differs between the sale of the shares in the business and the sale of the company's business and assets.

If part of your intention in buying the business is to move in turn towards selling at a later date, planning how to structure the business to best deal with these taxes may form part of your post-acquisition planning.

VALUE ADDED TAX

If the business is registered for VAT, when it sells either items of stock or service, or any business assets, such as plant and equipment or furniture, these are taxable supplies on which VAT (currently 17.5%) should be charged.

An exception is made where a business is being sold as a going concern to a VAT registered purchaser, in which case the business and assets can be sold without the need to charge VAT to the purchaser. HM Customs & Excise will have to be satisfied, however, that the sale is outside the scope of VAT. It is not uncommon, for example, in sales of business and assets by receivers, to find a clause included that the sale is of a going concern and it is therefore to be outside the scope of VAT, but in the event that it is ruled to be within the scope of VAT, the purchaser will have to pay VAT on the consideration.

In the event of a sale of the shares of a company, VAT does not apply.

STAMP DUTY

Stamp duty is a tax that applies to the sale of a wide range of assets at differing rates.

In the event of the sale of shares in a company, stamp duty of 0.5% is payable at current rates, whilst on the sale of a business and assets, stamp duty will be payable at varying rates on the varying classes of assets included in the sale.

One way to minimise the stamp duty implications of a business and assets sale is by looking to exclude assets from the transaction. For example, stamp duty would be payable if you purchase the business's debtor book, so it might be more cost-effective if the seller excludes debtors from the sale and retains these to collect in, thereby avoiding stamp duty. In this circumstance, the purchase price would obviously be less (as you are not getting the benefit of the collection of debtors) but if the seller retains this asset, they can collect the cash from the book as it comes in.

CAPITAL GAINS TAX

Capital gains tax is intended as a tax on the sale of assets which have been held over time (as opposed to income or corporation tax which is charged on the profits of trading on a regular basis). Both companies and individuals may be liable for capital gains tax.

The trend over recent years has been to reduce the impact of capital gains tax on business sales. Where a seller has held shares for over two years, the capital gains tax payable in respect of the value of those shares is reduced by a mechanism known as **tapering relief** down to an effective tax rate at the time of writing of approximately 10% on the sale of those shares.

If, however, the company sells its assets, any capital gain arising on the value of those assets will be chargeable to capital gains tax, subject to any reliefs at the company's rate of corporation tax (for example, 21%).

INCOME TAX

Where an individual has sold his shares in the company, there are no income tax implications as the entire taxation has in effect been dealt with through any capital gain that has arisen.

Where, however, the company has sold its business and assets, there then remains the problem of distributing the money from this cash shell to the shareholders. If the company distributes this by way of say, a dividend, then this distribution will obviously represent taxable income in the hands of the shareholders and may therefore be taxed at their personal tax rate.

There are mechanisms which can be used in order to minimise or eliminate the income tax due in respect of distribution of proceeds from the company to the owners. For example, a Member's Voluntary Liquidation (a solvent liquidation of the company carried out by a licensed insolvency practitioner) in which the assets of the dissolved company are simply distributed to the shareholders in settlement of their shareholding, can be used to reduce their tax exposure.

Of course, if there is any ongoing consultancy work or other payments following the sale, the seller is likely to be subject to income tax in respect of these.

INTERACTION OF INCOME AND CAPITAL GAINS TAXES

The most tax efficient route for the business owner is generally to sell their shares in the business, as if they have held these for over two years, they will only pay 10% capital gains tax. This compares, for example, to the company selling its business and assets (and paying capital gains tax on any profit on disposal), before having to distribute the proceeds by way of a dividend on which the owner will pay income tax.

This tax issue generally leads most sellers to prefer a sale of shares when disposing of the business. To minimise the risk of acquiring unknown or contingent liabilities, as has already been demonstrated, you are likely to prefer a sale of the business and assets. The type of sale therefore has a value to both the seller and you as buyer which must be reflected in the price paid.

The basic points are summarised in the table below, but the overriding rule must be to take professional advice at the outset as to how the deal can be best structured to meet your personal tax planning requirements.

Taxation of a business sale in summary

	Sale of shares	Sale of assets
Value Added Tax	n/a	17.5% on taxable supplies (if registered) unless transaction is a sale as a going concern.
Stamp Duty	0.5%	Range of charges dependent on asset sold.
Capital Gains Tax	Taxed at personal rate, but if held for more than two years, tapering relief applies, reducing tax rate to 10%.	Company chargeable to tax at its effective rate of Corporation Tax on profit on disposal subject to any reliefs.
Income Tax	n/a	Distribution of proceeds to shareholders (e.g. by way of a dividend) means taxable income for the shareholders at their effective personal rate of tax. An ongoing consultancy payment to the seller post sale will be subject to income tax in the normal way.

Phase 5: Making it Work

17

Taking Control

THE TIMESCALE AND NEED FOR SPEED

So you have completed a deal, congratulations! Take your partner out for a good dinner to celebrate and to thank them for their support in the process so far. But make sure that they understand that it is only the process so far. Because now comes the difficult part, which will determine whether it is all worthwhile or not – making the business work.

The reason for failure of most purchases is not because the due diligence missed a major looming problem which took the new owners by surprise, but simply because the new owners fail to make the acquisition work.

After all, you will have put a lot of time and effort into checking out the business before you bought it and ensuring that it has good products, good relationships with customers and is delivering value. All other things being equal you would hope that following the purchase this will continue to be the case, so if you bought a good business the only reason that it could become a bad business is as a result of the actions you take in buying it.

The process of taking control

The process of taking control of the business can divide into three phases:

- ◆ taking the business over on day one, which will involve a mixture of both completion activities and initial meetings that generally are immediately internally focused

- ◆ taking control in the first couple of months, when it is important to get out to meet the clients and key suppliers as quickly as possible; as well as pushing through any changes required to restructure the business in the way you want it

- ◆ running the business for the longer term.

To make this process as successful as possible you need to take into account that the fact that you have bought the business means that it is going to change as staff, customers and suppliers all adjust to the fact that a transaction has taken place and that you are the new owner.

Planning for change

You need to take advantage of this inevitable degree of change to ensure that the changes you actively want to put through happen as quickly and as efficiently as possible so as to minimise inevitable disruption. To do so you need to be as prepared as possible before plunging into the change process and to arrive with a plan at the outset.

Of course, as in the old saying, no plan survives first contact with the enemy and you will soon find that any process of changing the business will not run smoothly along the lines of your plan, which will inevitably become out of date. You will therefore need to be prepared to be quick thinking and adaptable in reacting to the inevitable changes in circumstances that you will be faced with on a day-to-day basis.

In practice, whilst a detailed proposed implementation plan is a useful starting point and guide as to how to set out, what you will find most of use during the process is:

- a very clear focus on the eventual outcome you're aiming to achieve as a result of your overall strategy

- a willingness to adapt your tactics in order to achieve that strategy

- a strong drive to put the strategy in place as quickly as possible.

So take as your motto a quote attributed to General Douglas MacArthur: 'Have a plan. Execute it ruthlessly. Start today.'

Approaches to avoid

In contrast, the approaches to avoid if you wish to achieve a swift and effective transition are:

- **failing to communicate** – you need to communicate real information to people about the real issues they are interested in and not simply expect to blind them with PR and hype

- **failing to provide real leadership** – you need to address head-on such issues as culture clashes, political battles amongst managers in the business and tying in the rewards for managers to the behaviours that you want to see

- **death by detail** – you concentrate on driving through the big picture and avoid becoming bogged down in minor details; and its allied failing of

- **death by committee** – you need to identify clearly the people responsible for driving projects through and empower them both to get on with it and to communicate what they're doing.

It is also worth remembering, however, that once you've got through a period of change you will then need to bed the business down to run on a more stable basis, and managers who are good at pushing through a major change programme may be poor at managing a business in a more steady state. You may therefore find that you will want to employ different managers for different parts of the process.

Example

One acquisitive industrial conglomerate developed a standard approach to managing businesses that it bought which became nicknamed 'the black BMW approach'.

The post-acquisition team would arrive on site the day after completion driving their black BMWs. This team's job was to continue to run the business 'as is' and to investigate it thoroughly but not to make any major changes whatsoever. Instead the team was to come up with the plan for what needed to happen to the business, and also to identify the person either within the business or to be brought in from outside to run it and to make the changes happen. As soon as that person was found and put in post, the 'black BMW' team disappeared off to the next assignment and the new managing director of the business was the person who had the job of making changes happen.

FAST OR SLOW INTEGRATION?

The 'black BMW approach' discussed above in some ways falls into the school of thought that suggests that a business sale is a disruptive event and that a purchaser should allow a short period of consolidation to take place before starting to make changes (graph A below).

Waiting before making changes

This approach allows you to 'play yourself in' in order to find out how the business actually operates and to establish working

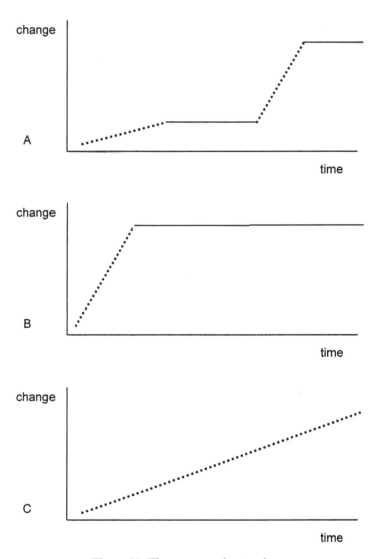

Figure 11. Three approaches to change

relationships with your key customers and staff. It is then felt that you are on safer ground in starting to make changes, since the information that was gathered during due diligence by you and your advisers was done so as an outsider and there is nothing like working in the business to refine your understanding of how it operates, particularly in respect of issues such as culture, the informal power structures and who has the key knowledge.

You can then start to make changes from a position where you have:

- stabilised the business after the impact of your acquisition and made sure it is under your control before commencing major change

- confirmed your understanding of the state of the business and the changes that you wish to make, based on not only the work you've undertaken from outside when doing your due diligence but from having had a chance to run the business for a while to see how it works from the inside

- met and established a relationship with the key employees, customers and suppliers so when you do start to make changes you are better able to communicate your intentions and achieve co-operation in implementing them as quickly as possible.

The disadvantage of this approach is that by implication you will have two periods of change, the sale and a subsequent restructuring, together with a period of uncertainty in between. Since there have been two periods of change there may also be a lingering question as to when the next set of changes will come along.

Making changes immediately
In contrast some buyers, including perhaps most famously John Moulton of the venture capital firm Alchemy, seem to favour taking advantage of this disruption to make changes immediately with the maximum 'violence', so they can be got through as quickly as possible to then allow the business to settle down (graph B).

The disadvantages of this approach are essentially the opposites of the advantages listed above, in that you will be embarking on a major change process *without* having:

♦ stabilised the business

♦ checked your understanding of how it operates; *or*

♦ established your communications with all the key stakeholders and obtained their support for your plan.

The advantage is that there is only one period of major change and that once it is complete it should therefore be easier to convince all the stakeholders the business is now stable and they have no further significant disruption to fear.
As the skills involved in managing a major change and the personality types best suited to do it can be very different from those required to run a business in a longer smoother growth phase, this approach also lends itself to the use of a specialist manager such as a 'company doctor' to lead the initial process (try the 'local help' facility at www.turnaroundhelp.co.uk for referral to an experienced company doctor). They can then hand the business over to someone else to run the business for the longer term in a more consensual or consultative and business development focused mode. This divorces the period of violent or radical change from the boss who is taking the business forwards.

Gradual change
There is a third approach (graph C) which is to attempt to avoid a step change so as to present a picture of business continuity and to avoid as far as possible upsetting any of the key stakeholders. This can lend itself for example to a simple succession sale in a family business, but is really only an appropriate approach if you do not have any major changes you

want to make. If you do have major changes you wish to make then this approach can be highly counterproductive as it will eventually result in the perception of continual drawn out change and confusion with no clear start to the process or sense of completion and return to stability afterwards.

Coping with uncertainty

Whichever approach you adopt, it is true to say that until the business has settled down, staff will be distracted from focusing on what you need them to do, which is to make the business a success by delivering good value to customers. Instead, time will be spent speculating on what is going to happen or worrying about their future. As a result staff will tend to concentrate less on their tasks, leading to greater rates of errors, quality returns and lost productivity. When people are worried about internal matters the relationships with outside parties such as customers tend to suffer, providing a great opportunity for competitors to move into the business's customer base and take advantage of disruption.

In the case of extreme uncertainty the best and most marketable employees will be the most tempting targets for competitors to poach. Salespeople for example may become concerned about their ability to sell and therefore earn bonuses as a result of the internal disruption in business and once poached can do significant damage.

And once into a prolonged change process, it is amazing how the costs of delay can rack up across all areas of the business.

By contrast a speedy change process that quickly delivers results – and, more importantly for the employees, certainty that the main period of change is now over and they can get on with their lives knowing where they stand – minimises these effects.

Compare the effects on employee morale of the following two approaches:

- an announcement that says 'having completed our strategic review we are restructuring the business and unfortunately have taken the decision to close the outlet in X with 20 redundancies at the end of the month. We are happy to confirm that this action will complete our restructuring and it is our intention to keep all other outlets open'

- a situation where over a period of six or nine months, 20 staff are made redundant in ones and twos.

In the first situation employees are given the bad news in one go, there is a clear rationale communicated as to the reasons why, and there is also importantly a clear assurance that the process is now completed and employees can stop worrying about whether their own jobs are at risk.

In the second situation there is no such certainty from the employees' point of view, just a drip drip of an extended period of job losses with the resultant uncertainty about individuals and futures. Even once you've completed making redundancies it is likely to take a significant period before this fact is actually accepted by the workforce.

Deciding on your approach
Which of these approaches you decide to take is a matter of business judgement, which should be based on:

- the complexity of the business being taken over

- how confident you feel in your understanding of how it operates

- how confident you feel in your ability to push through the changes immediately

- the degree of complexity of changes you think you wish to make

- your assessment of the degree of disturbance that the sale will have on the stakeholders

- how urgent the need is to change radically the business's performance.

Of course this is all in many ways an oversimplification, in that you are not simply going to make one series of changes in the business immediately after acquisition and leave it at that. As you move the business forward the business will of course be in a continual state of incremental change as you adapt it to meet new trading circumstances and develop it in the way you wish. This incremental ongoing change should be part of a normal business improvement and development programme, however, where the pace of change may be slower and the approach much more consensual than that needed to achieve a quick major step change.

All of the above tends to suggest that whether a change process starts immediately or after a period of consolidation, it should then be swiftly executed.

If you believe that it should start as soon as possible after the sale, then making it work means working on it in advance so that you arrive with a plan.

YOUR PLAN

This is where your work during due diligence on the business – its markets, its key customers, its suppliers, its key staff, culture, organisation and processes – should really pay off. As a result of this work you should have in place a plan for what you want to do to change the business before you walk in through the door.

Having this in place means that you know what to get on with, you know your priorities and you can also give clear leadership and a strong sense of direction to your new employees, which will help to settle much of the nervousness occasioned by the change of ownership. And so long as your plan is sensible and clearly communicated it will help keep staff motivated and enthusiastic as they become confident that their future is secure.

The areas that your plan needs to cover include:

◆ taking control

◆ communications and announcing the news both internally and externally

◆ how you are going to manage any major change programme

◆ how you will structure the new entity to manage risks (a 'bulkhead review')

◆ the financial management of the business, management information, and your plans to improve profit and cashflow

◆ the way in which you are going to manage the business for value and the degree to which you are going to integrate it with other operations that you may own (whether this is going to be a 'hands off' management style when the business manages itself against its financial targets or a 'hands on' one where it is closely integrated and controlled from the centre)

◆ how you can extract maximum value from the acquired business, such as by disposing of unwanted sites or business units for the greatest value.

This is all in addition to managing the necessary detail that you may have to arrange such as new stationery, new packaging or providing access to books and records.

This chapter covers the issues of communications and change management, while the financial and commercial management aspects are covered in Chapter 18.

COMMUNICATIONS

Uncertainty and disruption are your biggest enemies after the purchase, and effective communication is your best tool with which to fight these. Part of your plan should be a communications strategy, both internal and external, covering everything from the announcement of the deal and what it means, to your plans for moving the business forward and developing it.

Think of this as both a selling document to your staff and customers designed to maintain and develop confidence in you and the business going forwards; as well as a template that sets out the path that the business is going to take which puts the changes you are planning into context.

To design your approach to communication you need to understand:

◆ **who you are communicating with** – which will include both employees inside the business and people outside the business, principally your customers and suppliers

◆ **what you are trying to achieve by communicating with them** – which is generally to obtain support for the changes you are planning to make and to reduce any potential damage to the business by removing uncertainty

- **what you need to do to communicate effectively** – which is to understand what it is that the people you are communicating with will want to know, and provide them with a meaningful answer.

The groups of relevant people and the sorts of issues that they are likely to be concerned about include:

- **Employees** – who will want to know what's happening about jobs, who's going to be in charge of their department, when they will know about changes in procedures, what the plans mean in respect of the projects they are working on.

- **Customers** – who will be concerned as to whether quality will be maintained, whether they will still have the same point of contact, what will happen to prices, whether the new products in the pipeline will continue to be developed.

- **Suppliers** – who will be asking whether you will continue to use the existing suppliers, whether you will look to renegotiate prices, whether they can rely on being paid, on time.

It follows from this that you can easily adopt a systematic and structured approach by using a pre-prepared 'Q & A grid'. To do so, identify all the interested parties across the top of a sheet in as much detail as you think you will need. Then you should think up all the basic, rude, blunt questions that any of them might want to know and list these down the left. This provides you with a grid to fill in where each box will require an answer that can be communicated to the relevant parties.

In each case you should consider carefully the best medium for the message you want to put across to a particular audience, as the means by which people are provided with information can significantly affect the way they react to it. For example, if the plans unfortunately call for the closure of a factory this needs to

Issues	Interested parties			
	Employees	Customers	Suppliers	Public
Will there be redundancies?				
Will new products be launched?				
What will happen to the Wales factory?				

Figure 12. Communication grid

be communicated to those employees by way of a face-to-face meeting rather than announced as a press release to local media.

However, once the news is out, as a general rule you should put the answer out as widely as possible. It doesn't matter if someone hears it three times, as long as everybody that needs to hears it at least once.

This approach ensures that as far as possible you have a consistent and coherent message on any topic.

Of course this grid will never cover every question that you may be asked and there may be boxes in the grid for which you do not initially have an answer. The rule then must be to answer these questions as honestly and openly as possible whilst avoiding giving hostages to fortune or over-promising what can be delivered, which will undermine your future credibility. If you don't know the answer to a question you should say so, but try to give an indication of when you will know.

Communicating with staff
The two absolutely critical groups are your staff and customers, and your communications process usually starts immediately on

completion by holding a meeting with the staff. At this the old owner is likely to want to introduce you to announce that the sale has taken place. Having the old owner do so can help to reassure staff; and do not forget that as a result of the need to maintain confidentiality many of them will either not know of it at all or only recently have found out as part of the process of completion, which may have come as a shock.

You should have a positive message ready for this meeting to maintain enthusiasm, and having worked through your communications matrix be able to deal with any questions that arise or give a timetable for when things will be made clear.

There will often be questions about the likelihood of changes or redundancies, as a prime concern of employees will be whether any of them will lose their jobs. The rule here is as far as possible not to give hostages to fortune. The honest answer is often that:

♦ once you have taken over, yes, there are likely to be changes and you can never give any guarantees of jobs, but

♦ you have bought the business because it is successful and it has been so because of the way staff keep the customers satisfied

♦ to keep the business successful you will want to keep the customers happy and keep the staff who do so

♦ therefore, the best way to keep the business successful and to keep jobs secure is to continue to provide customers with excellent service.

If this is a succession sale within a family firm, you can emphasise that the sale has ensured there will be continuity in the business going forwards, which will therefore help safeguard jobs.

In addition to any general meeting, you will also need to meet the key players within the management individually as soon as possible post sale and confirm to them personally their importance to you in order to make sure you retain them.

It is a very natural reaction to focus the majority of your initial effort on communicating with the employees. This is because being inside the business they are very visible to you as the new owner and therefore the impact of any problems or issues can be very apparent to you. You will also rightly have a perception that your employees are a key channel for getting the message across to the customers as they represent the business to them. However, simply relying upon your communication with the employees to filter through in a secondhand way to the customer base is asking for trouble.

Communicating with customers

Your customers are the lifeblood of your business and your new competitors will be talking to them direct to suggest that the business sale and the changes that this will mean for the business are likely to have an adverse impact on the quality of service they are receiving (about which they may well be right as there is inevitably some risk of disruption). And if any disruption is prolonged, the people working for your competitors who are doing the talking to your customers may well be your own ex-sales people who are looking to take their relationships with them. It is therefore vital that you have a direct communications campaign to your customers to explain what has happened to the business and to ensure that you retain them through any changeover period.

You should arrange visits to each of your top customers as quickly as possible after the sale (or if at all possible before) so that ideally you can be speaking to them before knowledge of the transaction leaks into the marketplace and competitors start their attempts to poach.

You should ask the existing business owner to set up a series of meetings with the top customers, preferably over the first week or so, in order that they can introduce you to them. You can then make your pitch, which is usually based around the message of 'business as usual'. This also gives you an opportunity to open a direct dialogue with customers over any concerns they may have regarding issues that you may need to prioritise in your plan, as well establishing a new direct personal contact as quickly as possible.

Communicating with other stakeholders

Going forwards you should try to obtain good sources of information as to what questions all the main groups of people with any interest in the business (or 'stakeholders') are asking. This list ranges from shareholders, directors, managers and employees, through to suppliers, bankers, landlords, local authorities, customers and in some cases the general public.

Each group will have their own interests and issues of concern in the business that may have to be dealt with. So you should meet with suppliers and customers on a regular basis and encourage a dialogue with staff, possibly by using focus groups if the business has a large number of employees. And when you identify a question that is causing people problems, you should deal with it quickly.

Try also to identify the key opinion formers within each group. It may quickly become obvious, for example, which employees are the ones that the rest listen to; and so for your message to be effective, you need to ensure that these individuals are convinced. You should also ensure that your middle managers are brought into the process and used as effectively as possible to communicate to the workforce, as they will usually be seen as the normal channel through which such information is officially distributed to employees.

Your communication with all stakeholders needs to be both full and frank and an ongoing process. It is likely, for example, that any plans you have for the business will change over time. To maintain your credibility with the stakeholders you will therefore need to communicate actively how your plan is progressing, as well as the reasons for any changes to the plan in an open and ongoing way.

CHANGE MANAGEMENT

When it comes to making changes in the business there are really two questions:

◆ What types of changes to you want to make?

◆ How do you make change really happen on the ground?

In some ways the first is actually the easier question to answer, with some general rules:

◆ **Don't forget the detail, but stay focused on the big picture** – there will be a huge amount of detail and a wide variety of changes you may wish to put through. Don't lose sight of these but ensure you remain focused on making the relatively small number of key strategic changes you want to make as quickly and as efficiently as possible so that the business is rolling forward on the track you want. You will have time later to deal with the rest as part of an ongoing business improvement process.

One way to prioritise actions is to use a matrix like the one below to plot your estimates of which actions will have the largest/fastest relative effects so that you can focus on the ones that will make a real difference.

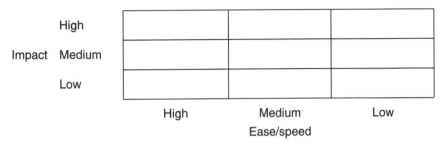

Figure 13. Prioritisation matrix

◆ **Focus on your long-term plan for the business** – so for example if the long-term plan is to build and sell the business then you should have your exit strategy in mind in considering every change to the business.

◆ **Don't make unnecessary changes** – don't change the business name just to see your name in lights. You bought a business with an established market reputation so you have acquired all its investment over the years in advertising itself and getting its name recognised amongst its existing and potential customers. Why would you want to throw all this overboard just as you are at the most risky time for the business in terms of losing customers?

◆ **No cost is too small to cut** – it is worth reviewing all the overheads and suppliers for a number of reasons. Firstly this ensures that all the members of staff know that costs are going to be actively watched and managed. As well as establishing financial discipline generally, if it is known that the new boss is reviewing all purchase orders and asking awkward questions, this can make staff think twice about what they need to buy, which will help to reduce outflows in the initial phase.

But it's also worth reviewing suppliers in general as many businesses are not good at purchasing and get into the habit of buying from the same suppliers without regularly tendering to check that they are getting the best price. Purchasing staff will also naturally build up personal relationships with suppliers and can as a result become unwilling to bargain hard or seek cheaper alternatives. In the worst cases these relationships can become actively corrupt with kickbacks that cost the business real money. So it is always worth undertaking a review of your key suppliers of both materials and services, as well as normal overheads such as utilities as a fresh and aggressive look may well enable you to make some quick cost savings.

◆ **Avoid death by a thousand cuts** – if you do have to make redundancies, it's generally best practice to do it once, in order to get it over with. A drawn out process of redundancies saps employee morale as in this situation no member of staff knows whether their job is safe from day to day in which case the best employees are usually the most marketable ones. And you may well find that the employees you really wish to keep jump ship to your competitors, leaving you in the worst case with a demoralised workforce of poor performers.

If you are having difficulties in prioritising tasks or in thinking through the linkages between tasks and issues that will need to be addressed, try using the 'sticky note consultancy' approach:

◆ Buy a pack of different coloured sticky notes.

◆ Have members of staff brainstorm individually without discussion as many suggestions as possible regarding issues facing the business onto yellow sticky notes (if it helps you can set a target for a minimum number of suggestions). The suggestions can be single words or short sentences.

◆ As a separate exercise that can run alongside this approach and be referred back to the discussion as you go through it, try handing out different coloured sticky notes and asking each member of staff to answer the question, 'If there was one thing I would change about this business to make it more successful it would be . . .'

◆ Collect all the notes in, read them out to the group, and try to consolidate them into similar topics. Then use a different coloured note to summarise the subject of each topic into a single phrase.

◆ Taking each topic then discuss with the group the degree of impact that dealing with the issue will have and the ease and speed with which it can be dealt with, so that agreement is reached as to where the topic lies on the matrix shown above.

◆ Taking the high-impact high-speed segment as priority you should then be able to focus on a limited number of high-value priority projects on which you can then again brainstorm, each time using different coloured notes and grouping ideas generated into topics:

– all the actions that can be taken in respect of these specific issues

– all the blockages, difficulties or problems that might be associated with any of these actions

– all the solutions to the blockages.

◆ Compare the actions that you generated through this exercise with the staff's ideas as to the one thing they would change. Consider how the results compare and why.

For each project generated by this approach, appoint a champion with responsibility for delivery and have them use the material created to produce a project plan with a defined timeline and key milestones. This should then be published within the business, for example by being written out on a length of brown paper and posted up in the business, and updated by the champion so that staff can see when the milestones are achieved.

MANAGING PEOPLE AND THE PROCESS OF CHANGE

You have now set your business objectives, you have decided what changes are needed. Is this enough? Will the changes simply happen? Or not?

The answer is that unless you make them happen, there will be no changes. And making them happen can be difficult because there are many barriers to overcome, which tend to break down into the following major categories:

Problem	Issue	Solution
Staff don't know they have to change	Lack information	Communication of plan, goals and actions
Staff can't change	Lack knowledge of what they need to do	Communication of plan, goals and actions
	Lack knowledge of how to do it	Training and support
	Lack resources (time, money, people, equipment) to allow them to do it	Project management skills
Staff won't change	Do not wish to make the changes	Understand motivation Manage culture change

Figure 14. Change issues

Or, in many cases, a combination of all three.

You will need to recognise that it is very difficult to change people's beliefs. But by planning rewards and managing people you can significantly change their behaviours. And since it is their behaviours that actually have an impact on the business, this is what you want to focus on.

The overall approach to managing change is to:

- **Take active steps** to break old habits and introduce new ones.

- **Provide clear objectives** that are communicated to staff clearly so they know what they are.

- Give them **role models** that they can follow, people who live the behaviours that you want who are placed in very visible positions so everyone can see them. This, by the way, implies that the culture and behaviour of staff must become one of your key recruitment and promotion criteria as opposed to purely technical merit or other qualifications.

- Give **meaningful, generous and very public rewards** – financial and recognition, promotion and new work opportunities to people who show the required behaviour.

- **Be consistent** and keep the messages (e.g. 'be customer focused') and your policies (e.g. managing people to ensure that they are very compliant with detailed company rules and procedures) consistent with each other (so how does a member of staff know what to do if satisfying a customer complaint involves doing something that goes against company procedures?).

HOW CAN YOU MAKE CHANGE HAPPEN?

Existing habits are hard to break. Making change happen requires applying effort to overcome often deep-seated resistance to change, in order to break out of existing ways of doing things and create new healthier habits.

Creating effective change therefore usually entails going through a process as illustrated below:

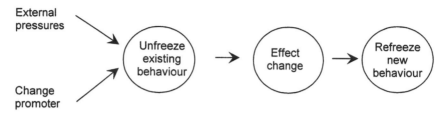

Figure 15. Making change happen

Your staff can be reluctant to change for a wide variety of reasons:

◆ **psychological** – uncertainty, fear, disorientation (so change needs to be as swift as possible to avoid nagging doubt, but slow enough to bring everyone with it)

◆ **personal attitudes and beliefs** – 'We cannot deliberately underquote in the initial stages of an assignment (like everyone else in the industry does) to get the work as it just isn't right'

◆ **group loyalty** – the sales team may fight like cats and dogs but just watch them stick together if you try to put production in charge

◆ **habit** – 'but we've always done it this way'

◆ **politics** – 'not if Joe is going to be in charge'

◆ **physiological** – the new roster of 20 consecutive night shifts is unacceptable.

To unfreeze existing behaviour you therefore often need the heat of external pressure (a 'burning platform') before people will realise the need to move to a new position. But you cannot simply rely on external forces to provide sufficient pressures, as few of your staff will have a real immediate appreciation of your position.

You will therefore also need to signal major change and make it real by doing something that really makes people sit up and take notice.

'Barnstorming ideas' and shock tactics (and the messages they convey) can include:

- **slaughtering sacred cows** – everything in your business is potentially up for radical change

- **killing something big** – is there a large visible project that can be axed (without threatening future development)?

- **clearing out non-performers** – you cannot afford passengers

- **breaking a blocker** – if someone is actively blocking change, they cannot be allowed to win; either they are with the changes and where we are going or they are against us.

Obviously, if you can get your staff to *want* to change ('buy in') they are obviously a lot easier to manage and motivate than if you need to force them to change. Unfortunately the management style required to get change to happen tends to be dictated by the degree of urgency and speed of response needed.

In the initial phases of a takeover, speed of change tends to be of the essence and periods of uncertainty have to be minimised. This tends to require a highly centralised and directive management style to deal with this phase, which then needs to evolve to a more empowering one allowing more autonomy and room for employee innovation and experimentation.

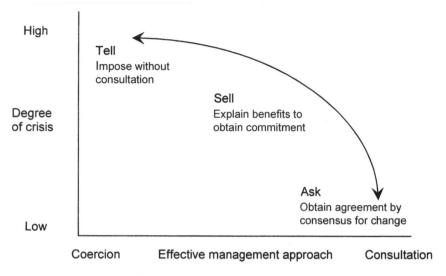

Figure 16. Management style by type of change

A compromise approach that can be very effective in empowering a team to direct a swift pace of change is the 'weekend workshop', where you get your line managers together as a group for a summit. There the team really thinks out, in a concentrated and intense atmosphere, what the situation is, what needs to happen, and who is going to do what. When this is done right, the team becomes a powerful committed force and never forgets, 'Our twelve-hour day when we sorted out how we were going to really fix this business.'

You will need to give the team time to gel, however, as to become a team, the group has to go through a team building process of forming, storming, norming and performing as discussed in Chapter 3.

As you move through the process, the ways of effecting and fixing change will start with a very directive style of fixing new habits, by for example:

◆ issuing instructions; and then

- checking up every day for 21 days that the instruction is being followed that day.

By the end of three weeks:

- the new way of doing something will have become the new habit

- your staff will know that once something has been decided, they need to do it because there is no hiding place and you will not be going away.

You can then relax your enforcement and policing on this item significantly.

This approach is highly time consuming and your efforts will therefore need to be clearly prioritised, but in a small company which does not have a tier of strong operational management there really is little alternative but to be involved on site every day to make any changes stick.

Over time you can move to a more empowering mechanism for changing the culture using other skills to manage the culture:

- **Walk the talk** – leading by example.

- **Shared values** – including attitude as a basis for recruiting like-minded staff to reinforce the culture. Defining 'antisocial behaviour' (e.g. rudeness to customers, laziness) for 'our culture'. If everyone is living the culture, the 'antisocial' can be dumped without remorse or protest.

- **Training** – the values of the organisation should be specified and incorporated into training and staff development.

- ◆ **Rewards** – reward employees who act the values.

- ◆ **Value staff** – treat them like winners and care.

- ◆ **Celebrate success** – identify wins (especially early quick ones), make success very visible (e.g. a bottle of champagne to people who achieve targets).

- ◆ **Celebrate creative failures** – better to try and not succeed than not to try at all, so long as the risk and downside of failure is limited.

- ◆ **Cultivate identity** – promote the values as part of your brand and make it real by way of uniforms, corporate colours, emblems and slogans (visit a Kwikfit).

- ◆ **Customers first** – make the job worthwhile.

- ◆ **Tight culture, loose management** – give staff discretion but within the bounds of a firm set of corporate values.

MANAGING AND MOTIVATING STAFF TO CHANGE

When managing staff it is important to recognise that your staff will have a variety of personality types and will be motivated by, and fear, different things.

Two types of employees – 'round pegs' and 'square pegs'

You as an entrepreneur may be driven by success (and fear failure). Some of your staff may seek praise and recognition and fear rejection. Both you and these types of employees may often be quick to take decisions, and are restless, active and open for change (call them square pegs). Others of your staff, however, will value security and structured policies within which to work ('so they know where they stand') and fear change, uncertainty or conflict (call them round pegs).

You therefore need to be careful in normal times that you manage your staff in a way that is appropriate to them. So your production staff may be round pegs, in the round holes of structured work and be managed in a round peg way (e.g. with detailed instructions on how to do their particular job). Your sales staff, however, will tend to be square pegs, in square holes, who need to be managed in a square peg way (e.g. with clear targets of sales to achieve and lots of praise for success).

This also means that you need to manage the way you go about changing things to match the needs of your staff:

Your pace of change	Square staff	Round staff
Fast	You will move at a speed they feel comfortable with	Your rush to change things will frighten these staff. You (and your other square staff) will need to slow the pace of change and provide more support so that these staff feel secure in their ability to handle change
Slow	Will be frustrated by your pace. You need to speed up your pace of change to keep them with you	You will move at a pace that they feel comfortable with

Figure 17. Matching pace of change to staff

Particularly with 'round' staff, managing change can be about building confidence in their ability to change. This is helped by:

♦ providing support through training and information

♦ building trust through two-way communication, avoidance of criticisms of the past, allowing failures, and appreciating that success may take time

♦ providing appropriate rewards.

Different motivations

Rewards are not always a simple matter of cash recognition. Different things motivate different people, and security, a feeling of being valued, or a team atmosphere can each be as important for some people, if not more so, than cash. You should therefore reward people in the way that is most motivating to them. So ask yourself:

◆ What reward structures do you have in place to encourage specific behaviours (by making it in your staff's interests to do what you want them to do), e.g. commission for salespeople?

◆ Do you understand what motivates your workers? Which of praise, security, power, excitement or cash will motivate which best?

◆ Have you identified which of your staff naturally tend to fill which team roles in a team (the new ideas person, the boss, the project manager, or the tidier up of loose ends)? Are you using them to their best advantage?

◆ Are there personality issues which are leading to conflicts (e.g., where the salesman who hates paperwork drives the production department up the wall because of failure to properly record and specify what the customer wants)? What are you doing to manage these sorts of issues?

◆ What is your natural management style? Direct (a spade is a spade, be it good or bad); influencing (lots of praise for good behaviour, coaching for bad); formal, by the book, with written memos, etc.? Does your style work equally well on everyone, or would it be more efficient for you to use different styles to manage different personality types?

Businesses run most efficiently:

- with round pegs in round holes

- when managers know who is round and who is square, and manage them in round and square ways appropriately

- by ensuring that systems mean that round and square individuals are used to complement each other and not to cause conflict.

This can best be achieved by using some basic psychometric tests to assess personality types and preferred team roles.

REDUNDANCIES

In some cases there may be no option but to make redundancies and if so you should consider in advance what the cost implications of these might be.

The cost of redundancies comprises a basic level of statutory payments, together with any contractual arrangements that are on top of this. The DTI publishes a guide which will allow you to calculate the statutory payments (which is available from www.dti.gov.uk/er/redundancy/payments-pl808.htm). Part of your due diligence exercise should be to obtain the required information for employee contracts to calculate redundancy costs in respect of each employee in case they are ever needed.

When making redundancies you will need to take care to meet current standards and legislation in respect of:

- consultation with employees
- grounds for redundancy
- selection of employees.

The consultation process

If you're planning to make 20 or more redundancies from any one establishment, the employer has a statutory duty to consult a recognised trade union or in their absence, appropriate elected representatives of the affected employees. The greater the numbers of employees being made redundant the longer the period of consultation required.

The consultation process involves the provision of disclosure, giving:

- the reasons for the redundancies

- the number and descriptions of the employees that are to be made redundant

- the total number of each type of employee at the establishment in question

- the employer's proposals for:

  - selecting the employees to go

  - carrying out the redundancies

  - timing of the redundancies

  - calculating any payments other than the statutory minimums.

The consultation must be conducted in good faith and include discussion as to any ways in which the redundancies can be avoided or minimised and the effects mitigated. Failure to conduct consultation in line with the legislation can mean that any dismissals will be deemed unfair and the company liable to pay a protective award to each redundant employee. And if a complaint is brought to an industrial tribunal it is up to the employer to prove that the relevant rules have been satisfied.

It is best therefore to obtain up-to-date advice from your solicitor or a specialist firm of employment advisers such as Peninsula (www.peninsula-uk.com).

Since employees generally have the right to bring a case to an employment tribunal within six months of dismissal at little or no cost to themselves there is always a risk that, even having followed all appropriate procedures, the company may still find a claim being made.

One way of avoiding this is by use of a compromise agreement where under a contract the employee agrees to give up their rights to bring such a claim, in return for some consideration. For such an agreement to be effective the employee must have taken independent legal advice, and it is normal for the employer to agree to pay for a solicitor to advise the employee on the agreement.

GOLDEN RULES

25. Successful business acquisition is not just a matter of successfully buying a business, but a matter of making a success of the business that has been bought.

(18)

Financial Management

MANAGING BY THE NUMBERS

Once you have bought the business and dealt with the immediate issues of taking control and undertaking any major change programme concerning the way the business operates, do not forget to look at how best to structure and manage the business from a financial point of view.

This chapter covers four main areas:

◆ the business or group's corporate structure

◆ management information

◆ profit improvement and extracting value from the business

◆ cash flow improvements.

GROUP STRUCTURE

The corporate structure within which assets are held can be important in a number of respects, particularly in groups, including:

◆ **clarity of management information** – where having a specific area of business clearly segregated and reporting as a specific business entity can make it easier to monitor results from different areas of the group's operation

- **creating 'lots' of value** – whereby the dividing up of a business into its component parts, each separately held within its own corporate entity, can sometimes increase the realisable value of the businesses as a whole, as it makes it easier to segregate different parcels of businesses and business assets for disposal to different parties

- **risk management** – splitting different trading businesses and assets of value into different limited liability entities can offer a degree of protection in that if one part of the business gets into difficulty it will not necessarily drag the others down (albeit that banks will tend to insist upon cross guarantees between different companies within a group to support any borrowings). This approach is known as a 'bulkhead' defence.

The structure will also have implications for how the tax liabilities of the various businesses are dealt with, for which you will need to take appropriate professional advice.

So you should look at the overall corporate structure of the group or business, since it may well be appropriate to use the opportunity of the takeover and any necessary restructuring to reallocate businesses and assets in order to put in place an appropriate bulkhead defence and/or to restructure the business into its component entities.

Example
The group was a construction contractor which also had a significant property portfolio. Despite the fact that there were a number of companies in the group, both the property portfolio and the main trading business were in the same limited liability company.

Unfortunately the trading side of the business got into difficulty. While the company had a strong asset base and was solvent on the basis of its balance sheet, the losses incurred on the trading activity meant that it was becoming insolvent from a cash flow point of view. If the business failed as a result, then an insolvency practitioner would have been appointed to sell all the assets.

Fortunately the trading business was turned around and restored to a solvent cash flow position. Thereafter the directors restructured the business so that there was a holding company with one subsidiary being a trading company, while another held the property assets.

Once this process had been completed, the effect was that should the trading business get into trouble at some point in the future, the property assets would not be at risk because of the failure of the trading business because they would henceforth be held in a separate company.

In the same way, it may be appropriate to look at the business you've bought and consider whether it is appropriate to split out one or more of the trading businesses into separate companies, as well as a separate company to hold property and other assets such as significant plant and equipment or intellectual property, as a way of managing risks within the business (contact ghm@enable-net.com).

CLEANING UP THE GROUP STRUCTURE

If you're buying what is essentially a small group of businesses, you may also find that the group's corporate structure has become 'cluttered' over the years with unnecessary subsidiary company shells. These may have arisen from past acquisitions, companies incorporated as special purpose vehicles (SPVs) from completed projects, old joint venture vehicles, or as a result of the restructuring of operations. You may of course further increase the number of such shells as a result of any action to restructure the business or install bulkhead defences.

And whilst these subsidiaries may be dormant, there is a real cost in continuing to maintain such shells in increased professional fees in preparation of accounts, statutory returns and tax returns, as well as in-house management time.

Advantages of cleaning up group structure

Arranging to 'clean up' the group structure of such companies as part of your post-acquisition restructuring is usually sensible, as while it will incur a small degree of professional costs to achieve, it usually results in:

- improved utilisation of company secretarial and finance staff

- reduced ongoing external professional costs in dealing with accounts preparation and tax affairs

- simplification of the group's tax returns as old intercompany trading positions are cleared

- simplification of group VAT work

- clarified lines of ownership and corporate structure for reporting purposes

- a clearer and more transparent group structure, usually giving rise to better value in the event of any subsequent disposal of the business.

The last point is particularly important if your overall strategy is one that envisages selling some or all of the businesses on again within the next few years, as undertaking this process of group structure cleanup should in any event be part of your grooming process.

The best way to conduct such a cleaning exercise on a group's structure is by the use of solvent Members Voluntary Liquidations, as these ensure that all potential tax and other liabilities have been dealt with, and all assets distributed to shareholders in a tax efficient manner, before the company is struck off. This work should be conducted by a licensed insolvency practitioner experienced in dealing with the issues that arise, such as the need to restructure any technically insolvent subsidiaries to solvency, protect trading names, deal with any residual assets and liabilities as well as liaising with the group's tax advisers to obtain the necessary clearances. Marchands Associates LLP (contact Martin Shaw or Charles Brook at info@marchands.org.uk) provide fixed price quotes for such work.

Example

An overseas based company purchased a UK manufacturing organisation. They then identified that there were over 30 non-trading and apparently solvent companies within the group's corporate structure, which needed to be cleared out in order to simplify group reporting and risk management.

Investigation showed that a number of these were in fact insolvent and required other group companies to write off intergroup debts, leading to a need to obtain tax clearance in respect of the effects across the group in order to allow the liquidations to be completed.

MANAGEMENT INFORMATION
To run a business properly you need information about how it is performing so that you can take the appropriate actions to address problems and continually improve its performance.

What management/financial information do you need?
To be useful, management information should be:

- **Regular** – prepared on a regular basis, e.g. weekly/monthly.

- **Consistent** – as far as possible prepared on a consistent basis and presented in a consistent way for ease of comparison and spotting trends.

- **Timely** – monthly management accounts should be ready by at least week two or three of the following month. Any longer and they are history lessons, not management tools.

- **(Materially) accurate** – for use in making management decisions, the information needs to be accurate (or accurate enough that the difference does not matter).

- **Understandable** – they need to be clearly laid out, with the assumptions clearly stated and the key points easily identifiable. Wherever possible the key points should be kept to one or two pages of summary figures (with the rest available for drilling down as required). Many people are uncomfortable when faced with sheets of numbers, so if practical and helpful, graphs should be used as an alternative way of displaying information (this is particularly good for showing trends).

- **Circulated** – the relevant people need to see the relevant information if it is to be of any use.

◆ **Used** – the information should be actively used to manage the business.

In a particular month, a financial information pack for a business might comprise:

◆ profit and loss (including variance analysis, see below)

◆ month end balance sheet

◆ aged debtors and creditors

◆ rolled forward profit and loss (see below) and cashflow forecasts.

But financial information is only part of the story. Your management information should also tell you the key facts on:

◆ **Sales**, such as:

  – actions – prospects, sales visits planned

  – performance – average and value, broken down by product, customer/product values, order pipeline, conversion rate per sales visit.

◆ **Operations**

  – key performance indicators showing utilisation and efficiency

  – stock outs (number of times you are out of stock)

  – customer satisfaction.

Using management accounts

Companies J, K and L all have identical results for the first quarter and identical year end targets.

Company J produces no management accounts ('We know how we are doing').

Company K produces a normal, accurate and timely set of accounts.

Company K	£000	£000
	Month 3	**Profit & loss**
	Month	Year to date
Turnover	100	325
Cost of sales	(40)	(130)
Gross profit	60	195
Gross profit %	60%	60%
Overheads	(50)	(150)
Profit	10	45

Company K's results tell management how they have done so far. But they do not really help the directors to manage the business.

Company L produces a fuller pack of monthly information comprising two reports.

Report 1 is a variance report showing how well or badly the business has done against its budget and why.

Company L –	**Month 3 profit & loss report (£000)**			
Report 1	**Month**	**Budget**	**Variance**	**Explanation**
Turnover	100	150	(50)	Widget sales
Cost of sales	(40)	(60)	20	poor due to
				competitor
Gross profit	60	90	(30)	X's
				promotion

Gross profit %	60%	60%	60%
Overheads	(50)	(50)	–
Profit	10	40	(30)

Report 2 is a rolling forecast that is updated each period for the actual results for the month and then the forecast for the rest of the year is revised.

Company L – Report 2	Actual to end Month 3	Month 3 rolling forecast (£000)				
		Qtr 2	Qtr 3	Qtr 4	Total	Target
Turnover	325	400	500	700	1925	1800
Cost of sales	(130)	(160)	(200)	(280)	(770)	(720)
Gross profit	195	240	300	420	1155	1080
Gross profit %	60%	60%	60%	60%	60%	60%
Overheads	(150)	(200)	(175)	(150)	675	(600)
Profit	45	40	125	270	480	480

Comment: The forecast overheads have been adjusted to show an extra spend of £50k and £25k on promotion in quarters two and three respectively to drive up sales to get back to hitting target.

Company L's monthly management information actually helps the directors to manage the business because:

◆ **there's no hiding place** – the profit and loss report's inclusion of a variance analysis identifies quantified differences between actual and planned performance that require investigation and act as a prompt for action

- **they are forward looking** – the monthly revision of a rolling forecast enables the directors to use the information on current performance to look forward and plan the steps that need to be taken to continue to manage performance towards the target for the year.

Setting financial targets

The finances provide a reasonable objective measure of the business's performance for comparison between one period and another. Setting realistic but challenging financial performance targets to be met by specific dates is therefore a vital part of putting in place a meaningful set of 'SMART' (Specific, Measurable, Achievable, Relevant, Time bounded) objectives for the business.

These can relate to both profit and loss and balance sheet items, e.g.:

- Achieve turnover growth of 30% per annum (probably the maximum normally sustainable level of growth for most businesses).

- Bank borrowings at a level with which the bank will feel secure (say 45% of debtors less than three months and 20% of fixed assets).

You can use a checklist such as the one below to decide what sort of financial targets you're aiming to meet:

Financial targets

	Current	Ideal
Profitability (%)		
Growth (%)		
Stock days		
Creditor days		
Debtor days		
Liquidity		
Gearing (%)		

Now you can use this information to quantify the financial targets you set for your business:

Profit and loss

	Now	3 months	1 year	2 years	5 years
Turnover					
Gross profit					
Gross profit %					
Overheads					
Net profit					

£000

	£000				
	Now	3 months	1 year	2 years	5 years
Balance sheet					
Fixed assets					
Stock					
Debtors					
Cash					
Trade creditors					
PAYE/NI VAT credits					
Other finance/loans					

This exercise can quickly lead you into starting to consider:

◆ How quickly can the business achieve the ideal situation?

◆ What do you need to change in how you operate your business to achieve these targets?

And as a way of summarising the steps you need to take to improve profitability in order to achieve the targets, you can then complete a profit improvement plan that specifies the steps that you are expecting to take and their likely impact.

This is sometimes known as a 'profit bridge', as it shows what gets you over the gap from where you are now to where you want to be.

Profit bridge

	By date	£
Current profit		_____
Steps to be taken		Effect
1 _____	_____	_____
2 _____	_____	_____
3 _____	_____	_____
4 _____	_____	_____
5 _____	_____	_____
6 _____	_____	_____
7 _____	_____	_____
8 _____	_____	_____
9 _____	_____	_____
10 _____	_____	_____
Required profit	_____	_____

PROFIT IMPROVEMENT

So what are the steps that will deliver improved profits?

Fundamentally improving profits requires achieving some combination of the following, concentrating your efforts on the areas that will have the highest impact and which are the quickest or easiest to put in place:

- **increasing turnover** – by increasing some or all customer numbers, value of spend per customer or frequency of spend

- **increasing margins** – by reducing costs of sales

- **reducing overheads** – which includes dealing with any under-performing parts of the business.

The basic steps to consider in each of these areas are:

Increasing turnover

- Can you **raise prices**? Check how sensitive your sales volume will be to price first. If you produce a 'commodity' (e.g. pencils), customers will tend to buy largely on price. As they can get exactly the same thing from Joe down the road if he is cheaper, raising prices above market rates will lead to a major loss of sales. If your product or service is 'differentiated', where customers cannot buy exactly the same thing from Joe, the position is a more complex question of perceived value and you must judge how much you can increase your price before customers decide that Joe's cheaper product will do well enough for what they want.

- What opportunities can you identify to quickly, cost effectively and relatively certainly **increase volumes** by attracting more customers, or getting them to come back more often, or spend more while they are buying from you (e.g. do your staff ask customers whether they want a new oil filter when they come in to buy oil?).

Increasing margins

- Identify the key constraints on the business (e.g. you only have one XYZ machine, which is a production bottleneck) and **ensure that profit is maximised for that constraint** (i.e. you should seek orders for product 1 as you make more money per hour of XYZ machine operation than you do by producing product 2).

◆ **Improve your productivity/output** by looking at your processes, although capital expenditure (e.g. increased automation) tend to be long-term issues.

◆ **Improve your efficiency** in control of purchasing, distribution, contract control, quality assurance or waste management. Look for any opportunities to reduce the cost of goods sold (e.g. reduce raw material prices, reduce scrap, change materials, lower labour component).

◆ **Reduce wage costs** by a redundancy programme (compare your head count to competitors or to that of two or three years ago).

◆ **Reduce bought in costs** where a change of ownership is an ideal time to review all purchasing decisions, institute new competitive tenders, etc.

◆ **Rationalise your customer and product base** to focus on the customers and products that generate you the most profits, and eliminate those on which you lose money.

Reduce overheads

Remember, overheads have to be covered by contributions from sales, so if you have a 25% gross margin, a £1 reduction in costs is equivalent to a £4 increase in turnover. No cost in your business is too small not to think about how can it be cut.

Are your selling, general and administrative expenses in line with industry standards? Can you look for savings in some of the following areas:

- **Premises costs** – can you consolidate and lease out extra space?

- **Vehicles** – can you eliminate the car fleet, or have your employees bear the costs of cars?

- **Professional costs** – can you reduce the costs of accountants, lawyers, etc?

- **Postage** – do you really need overnight couriers, etc?

- **Stationery** – is it properly controlled or are staff using large quantities of company stationery?

- **Telephone costs** – is the business paying for personal phone calls, Internet use, etc?

- **Advertising and promotion costs** – is all your advertising cost effective? How do you know what return you're getting?

- **Selling expenses** – can you cut the size of the sales force or the number of sales offices without significant short-term costs?

Consider closing or selling any of the business's subsidiaries or branches which have net cash outflows or are unprofitable. Once you have made the decision to exit a non-core sector or close an under-performing business you can face a number of problems such as:

- How do you maximise the value for shareholders from the exit process?

- How do you manage your way safely through the thicket of consultancy requirements and employee protection legislation as you wind down a business?

- How do you minimise the impact and bad press of a closure?

- Are your best managers experienced in handling closures and redundancy programmes, and anyway don't you want to keep them focused on and motivated by driving forward the core business or integrating the best bits of new business?

A number of businesses in the turnaround and restructuring field offer services to manage this sort of disposal for you, although ironically, because of the need for discretion you are unlikely to have heard much about the activities of the more successful practitioners in this field. An example is the 'CEASE' (Controlled Exit And Sale Execution) service from Resolution Inc (info@resolutioninc.biz) which uses experienced executives to manage anything from full-scale disposal programmes to discrete wind-downs and closures.

Taking this idea one stage further, consider whether there are any opportunities whereby you can extract value from a group of businesses acquired by disposing of parts which are profitable and valuable but which do not fit with your core business. In some cases, when carefully managed, such disposals can bring in a significant repayment of the total purchase price, leaving you with the parts of the business you actually want for a much smaller net payment.

Again, however, you will face similar problems as outlined above in that for example integrating the newly acquired businesses that you wish to retain effectively into your existing organisation is a critical task which you will presumably want to entrust to your best managers. These managers may also have to keep their existing 'day jobs' in whole or in part in order to keep your core business functioning.

At the same time managing the disposal of a recently acquired business for good value can be a complex and pressured task requiring great attention to detail of the business with which you have had little track record. This in turn appears to demand that you place your best managers in charge of the operation to achieve the result required. Is it realistic to expect your managers to be able to achieve all of these tasks at once?

Again there are specialists who offer a service in managing such disposals, such as Resolution Inc's Post Acquisition Realisation Team 'PART' (info@resolutioninc.biz).

CASHFLOW MANAGEMENT

Improving cash flow starts by a process of forecasting your cash flows (which also produces a document which is vital to managing your ongoing relationship with your bank). Preparation and monitoring of this forecast then enables you actively to manage your cash to improve your position.

Cashflow forecasting should be done on a monthly rolling basis at a minimum and preferably on a 13 week rolling basis. It's normally only necessary to move to a daily basis in the event of some cash crisis.

Cashflow forecasting is essentially straightforward as you are dealing with real cash movements into and out of the company, not more abstract 'accounting' transactions, such as accruals, prepayments or depreciation.

For a monthly forecast, all you are looking to calculate is:

- the cash you are going to get **in** that month

- less the cash you are going to pay **out** that month

◆ to give a **net** movement ('**flow**') of cash into or out of the company.

Adding the net inflow (or deducting the net outflow) of cash to the balance held at the start of the month gives the balance at the end of the month, as shown below.

	Period 1	**Period 2**
	£000	£000
Cash in	100	100
Less cash out	(50)	(125)
	———	———
Net cash in/(out)flow	50	(25)
Balance brought forward	25	75
	———	———
Balance carried forward	75	50
	———	———

An example of a 13-week cash flow forecast for Company M follows on pages 384–5. This type of forecast can be set up on a spreadsheet or filled out manually, and the headings shown should be sufficient to cover the main receipts and payments of most companies.

The best approach to cash flow forecasting is to keep it simple and to work methodically and logically down the page through all the cash coming in and going out of the business.

For example, your **cash received** will come from:

◆ **Existing debtors** who pay during the period. Look down your list of debtors, decide who is likely to pay in which period, and fill in the boxes.

- **New sales for cash.** Prepare a simple sales forecast by branch, line of business, contract, customer, or whatever is most appropriate. Then calculate how much of these sales will be for cash (in Company M's case, 40%) and fill in the boxes (remembering to add VAT as your receipts will be gross).

- **New sales on credit** where the customer pays within the forecast period. Once you have forecast sales, those that are not for cash must be made on credit. How long a credit period are you allowing your customers, and how long are they really taking to pay? Use this as a guide to plotting the likely receipts from these new sales (again gross of VAT).

- **Any other sources.** Will you be selling any assets, injecting any new funds, receiving any insurance payouts, like Company M, or generating any other cash from anywhere at all? If so, estimate how much and in which period (don't forget VAT where it applies), and enter the figures.

You can now total all these to obtain your estimated total inflows.

- **Outflows** are calculated on exactly the same principles.

- Do you pay the **wages** weekly or monthly? Write in the net amounts when they are due to go out.

- **PAYE** is due once a month, the **VAT** at the end of the month following the end of the quarter, so predicting the dates of these payments should be straightforward.

- Your purchase ledger/trade **creditor list** also tells you who you owe money to for purchases. So in the same way that you forecast receipts from debtors, go down the list and plan when

Company M cash flow forecast (£)

	Opening balance	1 Actual	2 Actual	3 Actual	4	5
Sales						
Branch 1		10,346	9,521	10,167	10,000	10,000
Branch 2		4,572	5,386	5,297	5,000	5,000
Net sales		14,918	14,907	15,464	15,000	15,000
VAT		2,611	2,609	2,706	2,625	2,625
Gross sales		17,529	17,516	18,170	17,625	17,625
Cash inflows						
Existing debtors	16,877	8,126	7,543	198	1,010	
New cash sales actual		6,813	7,334	7,390		
New cash sales forecast					7,050	7,050
New credit sales actual			1,026	9,386		
New credit sales forecast					10,485	10,781
Any other receipts						
Total inflows		14,939	15,903	16,974	18,545	17,831
Cash outflows						
Wages/salaries net					11,250	
PAYE/NI – existing	4,439		4,439			
PAYE/NI – new						
Trade creditors – existing	42,349	10,256	9,469	10,950	11,674	
New purchases						10,517
VAT – existing	15,796				15,796	
VAT – new						
Property costs (mortgage/rent/rates)					987	
Repairs and maintenance			36		15	15
Utilities (heat/light/power/water)		137		369	137	
Promotion					90	
Telecom			436			
Stationery		12	5	30	20	20
Motor vehicle running costs		156	167	170	165	165
Professional fees						3,600
Bank charges						
Lease/HP/loan payments			110			
Insurance		65				65
Capital expenditure						
Other costs				15		
Contingency					1,000	1,000
Total outflows		10,626	14,662	11,534	41,134	15,382
Opening bank balance	−42,321	−42,321	−38,008	−36,767	−31,327	−53,917
Net in/(out)flows		4,313	1,241	5,440	−22,589	2,448
Closing bank balance		−38,008	−36,767	−31,327	−53,917	−51,468
Bank facility available		−50,000	−50,000	−50,000	−50,000	−50,000
Amount (over)/under facility limit		11,992	13,233	18,673	−3,917	−1,468

6	7	8	9	10	11	12	13	Total	Check total
10,000	10,000	10,000	10,000	10,000	10,000	10,000	10,000	130,034	
5,000	7,500	7,500	7,500	7,500	7,500	7,500	7,500	82,755	
15,000	17,500	17,500	17,500	17,500	17,500	17,500	17,500	212,789	
2,625	3,063	3,063	3,063	3,063	3,063	3,063	3,063	37,238	
17,625	20,563	20,563	20,563	20,563	20,563	20,563	20,563	250,027	
								16,877	
								21,537	
7,050	8,225	8,225	8,225	8,225	8,225	8,225	8,225	78,725	
								10,412	
10,575	10,575	10,575	12,338	12,338	12,338	12,338	12,338	114,679	
5,200								5,200	
22,825	18,800	18,800	20,563	20,563	20,563	20,563	20,563	247,429	247,429
		11,750					12,250	35,250	
								4,439	
4,500				4,650				9,150	
								42,349	
10,509	10,902	10,575	10,575	10,575	12,338	12,338	12,338	100,666	
								15,796	
								0	
		987				3,200	987	6,161	
15	15	15	15	15	15	15	15	186	
369			137		369			1,518	
		90					90	270	
								436	
20	20	20	20	20	20	20	20	247	
165	200	200	200	200	200	200	200	2,388	
								3,600	
1,200								1,200	
110					110		200	530	
				65				195	
2,000								2,000	
								15	
1,000	1,000	1,000	1,000	1,000	1,000	1,000	1,000	10,000	
19,888	12,137	24,637	11,947	16,525	14,052	17,063	26,810	236,396	236,396
−51,468	−48,532	−41,869	−47,706	−39,090	−35,053	−28,542	−25,042	−42,321	
2,937	6,663	−5,837	8,616	4,038	6,511	3,500	−6,247	11,032	11,032
−48,532	−41,869	−47,706	−39,090	−35,053	−28,542	−25,042	−31,289	−31,289	
−50,000	−50,000	−50,000	−50,000	−50,000	−50,000	−50,000	−50,000	−50,000	
1,468	8,131	2,294	10,910	14,947	21,458	24,958	18,711	18,711	

you are going to pay what to whom. Bear in mind that you will also need to continue to make purchases as you trade, so forecast these in the same way as you forecast sales and plan in the payments (gross of VAT) for when you are going to make them.

◆ You will need to plan payments for **overheads** such as rent, heating, lighting, power, telephone, and your other commitments in the same way, as well as remembering to estimate how much VAT will need to be paid, and when.

Points to remember

The keys to successful cash flow forecasting are:

◆ **Know where you are starting from.** As you stand today you have a balance at the bank; you are owed money by your debtors that you are expecting to receive; and you will owe money to trade creditors, the Inland Revenue, HM Customs & Excise, and so on. Use these figures as your opening balances. If you do not have exact figures (why not?) then use your best estimates.

◆ **Ensure you are consistent.** Forecast the balance at the bank assuming that all cash received is banked (rather than the balance in your cashbook) as this will give you the most useful information. So, enter the current balance from your bank statement as your starting bank balance, and add back all those unpresented cheques that have been issued or are sitting in the drawer to your opening creditor figure to show how much you really owe.

◆ **Be realistic** in your estimates of timings and amounts. Your forecast needs to take into account:

  – What level are sales/purchases running at now?

  – What changes are really likely to happen over the period?

- What have you experienced in prior periods? (How quickly do your customers actually pay?)

- What are your terms of trade? (What length of credit do you allow customers/are you allowed by suppliers?)

- What are your due dates for statutory payments? (For example, the 19th of the month for PAYE.)

- What are your periodic payments? (For example, quarterly bills for utilities and rent.)

- What capital expenditure are you planning?

◆ **When in doubt be prudent.** Be pessimistic about when and how much people are going to pay you and when you are going to have to pay others.

◆ **Make your assumptions explicit.** If you tell your bank manager that sales are going to increase by 20% the month after next, you can then also tell him that this is because your contract with XYZ plc comes on stream. Otherwise he may just think that you are relying on the 'new sales fairy' to wave a wand and make this happen.

◆ **Check that you are showing all aspects of any transaction.** Company M has taken on a new sales representative for branch 2 (wages and PAYE up) for whom it is buying a new van (a deposit shown as capital expenditure and a new monthly HP charge), which will require fuel (motor vehicle expenses). Of course the reason for doing so is to increase sales and hence debtor receipts, but these will also be reflected in increased purchases and hence payments for goods sold.

◆ **Experiment with sensitivities.** Flex some of your key assumptions (what if sales go up by 5% instead of 10%, what if customers take 60 days to pay instead of 45) to see how sensitive the forecast is to these fluctuations. Make sure that you fully reflect all aspects of any change, however! But remember the above point, if sales go down, then purchases should fall as well.

◆ **Think widely.** Check that you have allowed for all possible payments that may need to be made by comparing the type of items with last year's detailed profit and loss account.

– Have you allowed for corporation tax, redundancy payments, pension top ups, or repairs if any of these are likely to fall due in the period?

– Business sales tend to require professional assistance. Have you allowed sufficient to cover the accountants', lawyers' and bankers' fees?

– Go through some old bank statements and cheque book stubs. Have you allowed for all the types of payment that you find?

◆ **Check carefully to make sure it all adds up!** Company M's cashflow has 'check totals' built in at the end. These are simply sums adding up the elements of the table in different ways to ensure that nothing has been left out. An example of the principle is illustrated below, where the first nine is calculated by adding together the values of all the column totals, while the second is calculated by adding all the row totals. If the two checksum totals match, you can be confident that there are unlikely to be any basic arithmetic errors in the table.

1	1	1	3	↕
2	2	2	6	
3	3	3	⑨	⑨

◆ **Finally, remember that you do not have a 100% reliable crystal ball.** Build in a margin as a round sum contingency to allow for the things that will inevitably come crawling out of the woodwork. The more uncertain your starting point, the larger this needs to be, up to say 10% or 20% of payments in some cases.

Part of the reason for cashflow forecasting is to build the bank's confidence that you are in control of your finances. Having a contingency in place is not only prudent, but if it helps ensure that you beat your forecast cash performance, it will also help to ensure that the bank's confidence in your management skills will increase.

As has already been illustrated in Chapter 10, the golden rule is that you will always need more money than you think. If the deal goes:

◆ better than you were expecting with a higher level of turnover, then this will require more working capital to fund it

◆ badly, less profits will mean that less cash is being generated to fund trading (and possibly even losses will occur that will have to be covered).

Example

This technique can also be used to review any large contract or project that the company is planning to undertake.

Company N is a roofing business, with a limited ability to borrow on its overdraft of £50k and it receives news that it has won a large contract, the details of which are:

Contract value: £620k
Subcontracted labour: £300k at £50k per month over six months

Materials:	£200k, of which £100k is required in the first month, followed by £20k per month for five months
Giving a profit of:	£120k

While the company has one month's credit from its suppliers for materials, it has to pay labour monthly (but labour is paid gross with no PAYE deductions). There is no retention on the contract and the company is to bill at the end of each month for the materials delivered, labour and one sixth of the profit, and the client will pay at the end of 30 days.

The directors are jubilant, and are convinced that this is going to be the making of the company.

Undoubtedly, it is a profitable contract. But should the company take it? The answer lies in looking at the cash flow. To simplify matters, VAT has been omitted.

Projected project cashflow (£000) per month

	1	2	3	4	5	6	7	8
Receipts	–	–	170	90	90	90	90	90
Payments								
Labour	50	50	50	50	50	50	–	–
Materials	–	100	20	20	20	20	20	–
Total payments	50	150	70	70	70	70	20	
Net movement (out)/inflow	(50)	(150)	100	20	20	20	70	90
Cumulative	(50)	(200)	(100)	(80)	(60)	(40)	30	120

The answer then, is clearly no, not as it stands. The project's early cash outflows mean that the company will run out of cash by the end of the first month if it accepts the contract and starts work.

Instead, Company N must explore whether the proposed payment terms can be changed to speed up receipt of cash (e.g. an upfront payment), or whether greater credit can be obtained from the labour and material suppliers, and/or negotiate increased facilities with the bank to enable the project to be undertaken.

Once you have prepared your forecast, use what you have produced.

◆ **Review it critically.** Having prepared it on a prudent basis, now see what scope there is for moving payments or bringing forward receipts. Compare the balance at the end of each month with the facility you have with the bank. Do you have 'headroom' within your facility or are you going to be in 'excess'?

◆ **Use it to plan.** If you are going to be in excess, plan what you are going to do about it. Look at what payments or receipts you can change, and/or speak to the bank in advance about the excess to agree a temporary extra facility. Use the cash flow forecast to explain why the excess will occur, how much it will be, how long it will be for, and how you are going to then reduce your borrowing to return to your normal facility.

As a word of caution, however, don't run to the bank with your first draft cash flow forecast, as this should always show your 'worst-case' position (you have been pessimistic after all). Only discuss your forecast with your bank once you have had a chance to review it thoroughly to amend and adjust it for the things that you are realistically going to be able to manage to improve the position. You need to discuss a final working forecast that is challenging but realistic and prudent, not ultra pessimistic.

- **Use it to monitor.** Roll the forecast forwards, month after month, comparing what actually happens to your forecast. Ask yourself where they differed and why. Then ask what that tells you about your estimates going forward and where you can/should amend your forecast to improve your estimates. From Company M's actual results in weeks one to three, it seems that the contingency built in is too high, as the only sundry expense has been the milkman at £15!

CASH FLOW IMPROVEMENT

Once you have forecast your cash flows, improving them is then a matter of:

- controlling the cash you have

- improving the cash flow from normal trading by reducing your investment in working capital and reducing the cash going out of the business

- getting more cash in from other sources.

Controlling the cash you have

As you prepare a 'central' cash flow forecast it logically tends to follow that to efficiently manage the business's cash you should:

- **Centralise control of cash receipts, payments and forecasting** (and forecast regularly on a cleared funds at bank basis). You can then prioritise and schedule payments so the available cash is best used for the benefit of the whole business, rather than being used by individual mangers, sites or branches as they see fit.

◆ **Roll forward the cash flow forecast on a regular basis,** reviewing performance against forecast each time you do so to pick up any variances that need to be investigated or which can be used to improve the next forecast's accuracy.

◆ **Increase** where appropriate the **level of authority required for purchasing or payments** so that cash is not wasted or committed outside of the central forecasting regime.

◆ By preparing a cash flow forecast you may be able to **identify any areas where the cash is leaking out**. Are particular branches, sites or parts of the business losing cash? If so, target these areas for specific reviews and remedial action.

Improving the cash flow from normal trading

Many businesses have a surprising amount of money tied up in debtors who are not effectively chased for fear of losing future business. This ties up vital working capital and is often the first place to look for funds.

Review the debtors ledger and take action to:

◆ reduce credit terms to customers

◆ target and get in overdue debts.

If as a result you find that credit control procedure or practices are poor, mark this as an area for specific action as part of your post-acquisition business improvement plan. In the meantime, introduce tougher credit terms for customers.

Similarly businesses may have too much money tied up in stock:

- **Reduce finished goods stock** (e.g. by a sale of slow moving or old items), but be careful with such strategies and consider the risks and consequences (e.g. is dumping stock in your normal markets going to spoil your efforts to increase normal sales?).

- **Complete work in progress** and turn it into sellable finished goods as soon as possible.

- **Analyse** how often the individual lines of raw material stock are turning to identify slow-moving lines for inquiry and action. Why are you holding such stocks? Can these be disposed of or returned to the suppliers? Can you seek your supplier's agreement to provide you with consignment stock whereby they deliver your stock on-site which you pay for only as you use it? While you're talking to suppliers, are you actually getting the best credit terms available?

- **Review your production management.** (Particularly if you are building, say, batches of sub assemblies, does this mean that you are deliberately tying up cash in parts that will not become finished goods for a long time? Can you move to 'just in time' production?)

Just as with everything else in life, what you don't spend, you get to keep, so the cancelling of discretionary expenditure such as payments of dividends and the reductions in overheads that you may be taking to improve profitability will also help to improve the cash flow.

As capital expenditure on new plant and equipment tends to involve large sums it should be scrutinised carefully to ensure that both the affordability and the business case for making the investment stand up.

Getting in more cash or credit from elsewhere
Other than trading, other possible sources of raising cash if this
is needed are selling assets, raising new borrowings or obtaining
investment.

◆ Review the assets on your balance sheet to identify:

– surplus fixed assets (land and buildings, plant and
machinery, motor vehicles) that can be sold

– assets that could potentially be made surplus (and then sold)
by sub-contracting out your manufacturing processes

– essential fixed assets that can be sold and leased back to
provide cash

– under-utilised plant and machinery capacity that can be
hired out, or spare factory or office space that could be
sub-let

– separable and saleable investments, subsidiaries or any parts
of the business (e.g. a specific branch).

◆ Is there any equipment lying around that is not even on the
balance sheet that can be sold?

◆ Can you use asset based financing (including factoring or
discounting your debts) to obtain more borrowings against
your assets than are available from the bank under its
debenture values?

◆ Do you have any unpledged assets that can provide security
for new loans, such as brands, trademarks and other
intellectual property rights?

◆ Using your cashflow forecast, seek to negotiate an extension
of your existing bank facilities or other borrowings to cover

the forecast requirement. If appropriate, seek to agree deferment of loan repayments or to roll up interest for later payment.

If seeking to borrow further funds, always consider carefully your business's ability to meet the payments in both the short and long term before taking further money. If you are borrowing because the business needs cash, you do not want to dig yourself deeper into debt that you cannot afford to service.

(19)

Buying a Business to Turn Around

WHY BUY A BUSINESS IN DIFFICULTIES?

Considering the trouble that most people go to in the process of
due diligence to ensure that they are buying a business that is
healthy and with good prospects, why might you want to do the
opposite? The answer lies in the potential to add significant
value.

A business in distress or at a high risk of failure is unsurprisingly
less valuable than a stable business with good prospects. It
therefore follows that if you can find a business for sale which is
in a distressed condition, which you are then able to turn around
into one with good prospects and strong growth, then you
should be able to achieve a huge increase in the business's value.

Many people who believe they have the qualities to turn a
business around are therefore interested in finding opportunities
to buy businesses in this condition with a view to making a
significant capital gain.

There can also be other advantages in buying a business in
difficulty in that the business's problems may be very obvious.
Furthermore, if the business is already going through a formal
insolvency process some of these may already be being dealt
with, while the effect of washing a business through an
insolvency may in practice give the buyer of such a business a

much 'cleaner' and safer purchase, as most liabilities will be captured in the insolvency.

Against this, a business that has been in difficulty is likely to have suffered a significant worsening of its trading and strategic position, having lost its relationships with its suppliers, suffered severe problems with staff morale, with the most employable seeking positions elsewhere, and with its reputation amongst customers and market share severely diminished.

Businesses in difficulty will be in one of three states:

♦ In difficulty but not (yet) in a formal insolvency procedure. Of these some businesses will be refusing to recognise that they have a problem, some of them will be being actively advised by professional advisers with a view to rescue, and some may simply be in the process of heading into insolvency.

♦ In a formal insolvency procedure directed towards the rescue of the business or company such as a Company Voluntary Arrangement (CVA) or an Administration.

♦ In a formal insolvency procedure directed towards the realisation of the business' assets in order to fund a payment to its creditors, such as a compulsory liquidation ordered by the court, a voluntary liquidation by the company on grounds of insolvency (a Creditor's Voluntary Liquidation or CVL) or an Administrative Receivership appointed by a floating charge holder.

Which of these categories a business falls into will have a significant impact on how it may be sold, what will be for sale, and the risks involved in buying it.

Given the level of both technical detail and risks involved in buying a business in difficulty, this is an area more than any other where you will need good advisers. For referral to an appropriate contact in respect of any of the professional advisers discussed in this section, from lawyers and insolvency practitioners through to company doctors, please feel free to contact me by email at mark@theoss.freeserve.co.uk and I will be happy to help.

It's also an area where it is appropriate to direct you to some further specialist background material, in which respect I would recommend *Buying a Company in Trouble* by Ian Walker (Gower Publishing, 1992, ISBN 0-566-07289-0) as essential reading. You may also find my book *Turning Your Business Around* (How To Books, 2002, ISBN 1-85703-767-7) useful as it expands on many of the areas covered in this chapter (and some earlier financial management issues).

SO HOW AND WHY DO BUSINESSES START TO FAIL?

Business failures are a bit like fires. Something smouldering may be difficult to see but can be relatively easy to put out with little damage or risk if caught early. Once a fire is really ablaze, it is much more obvious but can be much more difficult to put out as it has become dangerous to deal with, consuming resources and, crucially, cash.

As the old saying has it, cash is king. And no one believes this more firmly than people who are involved in business rescue and conducting turnarounds, because fundamentally businesses fail when they run out of cash.

There are really four types of business failure. Firstly there is the start-up that never does. It's a well-known statistic that most businesses cease trading within their first three years. It is an inevitable result of the willingness of entrepreneurs to take risks that this results in many businesses being founded in the belief that there is a market for a product, which sadly turns out not to be the case. Given how difficult it can be to raise money in the UK for a new venture, there are also many businesses that have so few resources to start out with that a relatively small setback in the early years is sufficient to kill them, where a larger business would pull through.

Having got through these critical first three years or so, business failures then fall into three main camps.

♦ **Catastrophic** failures, where the business suddenly 'falls off a cliff', whilst often being high profile, are actually very rare and are usually due to the impact of some traumatic event such as a major fraud, lost litigation or sudden change in regulations.

♦ **Overtrading** is a relatively common cause of business failure in boom times as businesses grow faster than their cash resources can support.

♦ Most **normal** failures follow what has come to be known as the business decline curve, where a business that is underperforming starts to become distressed and as the decline steepens, falls into crisis and eventual failure.

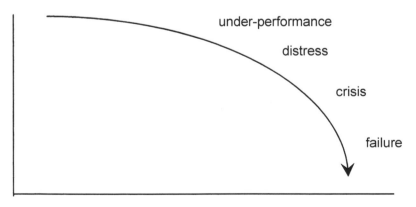

Figure 18. The decline curve

The frightening thing about the decline curve is how problems start to compound each other as the business descends the slope.

The under-performing business is making less profits than its competitors. With less profits it can reinvest less in keeping up to date or developing new products. Slowly, insidiously, it is starting to slip behind and over time market reputation and share start to be lost, resulting eventually in the first losses starting to be incurred.

As it has to fund losses, a business in distress starts to stretch and juggle its cash. The bank manager wants security and personal guarantees as the account starts to be constantly up against the overdraft limit and the business starts to delay sending in management accounts. It also starts to stretch payments to suppliers or make round sum payments on account as a way of eking out the available cash. The staff know that the business has problems and morale and quality of output sinks.

By the time it is in a crisis the finance director has either jumped ship or has gone off on long-term sick leave. It is on stop with its suppliers and the CCJs are starting to fly, so the business cannot get the materials needed to finish the order and bill the customer and it cannot collect the cash from the customer until it has delivered all of their order.

And if it cannot get the cash in to pay the rent or the wages at the end of the month, suddenly it's all over.

There seem to be five main contributing factors to most 'normal' business failures in varying degrees.

◆ **Management problems** such as the autocratic managing director whose drive has been vital in the past but is now driving the business into the ground while simultaneously

driving away anyone who tries to disagree; the board dispute
that has led to civil war; the lack of anyone who really
understands what the numbers are telling them; the family
company run in the interests of family members and not the
business's needs. Any and all of these sorts of issues can prevent
the business recognising or dealing with the problems facing it.

◆ The **big strategy challenges** that every business will inevitably
face, whether these are changes in the market and customers
demands; changes in technology that mean reinvesting and
moving on; or changes in the competition which require
improved efficiencies to keep the cost base competitive.

◆ **Lack of financial control** where it is usual to find that cash has
become tied up in excess stock or debtors; and that
management do not have accurate costings so they do not
really know how much margin they are making on the
different areas of the business.

◆ **Lack of operational control** of both hard issues such as
up-to-date machinery and efficient factory layout; and the soft
issues of organisational structure and staff management.

◆ **The 'big projects'** – the new computer system, the problem
acquisition, the new product launch, the premises move.
Anything that adds extra disruption to the business, while
taking away cash and management time can prove to be the
straw that breaks the camel's back.

So if you are looking to buy a business in difficulty the key
questions that you must answer are:

◆ **What has gone wrong?** Here the basic strategy analysis and
assessment outlined in Chapter 7 should enable you to
understand the reasons for the company's difficulties.

- **Is the business saveable?** This requires a more specific assessment of what needs to be done to fix the business and a judgement as to whether this is achievable. Even if you only buy the business assets rather than the company's shares, remember you may be buying the problems that are causing the business to fail.

To achieve a turnaround, you will generally need to have the following things present:

- **Viable business** – some core business that has future potential growth and profitability around which the business can be rebuilt.

- **Time** – turnarounds are not instantaneous and if started too late will either fail or require protection through an insolvency procedure.

- **Cash** – turnarounds need money, often there are costs associated with the initial restructuring (e.g. redundancy costs) and then to finance the future regrowth of the business, and this money must be found either from within the business ('bootstrapping') or from outside.

- **Vision** – a clear goal to which the business is to be directed, to provide both a target and motivation.

- **Management** – who have both the will to achieve the turnaround (it's your plan and vision) but also the skills (functional and situational) to make it happen, or access to external resources who can provide these skills when required.

- **Stakeholder support** – management cannot do it on their own, they need to take suppliers, customers, staff, bankers, shareholders and others with them.

- **Confidence in the process** – the stakeholders need to see how the company's management (who will be regarded as having got 'us' into this mess) are going to get 'us' out again, and this has to entail a structured approach in dealing with the problem, in which respect the introduction of a new external management team (particularly if they are putting money into the business) goes a long way.

But you must take a realistic and objective view of any turnaround opportunity; and whatever you do, don't just think of it simply as an opportunity to buy a bargain. Apocryphal evidence amongst IPs suggests that buyouts from receiverships and administrations are the most common sorts of buyouts to fail.

So no matter how good a company doctor you may be, while it may be possible to heal the sick, raising the dead is not an option.

In respect of businesses in insolvency it's worth noting, however, that in some cases the business in receivership or administration may not necessarily be in trouble itself. Since lenders will generally seek cross guarantees between all the companies in a group to support the group's borrowings, the failure of a group can result in perfectly viable trading businesses being pulled into an insolvency.

FINDING A BUSINESS TO TURN AROUND

There are a number of routes to finding a business in need of a turnaround before insolvency:

- The normal advertising process, in that if they have realised the difficulties they are in the owners may be trying to sell in order to get out before it's too late; although you will need to be able to spot that this is their motivation from your analysis of the business, as the sellers are unlikely to admit to the fact.

◆ Conducting research to spot signs of business or financial distress such as news in the trade press about problems or falling credit ratings. However, without access to some of the more specialised databases used to assess businesses for credit such as Company Watch (www.companywatch.net), you will probably find such financial research difficult. Even if you can spot a business in need of a turnaround you will then run into the problem faced by the banks of overcoming the directors' normal denial that there is any problem at all and that the value of the shareholders' stake in the business has declined to the level you believe it truly has.

◆ Identifying suppliers or customers that are getting into difficulty from how their dealings with your existing business are changing. Buying a customer that has failed owing you money can, however, be a case of sending good money after bad.

◆ Being invited in by a bank or VC house as a company doctor to sort out the problems. However, this requires a significant investment of time and effort in networking yourself to the various business support units of the banks and other financial institutions to become known and used in such situations.

◆ Be contacted as a potential buyer for a 'prepack' insolvency, which generally requires that you network yourself to both the insolvency and corporate finance partners in the larger accountancy firms who will deal with such situations.

◆ Join a business angel network with a view to spotting any potential turnaround opportunities that the network may see. In this respect you should firstly register with the Turnaround Equity Finder service (www.turnaroundequity.co.uk) as investor registration is free and this is the only nationwide network specifically set up to offer introductions into turnaround cases.

If you are considering making an investment into a business in difficulty, it goes without saying that you must look very carefully at the commitment you are making, the likelihood of recovery and the impact it will have on you should the business fail. You should always consider getting professional advice in these circumstances. You will find that businesses in difficulty often seek to raise injections of cash from outsiders as the management desperately try to stave off the inevitable failure.

When buying into a business in difficulty you should generally:

◆ never buy a minority stake, as you will want to ensure you have control over the business and how any cash you invest will be used

◆ never accept a directorship unless you're taking over active control of the company with a view to putting in place your turnaround plan.

Finally, if you are looking at buying a business that is in difficulty, always consider whether you are better off waiting with a view to buying the business out of a formal insolvency. Remember also that if you are in discussion with a business that is unwilling to accept your offer, you can always simply wait as you may soon have an option to buy it out of insolvency.

Once a business goes into a formal insolvency process, the appointed IP will be looking to sell it in order to get the best return for creditors. They will seek to do so by:

◆ directly marketing to potential interested parties that are identified by the business's management

◆ advertising the business for sale in the appropriate local, trade and national press such as the *Financial Times'* weekly businesses for sale listings

◆ dealing with any potential buyout by the company staff.

If the business has gone into liquidation then generally the IP will only be able to conduct a sale of the assets as their appointment as liquidator terminates all the employees' contracts, and businesses in liquidation therefore do not continue to trade.

If the IP has been appointed as an Administrator or Administrative Receiver then providing it makes commercial sense to do so (which generally means that by cutting costs and staff it can be traded in the short term on a cash positive basis) then the IP can continue to trade the business while they seek the buyer for it as a going concern.

BUYING A BUSINESS BEFORE INSOLVENCY

Buying a business that is in difficulty but which has not gone into a formal insolvency procedure is essentially the same process of investigation, assessment, negotiation and planning and execution of the post-acquisition strategy as has already been outlined in this book. Issues such as the transferring of employee liabilities under TUPE will be exactly the same as in any other business sale.

Of course, given that you know that the business is in difficulties, this general approach needs to be subject to the added degree of caution as discussed in this chapter so far.

Such transactions may also in practice be more difficult to finance.

◆ You may find difficulty in raising finance against the assets being bought as not only will lenders be concerned about lending into a business in difficulty (no bank likes to simply take on somebody else's problem loan) but you may also find a more fundamental problem in that you may have difficulty in obtaining a whitewash agreement in order to deal with the issue of financial assistance.

◆ Against this in some cases sellers, particularly if they are large corporates who are looking to dispose of an under-performing subsidiary in a way that avoids bad publicity for the main group, may be prepared to offer a 'dowry' to a new owner to take the business off their hands. It is rare but it does sometimes happen.

But for a business in difficulty, finance is a serious issue and you will have to look very carefully at how much investment it will take to restore a business to solvency. In particular, a business that is in difficulty is likely to have stretched its creditors, who will have been unwilling to give the credit terms that it is currently taking. You will generally find that as soon as you have bought the business, suppliers will seek to be paid up to date to recover their position. So in your working capital requirement planning you may have to allow specifically for funds to bring overdue creditors up to date to deal with this rush for payment.

To ensure that you raise the maximum amount of funding in as efficient and timely manner as possible you need to ensure you work with an appropriate finance broker as set out in Chapter 10. In addition, as the Turnaround Equity Finder service mentioned above operates to introduce investors into turnaround situations, you could use this to attempt to raise further turnaround equity for the business.

Given that there may well be issues of insolvency at the time that you buy the business there are also number of potential insolvency issues on which will need to take advice:

◆ What is the risk that the sale can be voidable in the future? If you buy the business and assets from a company which is insolvent at the time and which within two years of the deal goes into liquidation or administration, the IP appointed may be able to challenge the sale as a transaction at an undervalue. To do so they will need to prove both that the business was insolvent at the time and that the sale price was significantly less than what the assets were really worth.

◆ What is your potential exposure as the new owner and director of a business in difficulty to personal liability for its debts as a result of wrongful or fraudulent trading? If as a director you allow the company to continue to trade past the point where you know, or the court holds that a director should have reasonably known, that there was no reasonable prospect of avoiding insolvent liquidation, then a liquidator can apply to make you personally responsible for contributing towards the company's debts through an action for wrongful trading. If you've traded the business in a way designed to defraud creditors you can also be personally liable, as well as facing criminal penalties.

◆ What is your potential exposure as a director of the business to any deficit in the company's pension scheme? Under legislation that is being introduced at the time of writing it appears that directors may be at risk of being made personally liable for any deficits that final salary pension schemes may suffer in the event of insolvency.

◆ How can you protect your existing businesses from any risk of being dragged down by a poor purchase? This is a case where ensuring that you have a strong bulkhead defence in place is vital. You should, for example, try to ensure that there are no cross guarantees between the company that you use to buy the business in difficulty, and the other companies in your group.

BUYING FROM A RECEIVER OR ADMINISTRATOR

If an IP is looking to sell any form of decent trading business they will usually conduct a tender sale in which, having advertised the business, they seek best offers from potential interested parties (confusingly also known in the trade as 'IPs'). From an insolvency practitioner's point of view the best offer is not simply the highest offer but is the highest bid which the IP judges has the best chance of completing.

To ensure that you end up acquiring a business from an IP you therefore have to win the tendering process. To do so you should put in the highest bid that you wish to make and at the same time ensure that you have evidence that you have funds available with which to complete the deal.

Because the IP is under a duty to get the best available price for the assets they will generally not give you exclusivity until the deal is signed in case a significantly better offer turns up, and they will in some cases continue actively to solicit offers. The IP may also try to keep other counter bidders warm in reserve in case you drop out. In turn this means that until you've signed the sales contract, you are not bound in either.

However, in practice if the IP thinks you are serious you will start to move towards negotiation and sales contract with a view to completion; and the further down this process you get, the colder other counter bidders tend to become as the IP pays less attention to them and the deal gets older. The longer this process goes on before completion, the less options the IP may have of turning to other parties and the higher costs they will have run up on the case in managing to this point. As a result, IPs will seek to keep the period between agreement on offer and completion to a minimum and you will generally have very little opportunity to conduct any meaningful due diligence.

Some buyers therefore try to string the IP along for sufficient time for alternative bidders to have dropped out and then to reduce their offer to the level they actually want to pay immediately before the anticipated completion.

The dangers with this approach of course are twofold: firstly that the IP has either managed to keep another bidder interested, although you should be aware of the fact if you are in a 'contracts race'; and secondly that the delay in completing a purchase of the business means that it has suffered significantly more damage during the insolvency process than had you moved to a quicker completion.

Points to remember

When dealing with an IP there are a number of specific issues to bear in mind:

◆ The IP will usually only be acting as an agent for the company in selling and will only sell what right and title the company has to its assets. As they've not been in place for any meaningful period of time and will not have conducted any audit or verification work into the business affairs, IPs will in general offer no warranties whatsoever as to the assets included in any sale other than that as far as possible they will normally be happy to try to indicate the degree to which third parties are known to have an interest in the assets.

These third parties typically include HP and lease creditors with whom any new owner of the business will need to negotiate the adoption of the old contracts, as well as suppliers who may have effective reservation of title (ROT or Romalpa, after the case that established the principle) clauses under which ownership of the company stock does not pass to the company until a supplier has been paid for goods. The effect of this is that much of the raw material stock on site may not belong to the company.

♦ More crucially you will need to take a view as to how far you are likely to go to rely on any key contracts held by the business continuing. You are likely to find that many contracts entered into by the company have clauses in them stating that they terminate in the event of the company's insolvency. This is an area where often you are simply going to have to take a commercial decision and in many ways represents the riskiest element in buying a business from insolvency.

♦ If you're buying a business from an administrator or receiver you will usually be able to agree a purchase of the company's name with them (and you will find that they will usually change the name of the resulting shell company to ABC Realisations Limited). This can, however, be a problem if the company subsequently goes into liquidation and one of the directors of the company is also a director or involved in the management of your new company. This is because for five years from the date of insolvency they are prohibited from being involved with a company that is known by a 'prohibited name', which is any one that the company in liquidation used in the 12 months prior to its failure. In this event you can apply to court for permission to use the name.

♦ How far are you planning to rely on using the directors of the previous business in your new one? If the potential success of the business is critically reliant upon the continued use of the old directors you need to consider very carefully the risks involved. The directors of an insolvent company can, for example, be banned from acting as directors under the Company Directors Disqualification Act. They may also be facing personal liabilities under personal guarantees given the company's borrowings to its bank or landlord, or may even face actions for wrongful trading, each of which are likely to provide a major distraction to them if nothing else.

◆ While most liabilities of the business will be caught by the insolvency, remember that employee liabilities under TUPE will generally still transfer and so in taking on the business you will be taking on the liabilities for the employees retained and potentially be exposed to any claims for employees dismissed either by the business before insolvency or by the IP. In practice the level of such risks does cause some potential purchases out of insolvency to fail.

If you are buying a business out of insolvency you should use an experienced insolvency solicitor to help you. Such a solicitor will know the 'insolvency game' and you will save time as the solicitor will know what an IP will and will not do and will and will not sell, as well as being used to the very pressured and high-speed process involved. An experienced insolvency solicitor will therefore not waste time, for example, in seeking to try to negotiate warranties from the insolvency practitioner that the IP will simply not give, whereas an inexperienced general practice solicitor will often do so.

Given that insolvency is a relatively small world, a good insolvency solicitor will generally also know and deal with the insolvency practitioners in their area on a regular basis and will therefore normally have a reasonable working relationship with the IP on the other side of the table. Again, this can act to cut down the level of delays and misunderstanding as well as giving comfort to the IP that you are a serious purchaser.

Not all solicitors who specialise in insolvency will act on behalf of buyers of businesses, as some feel that this gives them a potential conflict of interest when dealing with IPs with whom they may be acting on other cases. However, some are happy to do so (try Jim James at jim.james@wardhadaway.com).

MAKING A TURNAROUND WORK

At its simplest, turnaround is about reversing the decline curve and by doing so restoring stability to the business and regrowing its value. There are generally four tasks to be undertaken in any turnaround:

◆ spotting the problems that need to be fixed

◆ surviving the crisis, as depending on how far down the decline curve the business has gone, there is usually the need to resolve some form of financial crisis so as to give time to carry out the turnaround

◆ putting together a plan, as having stabilised the business a turnaround strategy is required that sets out how the business is to be restored to health

◆ making it happen, as to really make a difference, the plan and all the changes that this means in how the business is run have to be turned into reality.

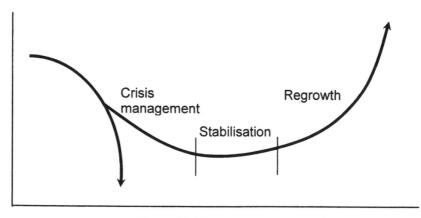

Figure 19. The recovery curve

Phases in the turnaround process

The turnaround curve divides into a number of distinct phases.

The early days of any turnaround are generally an exercise in crisis management and are focused on stabilising the financial position of the business. This involves taking firm control of the cash by taking charge of the chequebooks and installing strong cash controls and cash flow forecasting. The emphasis is then on getting as much cash in as possible by improving control of the debtor book and collections, reducing unnecessary stock levels and disposing of surplus equipment; whilst also strictly controlling the cash going out by reaching agreements with suppliers as to payment terms and shutting or radically restructuring areas of the business which are losing cash.

Once the bleeding has been stopped, sound foundations need to be laid for the subsequent successful regrowth of the company. This often involves a period of 'stabilisation' during which time the areas that are to be developed are identified and the necessary investment in people, operating efficiencies, new products, marketing and so on are arranged, as well as putting in place the necessary finance.

The final phase where all the pain becomes really worthwhile is the regrowth of the business and its value in accordance with the plan.

Necessary skills and experience

The difficulties of undertaking a turnaround should not be underestimated and they demand a particular mix of skills, experience and operating style. As discussed in Chapter 17 people who are good at managing the radical change needed during a turnaround often make extremely poor long-term managers, whilst very good managers for ongoing or growing businesses will struggle significantly with the chaos and difficulty of the early stages of a turnaround.

If you are looking to find a business to turnaround you should therefore think very seriously whether you have the skills to achieve the turnaround required. Have you:

◆ the experience of dealing with overcoming a cash crisis?

◆ experience of dealing with the insolvency issues around a business in difficulty?

◆ had to manage extensive redundancy programmes in order to cut costs?

◆ the confidence to lead staff during such difficult transition?

◆ had to deal with the business support arms of the banks and their approach to managing their risk position?

If not, you may need to obtain help from a turnaround practitioner (or 'company doctor') who is familiar with this type of crisis situation and who possesses the specific experience and skills needed to deal with it. Company doctors are generally highly experienced in the specific situational skills and circumstances involved in turning a distressed business around. They can therefore provide help with:

◆ analysis of the position, where they can provide an experienced eye to look over how deep is the crisis, assess the options and make an informed judgement as to whether the business is saveable

◆ being willing and able to act as a crisis manager who can deal with issues with the urgency and sometimes ruthlessness that they require

- coping with challenges and difficulties in a professional way

- having a body of specialist knowledge of commercial and insolvency issues such as wrongful trading and redundancy law to be able to both manage the risks, and to manage the interests of key stakeholders such as banks so that they will support the business through its difficulties.

The help provided by a company doctor is generally therefore extremely 'hands on' in nature. These are not professional advisers like the insolvency practitioner or the lawyer who, however close the relationship, will always remain outside advisers. Company doctors are the doers who become part of your business as directors to take charge and drive through change for the time needed to make the plan happen.

They often work alone but can usually also supply associates who are specialist interim managers able to deal with particular functional aspects of the business (e.g. a temporary finance director or production director) as may be required to turn the business's performance around.

For an introduction to a company doctor please either contact me at mark@theoss.freeserve.co.uk or try:

- The Society of Turnaround Professionals (www.stp-uk.org). STP is the UK's professional association of company doctors, the members of which have had to go through an accreditation process.

- The Turnaround Management Association (www.tma-uk.org for the UK chapter). TMA is in international organisation for professionals involved in turnarounds, including company doctors.

The Golden Rules

Introduction
1 Realise that this is a process – it's not doing a deal, it's making a deal work.

2 You are not buying a business for the sake of buying a business, you're doing it to achieve your objectives, whatever these might be.

Deciding you want to buy
3 Go in with your eyes open; make an honest appraisal of your reasons for buying a business and your strengths and weaknesses.

Deciding what to buy
4 Decide on your objectives (why you want to buy a business) and stick to them.

Beginning your planning and appointing advisers
5 Get good advisers – and take their advice.

Finding a business to buy
6 Don't get emotionally attached to any business until you have bought it.

7 Buy something that is not formally for sale and you'll have less competitors.

Before you approach
8 Do your research; be as well prepared as possible for your first visit.

Approaching the business

9   Understand why the seller is selling – how serious are they?

10   Only deal with serious sellers.

11   Don't buy on numbers alone, understand what the business is and what it does for its customers. 'Why people want to buy from this business and not its competitors?' is the most important question of all.

What is it worth?

12   Decide on your target and walk-away price and stick to it.

13   Trade price for certainty; the riskier the business is, the less it is worth to you.

14   First one to mention a price loses.

Financing the deal

15   You'll always need more cash than you thought you did.

16   Remember you need cash for not only the deal, but working capital and investment; don't leave yourself short.

17   Use a good asset finance broker to maximise your borrowing potential.

18   Work out what you can afford and sort out your financing early.

19   The seller is a source of cash.

Negotiating the price

20   Don't blow it by being too greedy once you've achieved your target price.

21   Understand what is important to the seller; it's often more than cash.

22   Terms are as important as price – sometimes more so.

Due diligence

23   Don't skip on due diligence – you'll pay for it later.

Commercial due diligence

24   Ensure you get a non-competition covenant.

Taking control

25   A successful business acquisition is not just a matter of successfully buying a business, it is a matter of making a success of the business that has been bought.

Useful Contacts

AUTHOR
mark@theoss.freeserve.co.uk

WWW.BAKERTILLY.CO.UK
Baker Tilly is a leading independent firm of chartered
accountants and business advisers that specialises in providing
an integrated range of services to the owner-managed business.
They provide their growing and established business clients with
audit, accountancy, personal and corporate taxation, VAT,
consultancy, corporate finance, financial services and business
recovery. The firm has national coverage through its network of
offices and is represented internationally through its independent
membership of Baker Tilly International. Contact 020 7405
2088.

WWW.CREATIVEFINANCE.CO.UK
Asset based finance brokerage able to assist in raising a range of
financing solutions for acquisitions as well as deferred
consideration bonding. Download their free 'FAQ' sheets or
contact finance@creativefinance.co.uk.

WWW.INSIGHTASSOCIATES.CO.UK
Specialists in improving financial management of businesses and
for providing 'outsourced' FD services. Contact Garry Mumford
on 01279 647447 or gmumford@insightassociates.co.uk.

WWW.MARCHANDS.ORG.UK

Boutique Corporation finance and insolvency practice which offers fixed price Business Hunter service and 'Corporate Structure Cleaning Service'. Contact Martin Shaw or Charles Brook on 01484 607444 or info@marchands.org.uk.

WWW.RESOLUTIONINC.BIZ

Provide experienced executives with the range of specialist skills and industry experience which you can use to support your post-acquisition plan as well as services for managing the disposal of unwanted parts of an acquisition for maximum value. Contact info@resolutioninc.biz.

WWW.TURNAROUNDEQUITYFINDER.CO.UK

Unique national introduction service focused solely on turnaround situations, bringing together equity investors interested in buying out or investing in turnaround opportunities with those businesses that want to meet them.

WWW.TURNAROUNDHELP.CO.UK

Specific advice and assistance on turning around a business in difficulties if required after acquisition. Contact help@turnaroundhelp.co.uk.

WWW.WARDHADAWAY.COM

Leading multi-disciplinary legal and corporate finance practice covering all areas of business sales. Contact Robert Thompson on 0191 204 4000 or robert.thompson@wardhadaway.com. For purchases from insolvency contact Jim James at jim.james@wardhadaway.com.

Glossary of Acronyms

BIMBO	buy in management buy out
CHOCs	client handles own customers
CID	confidential invoice discounting
CVA	company voluntary arrangement
CVL	creditor's voluntary liquidation
DTI	Department of Trade and Industry
EBIT	earnings before interest and tax
GAAP	generally accepted accounting practice
GRNI	goods received but not invoiced
IFA	independent financial adviser
IHT	inheritance tax
IPR	intellectual property
IRR	internal rate of return
MBI	management buy in
MBO	management buy out
OEM	original equipment manufacturer
OMV	open market value
PBIT	profits before interest and tax
PE ratio	price/earnings ratio
PG	personal guarantee
PII	professional indemnity insurance
ROT	reservation of title
SFLG	Small Firms Loan Guarantee Scheme
SPVs	special purpose vehicles
TUPE	Transfer of Undertakings, Protection of Employee Regulations
VC	venture capitalist
WACC	weighted average cost of capital

Appendix A

Sample Confidentiality Agreement

wardhadaway

Sandgate House
102 Quayside
Newcastle Upon Tyne NE1 3DX

THIS AGREEMENT is made the day of 200[ ]

BETWEEN

[*to be inserted*] ('the Owners')

[*to be inserted*] whose registered office is [*to be inserted*] ('the Target'); and

[*to be inserted*] whose registered office is [*to be inserted*] ('the Recipient').

RECITALS

A   [The entire issued share capital of the Target] is owned by the Owners

B   The Owners and the Target are the owners of Confidential Information relating to the Target and its business; and

C   To enable the Recipient to assess whether and if so on what terms it may wish to purchase the entire share capital or part thereof of the Target or all or part of its business but for no other purpose the Owners and the Target are willing to disclose the Confidential Information to the Recipient under conditions of confidentiality.

IT IS AGREED as follows:

1   Interpretation – In this agreement, the following terms shall have the following meanings:

1.1   'Confidential Information' means any of:

1.1.1   the information of whatever nature relating to the Target and/or its business or any of its subsidiaries which is or has been obtained by the Recipient and/or its Related Persons in written, electronic, pictorial or oral form

1.1.2   the information of whatever nature relating to the Target obtained by observation during visits to its premises by the Recipient, and/or its Related Persons

1.1.3   the analyses, compilations, studies and other documents prepared by the Recipient and/or its Related Persons to the extent that they contain or otherwise reflect or are generated or derived from the information specified in sub-clauses 1.1.1 or 1.1.2 above or both of them; and

1.1.4   this agreement, the fact that discussions or negotiations are taking or have taken place between the Owners and/or the Target and the Recipient and any of the information disclosed to the Recipient and/or its Related Persons as part of such discussions or negotiations

1.2   'Related Persons' means any officers, employers, agents, advisers or consultants of and/or any individual, firm, company, joint venture or partnership (whether or not having separate legal personality) associated or connected with the Recipient.

1.3   'Transaction' means the purchase of all or part of the business of the Target or the purchase of all or some of the share capital of the Target.

2   Exclusions – The obligations of confidentiality under this agreement shall not apply to Confidential Information or such of it which:

2.1   the Recipient can prove by documentary evidence was already in the Recipient's possession before its disclosure under this agreement [*within 8 days of the receipt by the Recipient of such information*]

2.2   is disclosed or has before the date of this agreement been disclosed to the Recipient by a third party who has not derived it directly or indirectly from the Owners and/or the Target in breach of any obligations of confidence; or

2.3   is or becomes generally available to the public through no act or default on the part of the Recipient and/or its Related Persons.

3   **Undertakings** – In consideration of the Target and/or the Owners making the Confidential Information available to the Recipient and/or its Related Persons (there being no obligation on the Target or the Owners to supply such information) the Recipient undertakes to the Owners and by way of further obligation to the Target that:

3.1   it will use the Confidential Information solely for the purpose of evaluating the Target with a view to deciding whether or not to enter into a Transaction and not for any other purpose and will not permit or assist a third party to make use of Confidential Information for any other purpose

3.2   it will treat and safeguard as private and confidential all the Confidential Information received or held by it at any time

3.3   except as may be required by law, the requirements of the London Stock Exchange and the Panel of Take-overs and Mergers, it will not (whether or not a Transaction is entered into with the Owners and/or the Target) at any time without the prior written consent of the Owners disclose or reveal or permit the disclosure of any Confidential Information, whether directly or indirectly, to any person other than its officers, senior employees and advisers who have previously agreed to maintain the confidentiality of such information in accordance with this agreement and who reasonably need to know the same for the purposes of an evaluation under clause 3.1

3.4   it will procure that its Related Persons strictly observe the terms of this agreement and the Recipient will be responsible for any breach of this agreement by any of them and shall indemnify the Target and the Owners in respect of all damage (including but not limited to legal costs) which may arise directly or indirectly from the unauthorised disclosure or use of any Confidential Information; and

3.5   upon written request from the Target or the Owners it will immediately return to the Target or the Owners, as appropriate, all documents, computer media and papers containing Confidential Information, destroy any papers referred to in sub-clause 1.1.3 above together with any copies and expunge all Confidential Information from any computer, word processor or other device or media containing it and [*the Chairman of the Board of*] the Recipient will confirm compliance with the above in writing to the Owners.

4   **Restrictions** – In consideration of the Target and the Owners making the Confidential Information available to the Recipient (there being no obligations on the Target or the Owners to supply such information) the Recipient undertakes (on behalf of itself and any of its subsidiary companies) to the Owners and by way of further obligation to the Target that it will not during the course of negotiations toward the Transaction or in the event that a Transaction is not entered into with the Owners it will not during the period of 12 months from the date of the latest disclosure to the Recipient by the Owner or the Target of any Confidential Information pursuant to this agreement either directly or indirectly:

4.1   solicit, endeavour to entice away or offer to employ any person who was at any time during those negotiations employed by the Target in any capacity, whether or not that person would commit any breach of his or her contract of service in leaving such employment

4.2   make contact with any client or supplier of the Target [*in connection with* [*specify a particular activity*]]

4.3   for the avoidance of doubt, the restrictions contained in clause 4.1 shall not apply to the placing of any general advertisement for the purpose of recruitment; and

4.4   each restriction contained in clause 4 shall be read and construed independently of the other restrictions and whilst the restrictions are considered by the parties to be reasonable in all the circumstances as at the date of the agreement it is acknowledged that restrictions of such a nature may be invalid because of changing circumstances or other unforeseen reasons and accordingly it is hereby agreed and declared that if any one or more such restrictions shall be judged to be void as going beyond what is reasonable in all the circumstances for the protection of the interests of the Owners and the Target the validity of any other restrictions contained herein shall not be affected.

5   **Legal Requirement to Disclose** – In the event that the Recipient, its Related Persons or anyone to whom the Recipient or its Related Persons transmits any Confidential Information (without prejudice to the restrictions contained in clause 3) becomes (or is reasonably likely to become) legally required to disclose any Confidential Information:

5.1   prompt notice shall be given to the Owners [*at the address given above*] so that the Owners and/or the Target may seek an appropriate remedy to prevent disclosure or waive compliance with the provisions of this agreement preventing disclosure; and

5.2   the Recipient or its Related Persons will be entitled to do so only to the extent so actually required and subject to prior agreement or if not practicable, consultation (if practicable) with the Owners in regard to the timing and content of the disclosure.

6   **Authorised Contact** – Neither the Recipient nor any of its Related Persons will contact or communicate with any directors, employees, advisers, agents, consultants of the Target [or the Owners] regarding the business operations prospects or finances of the same [or the Target] unless written consent has first been received from the Owners.

7   **No Representations or Warranties** – The Confidential Information made available to the Recipient and its Related Persons has not and will not have been independently verified by the Target or the Owners or their advisers and the Recipient will be solely responsible for making its own judgment and decisions on all Confidential Information. Neither the Target nor the Owners nor any of their respective officers, shareholders, employees, agents or advisers make any representation or warranty (express or implied) as to the accuracy or completeness of the Confidential Information or as to the reasonableness of any assumptions or projections which may be contained in it. If the Recipient subsequently decides to enter into a Transaction, the Recipient acknowledges that it will not have relief for any representation or warranty contained in any Confidential Information save as expressly incorporated into any written acquisition agreement. Neither the Target nor any of its subsidiaries nor the Owners nor any of their respective officers, shareholders, employees, agents or advisers will have any liability to the Recipient or any of the Recipient's representatives or its Related Persons resulting from the use of the Confidential Information. This clause 7 will not apply to the extent of any fraud or fraudulent misrepresentation by any of the Target, the Owners or any of their respective officers, shareholders, employees, agents or advisers.

8 **Entire Agreement** – This agreement constitutes the entire agreement and understanding between the Target, the Owners and the Recipient in respect of the obligations of confidentiality and restrictions accepted by the Recipient in relation to the receipt by the Recipient of all Confidential Information and the evaluation by the Recipient of the Target or its business and shall supersede and override any such obligations or restrictions included in any terms or conditions submitted by the Recipient.

9 **No Waiver** – No delay, failure or forbearance by the Target or the Owners to or in the exercise any of their respective rights under this agreement shall be construed as a waiver of such rights and shall not prevent the future exercise of such rights.

10 **Breach of this Agreement** – Without prejudice to any other rights and remedies the Target and the Owners may have, the Recipient agrees that the Confidential Information is valuable and that damages may not be an adequate remedy for any breach of this agreement by the Recipient. Accordingly the Recipient agrees that the Target and the Owners shall be entitled without proof of special damage to the remedies of an injunction and other equitable relief for any actual or threatened breach of this agreement by the Recipient.

11 **Enforcement** – The Recipient acknowledges that the rights and obligations contained in this agreement are enforceable by the Target or the Owners.

12 **Third Party Rights** – No person shall become entitled to enforce the provisions of this agreement who would not have been so entitled but for the enactment of the Contracts (Rights of Third Parties) Act 1999 and for the avoidance of doubt it is hereby agreed that the provisions of the said Act shall not apply to this agreement.

13 **Severance** – If at any time any provision of this agreement is or becomes invalid or illegal in any respect, such provision shall be

deemed to be severed from this agreement but the validity, legality and enforceability of the remaining provisions of this agreement shall not be affected or impaired thereby.

14   Assignment

14.1   This agreement shall be binding on the parties and their respective successors in title.

14.2   Neither of the parties shall be entitled to assign this agreement or any of its rights and obligations under it except as permitted in this agreement.

14.3   The Owner may assign its rights to any member [of its Group] or to a successful purchaser of the Target or its business and those persons will be entitled to enforce this agreement as if they were the Owner.

15   No Offer – No documents or information made available to the Recipient will constitute an offer or invitation or form the basis of any contract. The Owner and the Target shall be entitled at any time to decline to provide or continue to provide any Confidential Information to the Recipient.

16   Acting as Principal – The Recipient is acting as principal and not as a broker or agent.

17   Governing Law – This agreement shall be governed by and construed in accordance with English Law and the English Courts shall have [non]-exclusive jurisdiction.

This agreement is executed and delivered by the Recipient as a deed the day and year first before written.

Executed and Delivered as a Deed

Document provided by Ward Hadaway

Appendix B

Sample Legal Due Diligence Questionnaire

Introduction

To: The Directors of [*Target*]

From: Ward Hadaway

1   References in this questionnaire to the 'Company' are references to [target] and all of its subsidiary companies (if any). Please therefore reply to each enquiry for [target] and all its subsidiary companies (if any).

2   Please supply a copy of the documentation and/or supply the information requested in this questionnaire in relation to the Company and identify replies by using the same numerical reference system. In the event that there is no documentation or information in relation to a particular company, please confirm there is none in the reply to that enquiry.

3   In the case of any copy documentation, please ensure that each copy is complete and where a full understanding of the position cannot be obtained from the copy document(s) alone please also provide an explanation. Where details have been requested, please reply as fully as possible to avoid any further enquiries.

4   We suggest that you supply responses as and when the information is available rather than waiting until all the information has been collected.

5 [The replies to this questionnaire (and any further enquiries raised by Ward Hadaway) will form the basis of a formal legal due diligence report about the Company to be prepared by Ward Hadaway and issued to [ ] as instructed by you.]

6 This questionnaire is not exhaustive and supplemental requests for information and/or documentation may be made by the appropriate department of Ward Hadaway.

7 Please address all responses to and queries about this questionnaire to [ ] on [ ]; e-mail: [ ] or [ ] on [ ]; e-mail: [ ]

8 **Constitution of the Company**

8.1 Please provide a copy of the current Memorandum and Articles of Association of the Company and any amending resolutions in relation to the same.

8.2 Please provide the names and company registration numbers of the Company and all companies in which the Company holds, or has agreed to hold or to acquire, shares and, in the case of each such company, specify:

8.2.1 the authorised and issued share capital

8.2.2 the names of the shareholders and the number and class of shares held by them

8.2.3 the product manufactured and/or the service supplied; and

8.2.4 the general nature and scale of operations.

8.3 Please supply copies of all agreements relating to the ownership and/or control of the Company.

8.4 Please supply copies of all options and agreements relating to the issue or transfer of shares in the Company.

8.5 Please deliver the statutory books (and any separate minute book(s)) of the Company to Ward Hadaway. The statutory books will be returned following inspection.

8.6 Please supply copies of all declarations of trust and other deeds and documents governing the trusts upon which any shares in the Company are held, together with the names and addresses of all trustees.

9   Accounts

9.1 Please supply copies of the audited accounts of the Company for each of the last three years.

9.2 Please supply details of any changes in accounting policy over the last three sets of audited accounts.

9.3 Please supply copies of all unaudited draft accounts of the Company.

9.4 Please supply copies of the most recent Management Accounts of the Company.

9.5 Please supply copies of the current year's budgets.

9.6 Please supply copies of all current Business Plans.

9.7 Please provide a schedule itemising:

9.7.1 current debtors, period of debt and amount; and

9.7.2 current creditors, period of credit and amount.

10   Litigation

10.1 Please supply details of all prosecutions, proceedings, litigation, arbitration, mediation or other forms of dispute resolution in which the Company is or is likely to be engaged, or has been engaged in the previous three years.

10.2 Please supply details of all outstanding complaints or disputes (including any intimated by or intimated against) the Company in relation to:

10.2.1 any materials or goods (or class of materials or goods) supplied by the Company; and/or

10.2.2 any services (or class of services) rendered by the Company; and/or

10.2.3 any other aspect of the business of the Company.

10.3 Please supply details of any subsisting circumstances or grounds which are likely to give rise to:

10.3.1 any prosecutions, proceedings, litigation or arbitration involving or concerning the Company; and/or

10.3.2 any complaint or dispute (as referred to at 4.2 above).

10.4 Please supply details of all accidents at work which have or could have given rise to a claim against the Company (whether or not covered by insurance).

10.5 Please supply details of all material breaches that have occurred under any contracts or arrangements to which the Company is a party.

10.6 Please supply a copy of the Company's accident record book.

10.7 Please supply a copy of the Health and Safety at Work Act etc. procedures.

11   Plant and equipment

11.1 Please supply a copy of all up to date plant and machinery registers giving details of the location of this plant and machinery.

11.2 Please supply details of all plant and equipment (excluding computer equipment) used by the company subject to leasing, credit sale, hire purchase or similar arrangements.

11.3 Please supply details of any equipment used by the Company but owned by another member of the Company's group or any third party and details of the arrangement in respect of the use of such plant and equipment.

12   Business of the company

Finance

12.1   Please supply details of all banking and financial arrangements operated by, or available to, the Company, and please also supply copies of all agreements, facility letters and/or other documents relating to the same.

12.2   Please supply copies of the following:

12.2.1 all legal charges, debentures, mortgages or other financial or security documents affecting the Company, or other documentation relating to the same; and

12.2.2 all loan agreements affecting the Company or other documentation relating to the same.

12.3   Please supply copies of all hire purchase, leasing, credit sale, or deferred payment agreements or similar arrangements to which the Company is party.

12.4   Please supply details of any guarantees, sureties or indemnities (or assurances of a similar nature) which have been given by or for the benefit of the Company.

Insurance

12.5   Please supply details of all policies of insurance maintained by the Company, and a copy of the policy documents and any other agreements and/or documents relating to the same (including any insurances relating to life assurance, permanent health insurance and medical expenses insurance).

12.6   Please supply details of all insurance claims made by and against the Company – both current claims and those made by and against the Company within the last three years.

12.7   Please confirm that the Company has paid all premia on its insurance policies.

12.8   Please supply details of credit insurance effected and claims experience.

Grants

12.9   Please supply details of all investment, employment, local authority or central government grants which have been paid or awarded to the Company (including the terms and conditions of repayment) and please also supply a copy of all agreements and other documentation relating to the same.

Trading

12.10   Please supply copies of the following:

12.10.1 all agreements and written contracts terminable upon the transfer of shares in the Company

12.10.2 any outstanding quotations or tenders made by or to the Company

12.10.3 all standard terms and conditions of trading issued by the Company. Please also supply details of when and how such terms and conditions are used

12.10.4 all standard terms and conditions of trading issued by third parties which affect the Company. Please also supply details of when and how such terms and conditions are used.

12.11   Please supply copies of all agreements and/or other documentation relating to the following:

12.11.1 all licences or consents granted by, or in favour of, the Company

12.11.2 all registrations held by the Company that are necessary or desirable to conduct its business

12.11.3 all material or long term agreements or arrangements to which the Company is a party

12.11.4 all maintenance agreements or arrangements to which the Company is a party

12.11.5 all agency agreements or arrangements to which the Company is a party

12.11.6 all distribution agreements or arrangements to which the Company is a party; and

12.11.7 all factoring agreements or arrangements to which the Company is a party.

In the case of any such licences, consents, registrations, agreements or arrangements (referred to in 6.11.1–6.11.7) not reduced to writing, please supply a summary of their terms, including the names of the parties, commencement date, termination date, duration and termination provisions.

12.12 Please supply details of all arrangements between the Company and the Company's competitors (whether legally enforceable or not) and supply a copy of all agreements and other documentation relating to the same.

12.13 Please supply details of the trade associations of which the Company is a member, if any, including copies of any rules or code of conduct of such association(s) or agreements between members with which the Company should comply.

12.14 Please supply details of all agreements, arrangements or transactions to which the Company is or has been a party for the transfer of any assets at undervalue within the period of 2 years preceding the date of this questionnaire.

12.15 Please supply a list of major customers of the Company (ie those accounting for more than 5% of its turnover) and the value of sales to each in the last 3 years.

12.16 Please supply a list of major suppliers of the Company (ie those accounting for more than 5% of goods or materials purchased) and the value of purchases from each in the last 3 years.

12.17 Please provide details of any restrictions on the Business to conduct its business and copies of all agreements and/or other documents relating to the same.

12.18 Please supply details of any supplier or customer where the relationship is likely to change because of the sale of the Company or for other reasons (including full details of the last 12 months' purchases or sales and orders in hand).

12.19 Please supply details of any significant capital or reserve commitments.

13   Intellectual property

13.1   Please supply details of:

13.1.1 all patents or applications for patents vested in, or used by, the Company

13.1.2 all registered and unregistered trade marks, trade names and brand names vested in, or used by, the Company

13.1.3 all registered and unregistered service marks vested in, or used by, the Company

13.1.4 all registered designs vested in, or used by, the Company

13.1.5 all design rights vested in, or used by, the Company

13.1.6 any material in which the Company has, or claims, a copyright interest or database right

13.1.7 all other intellectual property rights vested in, or used by, the Company

13.1.8 all domain names owned or used by the Company.

In each case provide the date of application, date of grant, and registration number, and details of actual use over the last three years anywhere in the world, as appropriate.

13.2   Please supply copies of the following:

13.2.1 all agreements, licences or arrangements to which the Company is a party affecting or relating to the development of any intellectual property rights vested in, or used by, the Company or where such agreements, licences or arrangements are not in writing, please supply a summary of their terms, including the names of the parties, commencement date, termination date, duration and termination provisions.

13.3   Please supply details of any of the rights referred to above which are shared with any other members of the Company's group of companies.

13.4   Please supply details of any challenges or disputes relating to any intellectual property rights owned or used by the Company, including any challenges to the validity, subsistence or ownership of such rights.

13.5   Please provide details of the Company's Intellectual Property Rights (IPRs) policies including Internet and security policies and design protocols.

13.6   Please supply details of any notice(s) or claim(s) that the Company has received or is aware of alleging that the Company has or is alleged to have infringed the IPRs of any third party and, in each case, please provide:

13.6.1 details of the circumstances of the infringement, alleged infringement, or claim; and

13.6.2 details of the circumstances surrounding any infringement or claim.

13.7   Has the Company disclosed to any person any of its intellectual property or other confidential information or trade secrets and if so please provide details and copies of any relevant agreements.

14   Information technology

14.1   Please supply details of all computer facilities and other information technology hardware or systems (including make, model, specification and capacity) in the possession of and/or used by the Company in the operation of its business and in each case specify which is owned by the Company, which is the subject of any hire purchase, leasing, rental or deferred payment agreement, or which is otherwise provided by a third party.

14.2   Please supply details of all software (including nature, description, version, and the number of copies licensed) owned or used by the Company.

14.3   Please supply details of the author of any software owned, or used by, the Company.

14.4   Please supply copies of all software licences for computer programs licensed to the Company, any software and new media (including web sites and CD ROMS) development, commissioning, hosting and maintenance agreements used by or developed by or on behalf of the Company.

14.5   Please supply details of any web site operated by or hosted on behalf of the Company and any CD ROMs used by the Company in connection with the Business and the promotion of the Business, and any terms and conditions for the use by third parties of such new media.

14.6   Please supply a copy of the Company's Data Protection Act Registration and details of the nature of data stored by the Company and whether and to whom such data has been or may be transferred from time to time.

14.7   Please supply details of:

14.7.1 any and all of the Company's information technology systems that have been affected by millennium compliance problems or the introduction or use of the ECU and any: millennium/date compliance (Y2K) problems; and problems associated with the introduction and use of ECU.

14.7.2 the Company's policy and strategy towards the introduction or use of ECU; and

14.7.3 any audit carried out, or to be carried out, by or for the Company in respect of its information technology systems that are likely to be affected by ECU problems.

15 Directors

15.1 Please supply the names, addresses and job titles (if any) of each of the directors of the Company and the company secretary and, in each case, specify whether such officer is employed by the Company.

15.2 Please supply a copy the service agreement/contract or written statement of terms of employment for each of the officers of the Company and, in each case where there is no such written documentation, please supply details of the officer's:

15.2.1 obligations and duties

15.2.2 length of service

15.2.3 date of commencement of service

15.2.4 remuneration and fringe benefits (including any accommodation provided)

15.2.5 unexpired term of office (if employed for a fixed period); and

15.2.6 details of the notice period required to terminate the officer's employment (on either side).

15.3 Please supply details of all arrangements between the Company and any of its directors which relate to or affect the capital, business, property, assets or liabilities of the Company and/or any of its group undertakings, and supply copies of all agreements and other documentation relating to the same.

15.4 Please supply details of all loans granted by the Company and/or any group undertaking to any of the Company's directors, and/or vice versa.

16 Employees, consultants and sub-contractors

16.1 Please supply the names of all employees of the Company and in each case specify the employee's position, age, length of service, date of commencement of employment, contractual notice period (on either side), length of any fixed term contracts, salary and other contractual and non-contractual benefits such as entitlement to a bonus, company car, and medical insurance.

16.2 Please supply:

16.2.1 a copy of all standard terms and conditions of employment (if any) for the Company's employees and specify those of the Company's employees to which these are applicable

16.2.2 details of all employees of the Company who are not employed under the Company's standard terms and conditions of employment and, in each case, supply a copy of the employee's service agreement/contract or if there is no written documentation, supply details of the employee's terms and conditions of employment (including the details set out at 10.1 above)

16.2.3 copies of any staff handbooks and/or circulars

16.2.4 copies of any disciplinary and grievance procedures

16.2.5 a copy of any variations to employees contracts which have been notified to employees by means of notice/circular; and

16.2.6 a copy of all current organisation charts.

16.3 Please supply:

16.3.1 the terms of and details of those persons entitled to (together with details of their entitlement) participate in any share option, bonus, incentive or other scheme(s)

16.3.2 details of all bonuses paid out in the last 36 months; and

16.3.3 a copy of any scheme agreements or other documentation relating to the same.

16.4   Please provide:

16.4.1 details of any ex-gratia payments in the last 12 months and of any current or former employees in respect of whom the directors consider the Company to be under a moral or legal obligation to provide retirement or death, accident or sickness disability benefits; and

16.4.2 details of all voluntary pensions or payments and of any current arrangements (whether legally binding or not) for the making of any pension or ex-gratia payments to employees or former employees not covered within the reply to 10.4.1 above, or elsewhere in this questionnaire.

16.5   Please provide details of arrangements to provide paid holiday to each category of employee including calculation of holiday pay.

16.6   Does holiday pay include shift bonuses, overtime payments, performance bonuses or commission payments?

16.7   Please confirm the date upon which the Company's holiday year commences.

16.8   Please confirm the means by which the time worked by each employee, the rest breaks provided and taken by each employee and the holidays taken or holiday pay received, is recorded and in each case please provide an example of the records maintained.

16.9   Please supply details of any job vacancies which are currently, or are about to be advertised and, in addition, details of any job offers made or about to be made.

16.10   Please supply details of any employee absent on sick leave or maternity leave (or who the Company is aware is about to go on maternity leave) or authorised or unauthorised leave of any nature.

16.11   Please supply details of all employees who have resigned or had their employment terminated within the last six months.

16.12 Please supply details of any employee of the Company who has given notice terminating his or her contract of employment or any employee under notice of dismissal.

16.13 If any of the Company's employees work shift patterns, please provide details of the shift patterns worked including start and finish times of each shift, whether the workers perform variable shift patterns, details of rest breaks, daily and weekly rest periods provided and the categories of employees who perform work to shift patterns.

16.14 Please supply details of the systems in place to record compliance with the Working Time Regulations 1998.

16.15 Are there any collective or workforce agreements in place? If yes, please provide full details and copies of all relevant agreements.

16.16 Does the Company have any 'night workers' within the meaning of the Working Time Regulations 1998? If yes, please provide full details.

16.17 Since the Working Time Regulations 1998 came into force on 1st October 1998, has the Company complied with all the Regulations? If not, please provide full details of any breaches.

16.18 Please confirm that all employees who qualify for the national minimum wage have received the national minimum wage since the National Minimum Wage Regulations 1999 came into force on 1st April 1999. If there have been any breaches, please provide full details.

16.19 Please supply details of the systems in place to record compliance with the National Minimum Wage Regulations 1999.

16.20 Please supply copies of any agreement entered into between the Company and any employee in accordance with the National Minimum Wage Regulations 1999.

16.21   Please provide details of all disputes between the Company and any employee or ex-employee, including matters already referred to an Employment Tribunal and those that are expected to be so referred or settled by the payment of money.

16.22   Please supply details of the Company's redundancy policy.

16.23   Please supply the names and addresses of all consultants, sub contractors or other self employed persons retained/engaged by the Company.

16.24   Please supply a copy of all written agreements with, or written terms of engagement for, all sub-contractors, consultants and self employed persons retained/engaged by the Company, or where there is no written documentation supply details of the terms and condition of retainer/engagement (including termination provisions).

17   Pensions

17.1   Please supply details of all pension schemes effected by the Company or in which the Company or any of its directors or employees have an interest.

17.2   Please supply a copy of all Trust Deeds and rules (including any amendments).

17.3   Please supply a copy of all explanatory booklets or leaflets distributed to members.

17.4   Please supply a copy of all insurance policies (for insured schemes).

17.5   Please supply a copy of the two most recent valuation reports and details of any actuarial advice or certificates received.

17.6   Please supply a copy of the Trustees reports and accounts for the last 3 years.

17.7   Please supply details of any special arrangements/ augmentations for individual transferees.

17.8   Please confirm that the pension scheme operated by the Company is an Exempt Approved Scheme and, if it is, please confirm that the members of the Company are not aware of any reason why such approval could be withdrawn.

17.9   Please supply a copy of any contracting out certificate.

17.10   Please supply a summary of the deferred and pensioner members of the scheme and a copy of the latest available scheme accounts.

17.11   Please supply a list of the scheme's active members at the annual review date, including their sex, date of birth, pensionable salary and the date upon which each such member joined the scheme.

18   Taxation

18.1   Please supply details to date of tax returns which have been made.

18.2   To what date have tax returns been settled?

18.3   Please supply details of what matters are in dispute or under discussion with the Inland Revenue.

18.4   To what date has tax been deducted under PAYE/VAT and been accounted for and paid over?

18.5   Please supply details of any covenants entered since 6 April 1965 for annual payments of any nature.

18.6   Please supply details of the calculation of deferred tax relating to the last set of audited accounts.

18.7   Please confirm if the Company is, or has been, a 'close company'. If it is or has been, please supply details of any directions which have been made and which are outstanding, including details of any notice of intimation that any direction will be made?

18.8 Please supply an analysis of the tax provision in the latest accounts with explanation of key components.

18.9 Please supply copies of the last three years' tax computations.

18.10 Please supply details of any special arrangements with, or dispensations by, any tax authority.

18.11 Please supply details of any overseas trading via non-statutory entities or agents, and details of controls and procedures for compliance with overseas filing requirements.

18.12 PAYE: Please supply a copy of any recent or ongoing audits or investigations in relation to employee taxes and potential exposures in this request.

18.13 VAT: Please supply details of recent or ongoing audits or investigations in relation to VAT, sales taxes and customs duties, and potential exposures in this respect.

19   Properties

19.1 Please supply details of all property owned by, leased to, licensed to, or otherwise used by the Company, or in which the Company has any interest, and in each case specify:

19.1.1 the tenure of such property and provide details of areas of both freehold and leasehold title together with plans thereof

19.1.2 details of any disputes (including rent reviews and dilapidation claims) subsisting or imminent in relation to any properties

19.1.3 registration details.

19.2 Please supply details of any property transactions in the course of negotiation.

19.3   Please supply a copy of all survey reports or valuations received by the Company relating to any of the properties owned or occupied by it.

19.4   Please supply a copy of all title deeds relating to all properties owned by, leased to, licensed or otherwise used by the Company, or in which the Company has any interest.

19.5   Please supply details of any property, premises or other facilities shared or used in common with other persons and supply a copy of all agreements, licences and other documentation relating to the same.

20   Environmental

20.1   Please provide details of any land currently or previously owned, occupied, used or held by the Company which is used or has been used (by the Company's previous owners (if any)) for any of the following:

20.1.1 the deposit or treatment of waste

20.1.2 land filling or backfilling operations

20.1.3 any contaminate use which may result in the land being identified as contaminated under section 78B of the Environmental Protection Act 1990; or

20.1.4 any use requiring a waste disposal licence under Part II of the Environmental Protection Act 1990.

20.2   Please supply copies of any environmental, investigations, assessments, reports or audits which the Company has commissioned or which have been carried out in respect of the Company's operations or in respect of any land currently or previously owned, occupied or used by the Company, including any ground investigation surveys.

20.3   Please supply details (and copies) of all environmental licences relating to the Company.

20.4   Please provide details of any complaints or prosecutions made or threatened or brought against the Company and any infringements by the Company of any environmental regulations and/or laws including but not limited to:

20.4.1 the Control of Pollution Act 1974

20.4.2 the Water Resources Act 1991

20.4.3 the Environmental Protection Act 1990; and

20.4.4 the Environment Act 1995.

20.5   Please provide details of any procedures or operations carried out by the Company which involve polluted or contaminated materials.

20.6   Please provide:

20.6.1 details of any outstanding recommendations made to the Company by the Environment Agency, the Health and Safety Executive, local authorities or any other statutory body under any environmental or health and safety legislation and regulations

20.6.2 details of any site at which the Company carries on a process which will require authorisation under Part 1 of the Environmental Protection Act 1990, including details of whether the relevant process is within Schedule A or Schedule B and whether any indication has been received from the Environmental Agency or the local authority as to any works which the Company will have to undertake in order to obtain authorisation

20.6.3 details of any complaints or claims by owners or occupiers of any neighbouring land in respect of activities carried on by the Company or in respect of the condition of any land currently or previously owned, occupied, used or held by the Company

20.6.4   details of any waste disposed of by the Company including the type and amount of waste, examples of transfer notes, consignment notes and registered carriers certificates

20.6.5   copies of trade effluent consent relating to discharges from any land owned by the Company; and

20.6.6   confirmation that the Company does not need to register under the Producer Responsibility Obligations (Packaging Waste) Regulations 1997.

Document provided by Ward Hadaway.

Appendix C

Sample Financial Due Diligence Checklist

CLIENT NAME ACCOUNT DATE Reviewed by: Date:	Completed by: (initials & date)
STATUTORY AND GENERAL 1 The name, registered office and country and date of incorporation 2 The acquisition date, if applicable, and consideration therefore 3 Location and principal activities of the business over the last 2 years 4 Minutes of shareholders' and management meetings for the past two years to date 5 Memorandum and Articles of Association and other statutory records 6 A list of shareholders with details of classes of shares and share options 7 Details of shares held in trust and links to other shareholders	

8   Auditors and other professional advisers

9   Any outside shareholders' interests in subsidiaries, and details of other shareholders in associated companies

10 Guarantees and contingent liabilities

11 Copies of any joint venture agreements

12 Any current litigation or other disputes

ADVISERS etc

Provide names and addresses of:

a   bankers

b   solicitors

c   auditors

d   brokers, sponsors and other advisers

DIRECTORS AND EMPLOYEES

1   Details of management structure and division of responsibilities

2   List of directors and senior executives and particulars as to:

a   previous experience and connection before joining

b   qualifications and degrees

c   duties over the past two years

d   years of service and appointment to the Board

e   current remuneration package including benefits

f   details of any service agreements

g   any interests in transactions with the company

h   pension arrangements; and

i   other directorships held outside the group

3   List of former directors and senior executives who have left during the last two years

4   Number of employees analysed as to functions

5   Number of employees in each trade union and union arrangements with the company with details of any recent dispute

6   Outline of salary/wage payment structure and salary/wage reviews for all employees

7   Average rates of pay over the past year ended 200 . . . over types of staff

8   Outline of contracts of employment

9   Current training arrangements for employees

10 Staff welfare, social clubs etc

11 Details of bonus arrangements and payments over the past two years

PENSION ARRANGEMENTS

1   A copy of the pension trust deed together with pension literature available to members

2   A copy of the latest pension fund accounts

3   Any ex gratia pension commitments

PREMISES

1   Summary of premises showing tenure and area, and distinguishing if possible between offices, warehouse area, plant yard, servicing areas etc

2   Sight of any recent independent or internal valuations or insurance reports

3   Details of rents payable and sight of leases or tenancy agreements (with details of any onerous lease provisions, for example on dilapidations)

4   Details of any vacant or sublet properties

5   Comments on the availability of any spare land

6   Details of any grants of planning permission

INSURANCE

Details of all current insurance cover and premiums

MANAGEMENT CONTROL AND INFORMATION

1   Details of the structure of the accounting function

2   Details on the regularity with which all management reporting information is produced and persons for whom this information is produced

3   Copies of all management accounts and other monitoring information prepared for management for, at least, the last financial year and a reconciliation to the annual financial statements

4   Copies of all management accounts and other monitoring information prepared for management since the last annual financial statements

5   Copies of all annual and interim accounts, returns and responses to review visits submitted to regulatory bodies over the last two years

6   Details of the accounting systems in operation, procedures manuals etc

7   Copies of any audit management letters over the past three years

8   Details of the role of any internal audit department

9   Details of the computer applications and staff involved including plans to cover disaster recovery

10 Details of any treasury function, organisation and personnel

11 Profit/capital budgets over the past two years and comparison to actual

TRADING (details for the two years ended . . . unless otherwise shown)

Financial statements

1   Copies of the audited and supporting detailed accounts, directors reports and (where issued) chairman's statements for the last three financial years

2   Details of accounting policies adopted, together with changes (and their impact on the financial statements) over the last three years

Sales

3   Analysis of turnover by main product/service group

4   Analysis of turnover by main customers, identifying customers common to other members of the group and also sales to members of the group

5   Analysis of turnover by geographical area (UK [by broad area], overseas by country)

6   Analysis of turnover by employee/account executive

7   Details of current terms of trade settlement etc – any special terms

8   Details of contract arrangements with current major customers – any long term contracts

9   Who are regarded as the major competitors and any analysis made of the company's competitive situation in the industry

10 Customer age profiles at year end 200 . . .

11 Details of pricing policies

12 Examples of sales literature given to customers

Contribution/gross profit (information required if not already covered by management accounts, and again covering the past two years)

13 Analysis of contribution by appropriate department/service provided

14 Any significant fluctuations on a monthly basis together with reasons why they occurred

Costings

15 A brief summary of the costings used to substantiate pricing policies

16 A note of the way in which these costings are regularly monitored to management accounts, or

feedback of actual costs compared with the costs used for quotation purposes

17 How much does marginal costing feature in quoting selling prices

18 To what extent are costings a necessary part in compiling management accounts

Costs and suppliers

19 Within each principal cost making up the gross profit a summary of the major suppliers and the costs incurred

20 Details of general order and supply terms

21 Particulars of any long term agreements with suppliers

22 A note of alternative supplier arrangements that are possible for significant costs

23 Details of any specific financial arrangements

24 Details of any services provided by other group companies

25 Details of subcontract work where this is significant

ASSETS AND LIABILITIES (details at 200 . . .)

Fixed assets

1   Summary and description of the principal fixed assets and useful life (this could probably be a fixed asset register)

2   Details of any freehold properties owned by the company, its date of purchase and cost, any

subsequent improvements, recent internal and external valuations

3 Details of any leasehold properties and terms of lease

4 Details of any significant profits/losses on disposals in the last two years

5 Details of asset replacement policies

6 Details of any capital expenditure budgets for the future

7 Details of any asset revaluations

8 Details of significant hire purchase, leasing and rental agreements

9 Details of depreciation policy

10 Details of trademarks, licences etc

Current assets, current and other liabilities

11 A summary of the composition of stocks and any provisions

12 To have available for inspection the relevant stock sheets

13 A summary of trade and other debtors, and bad debt provisions

14 An aged list of debtors

15 A note of planned debt collection targets and the size and experience of the credit control department

16 A summary of cash/overdraft figures together with bank reconciliations

17 A summary of trade and other creditors

18 A list of trade creditors

19 A note of the policy for payment of suppliers

20 Copies of any loan agreements

21 Details of facilities and review dates of all borrowings

22 A summary of provisions for liabilities and charges

23 Details of any capital commitments, financial commitments and contingencies

24 A summary of the movements on taxation accounts over the past two years

Taxation/duties

25 Copies of the most recently agreed and subsequent draft tax computations

26 A note of any matters in dispute with the Inland Revenue

27 Details of any deferred tax provisions and potential tax liabilities

28 A note of the principal effects of VAT on the business and sight of VAT returns for the past 2 years

29 A note on the principal effects of customs duties and procedures to deal with them

PROFIT FORECASTS

1   Details of forecasts made in the past three years with a comparison to actual

2   Details of current forecasts for the . . . years
ended 200 . . .

3   Details of the assumptions made

CASH FLOW

1   Details of forecasts made in the past three years
with a comparison to actual

2   Details of current forecasts for the . . . years
ended . . . 200 . . .

3   Details of the assumptions made

PROSPECTS

Details of any business plans for the future (of which
the above forecasts form part)

NOTE: The above information is not exhaustive and there will inevitably
be some further requests as the work progresses.

Document provided by Baker Tilly ©

Appendix D

Summarised Sample Share Purchase Agreement

Dated 200[ ]

[Details of Selling Shareholders to be inserted]

and

[Details of Purchasing Company to be inserted]

Draft Acquisition Agreement relating to the Sale and Purchase of the Entire Issued Share Capital of *[Target Company to be inserted]* Limited

wardhadaway

Sandgate House
102 Quayside
Newcastle Upon Tyne NE1 3DX

This Agreement is made the day of 200[ ].

Between the seller ('the Seller') and the buyer ('the Purchaser')

Interpretation – Sets out the definitions of terms to be used throughout the contract, which are then usually shown with an initial capital letter in the text (e.g. Completion in 5 below).

Sale of shares – Defines what is being sold, e.g. specifies the shares to be transferred.

Consideration – How much is to be paid for the shares, typically a specified amount and then a reference to uplifts in respect of specific clauses (e.g. stock at value).

Conditions precedent – Any specific conditions required such as passing of a resolution to allow the sale, any reference to competition or regulatory authorities permissions etc.

Conduct of business pending completion – Sets out specific responsibilities in the period prior to Completion (e.g. that the seller will carry on trading as normal, keep the insurance up to date and not sell off major assets or make any other significant changes).

Completion – Details of how and when Completion will take place and what the parties have to do to allow this to happen and the fallback options if there are any problems in delivering documents etc.

Completion balance sheet – How (and when) the Completion accounts which determine the final purchase price (e.g. in respect of stock values) are going to be drawn up and what happens about any disputes.

Warranties and representations – The warranties given by the Sellers to the Purchaser which will generally include that: the Sellers have the power and authority to sell the shares; the Warranties given will be true, accurate and not misleading and will continue to be so at the time of Completion; each warranty is separate and independent of the others; if you qualify any warranty as being to the best of your knowledge, this is after having made reasonable enquiries; you accept that the Purchaser is relying on your warranties.

This will also set out that the Purchaser's rights in respect of any warranties given; will not be altered by any knowledge that they had (other than what is in the disclosure letter or any failure to claim immediately in respect of any breaches; that the warranties and representations are limited to those specified in the agreement; that the rights of the Purchaser to claim under the warranties will be limited by the terms of Schedule 5 (unless there has been fraud or misrepresentation).

Restrictive covenants – Sets out the commitment of each of the Sellers not to without the Purchaser's prior written consent: Engage in a specified type of business (directly or indirectly) for a specified period and/or within a specified area; Entice away employees (particularly key ones who may be specified); Solicit customers, business (or sometimes suppliers); Use a similar business name.

Confirms that these restrictions are separately enforceable and are considered reasonable to protect the goodwill of the business being purchased.

Retention and joint account – How the Retention account into which a proportion of the sales proceeds are going to be paid will be dealt with and how claims against this account by the purchaser should be made.

Payments – That all payments made under the contract should be made in full without any set offs.

Provisions relating to this agreement – General provisions about how the agreement is to be read and interpreted (e.g. that it is governed by English law).

Announcements and circulars – That no announcements about the sale other than any required by law or regulations should be made without the other side's consent.

Entire agreement – That this Agreement and its related schedules constitute the whole agreement and supersedes any other documents or agreements (which can only be changed by written agreement of both sides). Also used to ensure that each party acknowledges that it is relying solely on the documents referred to in the agreement and not on any other representations.

Subsequent sale – A non embarrassment clause that if the buyer sells on the company at a profit within a specified period, the buyer has to pay a proportion of the proceeds across to the seller.

Costs – That each party bears its own costs in respect of the agreement.

Notices – Details of where and how notices can be served on the other party and when they will be deemed to have been received.

Further assurance – A confirmation that where necessary, the sellers will (at the buyer's expense) execute any further documents that may be needed to complete the sale.

Schedule 1

The sellers' holdings – A table setting out the sellers' shareholding(s).

Schedule 2

Company details – A table setting out details of the company (Company number, date of incorporation, authorised share capital, directors, registered office, auditors, accounting reference date etc).

Schedule 3

The properties – A table setting out details of the freehold and leasehold properties owned by the company.

Schedule 4

Warranties – The detailed specific warranties that are being agreed, covering, in a typical agreement, say:

Memorandum and Articles – The copy of the Memorandum and Articles of Association of the Company attached to the Disclosure Letter are correct, that the register of members and other statutory books of have been properly kept, are up to date and the Seller has had no notification that there are any mistakes that need to be corrected.

Options – That there are no outstanding options or other rights to the company's shares.

Returns – That as far as the Sellers are aware the Company has complied with the provisions of the Companies Acts and has filed all statutory returns and notified all charges at Companies House.

Commissions – That there is no liability for a brokerage or other fee outstanding in relation to a sale of the shares.

Possession of documents – That the Seller has all the original copies of all relevant documents (e.g. title deeds).

Investigations – There are (as far as the Sellers are aware) no current or pending government investigations into the company (and no grounds for such an investigation known).

Accounts warranty – As far as required by the agreement, the accounts have been drawn up in accordance with normal accounting conventions, have been prepared on the same basis as accounts for the last three years, give a true and fair view and meet the requirements of the Companies Act.

Stock valuation and accounting policies – That the stock in the accounts has been valued consistently with prior periods, at the lower of cost or net realisable value in accordance with the relevant accounting standard (SSAP 9) with adequate provision for obsolete or slow moving stock.

Depreciation of fixed assets – That the fixed assets in the accounts have been depreciated consistently in the last three years' accounts in accordance with the relevant accounting standard (SSAP 12).

Accounting reference date – The accounting reference date of the Company is as stated in Schedule 2.

Book debts – None of the debtors shown in the accounts are overdue by more than 90 days old or have (or should have) been written off as irrecoverable or credit notes issued.

Books of account – Full disclosure of all matters has been made to the auditors in drawing up audited accounts and the books and records are accurately prepared and complete.

Capital commitments – There are no outstanding commitments to capital expenditure (or disposal of capital assets).

Dividends and distribution – There have been no dividends or other distributions paid since the last balance sheet date.

Bank and other borrowings – The Company has kept within its overdraft facility over the past twelve months and total borrowings have not exceeded any limitations imposed by its Articles, a debenture or regulatory requirements.

All loans and debts have been repaid as they fall due and the company has had no formal or informal demands or notice to repay from any lender.

The company has not created any loan capital or entered into any off balance sheet finance arrangements or discounted its debts.

Loans by and debts due to the company – The Company has not lent any money which has not yet been repaid to it, has not lent money other than in the normal course of business and has not made any loan or quasi-loan contrary to CA (this is targeted particularly at Directors' loan accounts).

Liabilities – So far as the Sellers are aware there are no liabilities outstanding (including disputed or contingent liabilities) other than those shown in the Accounts or incurred in the normal course of trading since the Balance Sheet Date.

No one has claimed any security over assets and there are no disputes relating to any assets.

Bank accounts – Details of all the bank accounts and other accounts of a finance nature operated by the Company are set out in the Disclosure Letter.

Continuation of facilities – Full details of all the Company's financial facilities (e.g. loans, overdrafts, letters of credit etc) are set out in the disclosure letter (with copies attached where relevant). The Seller is not aware of any default or demands for repayment.

Effect of sale of shares – The Sellers have no reason to believe that as a result of the share sale: any supplier or customer will want to cease trading with the company or wish to change its terms of trade; any key employees will wish to leave; the company will lose any specific rights; the company will breach any agreement or regulatory requirements; allow anyone to escape an obligation to the company; make any debts or loans fall due for immediate payment or lead to any lender exercising their security (e.g. by appointing a receiver).

Business since the balance sheet date – The business has been carried on normally since the balance sheet date with all transactions being recorded as normal, no major changes in the business's circumstances, customers, suppliers or turnover and the level of fixed assets maintained, no new borrowing taken on and all liabilities paid on normal due dates.

Licences – So far as the Sellers are aware the Company has all its necessary licences and permits required to conduct its business, the Company complies with their requirements and the Seller is not aware of any breaches or other reasons why these might be revoked.

Litigation – As far as the Sellers are aware neither the company nor any related party is engaged in any litigation and there is none pending against the Company or a related party (or any known grounds for proceedings).

There are no disputes with the government, no outstanding or potential employee claims and as far as is known, no pending criminal prosecutions against any officer of the Company.

Insolvency – The Company is not insolvent nor is it unable to pay its debts within the meaning of section 123 of the Insolvency Act 1986. There are no outstanding judgements or court orders against the company; no one has taken any action to commence insolvency proceedings against the Company (liquidation, receivership or administration) and there are no proposals for a Company Voluntary Arrangement or other compromise with creditors.

Insurances – Details of the insurance policies are set out in the Disclosure Letter, the premiums are up to date and the Seller is not aware of any outstanding claims.

Details of the policies of insurance currently effected by the Company.

Fair trading and restrictive practices – So far as the Sellers are aware the Company is not in contravention of any of the relevant competition legislation.

Material contracts – The Company has no contracts that are equivalent to more than 10% of its turnover or significant contracts that: the company is in breach of the contract terms; might be cancelled as a result of the sale; are loss making; were entered into other than as part of part of normal business; have significant currency or other risks; or carry onerous terms or cannot easily be fulfilled.

Grants – Full details of all grants and other such support are set out in the Disclosure Letter and the Seller is not aware of any grounds that would require repayment or forfeiture.

Compliance with contracts – The Company has complied with all contracts it has entered into and made all payments due.

Defective products – So far as the Sellers are aware the Company has not made or sold any defective products or had any notices under relevant consumer protection legislation.

Service liabilities – The Company has no outstanding liability (other than imposed by law) to service, repair, maintain or take back goods that are sold.

Data protection – The Company has registered under the Data Protection Act 1998 and complied with its requirements.

Guarantees and Indemnities – There are no any outstanding guarantees or indemnities given by the Company.

Directors – The directors details shown in Schedule 2 are correct.

Pollution – So far as the Sellers are aware the Company has complied with relevant Environmental legislation, holds relevant licences and has no Environmental claims or liabilities.

Employees and terms of employment – Full details of employees and their terms and conditions are set out in the Disclosure Letter. There are no other contracts (e.g. personal service contracts) and no binding agreements with trade unions or other body representing employees.

Bonus and other schemes – There are no bonus or profit share schemes or other discretionary payments made.

Service contracts – There are no contract containing notice periods of over one month or including payments on termination in excess of the statutory minimums.

Disputes with employees – There are no outstanding or potential disputes with claims against the Company by employees or ex employees as far as the Sellers are aware.

Agreements with unions – There are no agreements or other agreements (whether or not legally binding) between the Company and any trade union or other body representing employees.

Change in remuneration – There have been no significant changes in employees terms of employment or their pay made or discussed since the Balance Sheet Date.

Redundancies – No employee will become redundant and be entitled to a redundancy payment as a result of any provision of this Agreement.

Pensions – Full details of all pension schemes are set out in the Disclosure Letter (and there are no other such schemes), together with: copies of the relevant deeds and schemes rules; membership details; benefit entitlements; confirmation that: contributions are up to date; insurance is in place to cover benefits; all advisory costs have been paid up to date; there are no other liabilities and no actual or pending claims or litigation in respect of the scheme.

Assets and charges – The Company owns all the assets to be sold and there are no outstanding liabilities or charges attached to any of the assets.

Stock and work in progress – Levels of stock are adequate but not excessive, the stock is properly identified and is in good usable or saleable condition (except where already provided for as slow moving or obsolete).

Leased assets – There are no grounds under which leased assets are at risk of being repossessed.

Plant and machinery – The company owns and controls all the plant, machinery, vehicles and other equipment to be sold, subject to any leasing or HP agreements shown in the disclosure letter.

Tax provisions – The Company has made proper provision (taking account of the relevant Accounting Standards) for all tax and deferred tax liabilities.

Administration – All tax returns, computations and payments due have been made or paid by the due dates and are full and accurate. No material tax liabilities have arisen since the balance sheet date and the Company has properly operated its PAYE accounting system.

Taxation claims, liabilities and reliefs – Full details of any and all tax claims and that may be made by the Company any and all potential tax liabilities are set out in the disclosure letter.

Distributions and deductibility of payments – The Company has not redeemed any shares or paid any distributions or dividends since the Accounts Date.

It has not received or made any payments which may be disallowable for tax purposes or which would give rise to a capital gain.

Close companies – The Company has always been a close company as defined by tax legislation and has complied with the requirements for this type of company.

Group Relief and Surrender of Surplus Act – The Company has not been a member of a group or an associated company of another at any time in the last 6 years.

Capital allowances – All expenditure on plant and machinery qualifies for writing down allowances and has not elected to treat any assets as short life assets.

Transactions not at arm's length – The Company has not undertaken any transactions at undervalue or not at arm's length.

Base values and acquisition costs – The values used for capital assets will be such that no chargeable gains arise as a result of the sale.

Tax avoidance – The Company has not engaged or been a party in any tax avoidance schemes.

Unremittable income and capital gains – The Company has no income that falls within the category of 'unremittable income' under tax legislation.

Demergers – The Company has not been involved in a demerger.

Transfer of overseas trade – The Company has not transferred any part of its business overseas.

Sale and leaseback of land – The Company has not entered into any sale and leaseback of land arrangements.

Stock dividends and deep discount securities – The Company has not owned or issued any 'deep discount' securities.

Controlled foreign companies – There are no grounds for the Inland Revenue to direct that profits are apportionable to a foreign company.

Chargeable gains – The rules to be applied to determine the Company's potential corporation tax liabilities.

Capital losses – The Company has not incurred a capital loss involving a connected person.

Acquisition from group members – The Company does not own any assets purchased from a company with which it was in a group at the time

Replacement of business assets – The Company has not made claims under tax rules relating to roll over relief, replacement of business assets etc.

Gifts involving group companies – The Company has not received any assets by way of gift.

Gains accruing to non-resident companies – The Company has no gains that may be liable to tax as a non resident company.

Value Added Tax (VAT) – The Company has registered for VAT and: maintains accurate records; has complied with the requirements of the tax; is up to date with payments; has no outstanding penalties or notices; is not part of a group; does not operate any partial exemption recovery method; the disclosure letter gives full details of any bad debt relief being claimed.

Inheritance Tax (IHT) – The Company has made no transfers of value and there are no outstanding IHT charges.

Stamp duty – All stamp duty liabilities have been paid and no claims for relief have been made in the last five years.

Title – That the property details set out in Schedule 3 are correct, the Company has good title to any freehold land and is not occupying any properties not declared on Schedule 3.

Restrictions and encumbrances – The Company has full rights to occupy the properties and there are no onerous restrictions or covenants.

Town and Country Planning and related matters – The Properties are currently used for the purposes set out in Schedule 3 and this use is authorised under relevant regulations covering planning, public health, building regulations etc.

Adverse orders – No notices have been received adversely affecting the current use of the Properties.

Disputes and access – The Sellers are not aware of any disputes regarding boundaries or access.

Leasehold property – The Company is up to date with its rent, there are no rent reviews outstanding and has not contravened and material conditions of its leases.

Statutory obligations – The company has met all its obligations under all relevant law (such as Fire Precautions, public health, environmental protection, factories acts etc) and there are no outstanding notices.

The rateable value of the Properties is set out in the disclosure letter.

Intellectual Property Rights (IPR) – The Company is the sole owner of the IPR that it uses and where appropriate this has been registered in the company's name within the relevant countries and the registrations maintained.

That the company has kept its IPR confidential, has not given any third party rights over the IPR, is not aware of any infringements (and has not infringed any other parties IPR) and is not party to any secrecy agreements in respect of other parties IPR.

Shares – That the Company does not own (or is committed to buy) shares or bonds in any other company.

General – That all the information provided by the Sellers' Solicitors to the Purchaser's Solicitors as written replies to their pre-contract enquiries was and still is true and accurate in all respects.

Schedule 5

Warranty limitation provisions – The Sellers' maximum total liability is limited to the sale Consideration.

The Purchaser can only make a claim if the total liability exceeds a specified amount (but any such claim will be for the whole amount).

The Sellers have no liability where the amount is less than a specified sum.

The Sellers have no liability unless claims are made in writing (with full details) within the specified period.

The Sellers have no liability for matters arising out of actions taken after the date of completion or matters set out in the disclosure letter.

The Sellers have no liability if the purchaser fails to take their advice in dealing with any dispute or claim.

The Purchaser cannot make a claim arising solely from any changes in prevailing rates of taxation.

If the Sellers settle any claim that Purchaser is subsequently able to recover from a third party, the purchasers will reimburse the Sellers (net of costs).

The purchaser will advise the seller as soon as practical once the purchaser becomes aware of any circumstances that may give rise to a claim under the warranties and keep the seller notified of developments and provide copies of relevant information.

The Purchaser will take actions (at the seller's cost) that the seller reasonably requests to deal with any situation that may give rise to a warranty claim.

The Purchaser cannot settle any matter giving rise to a Warranty without having complied with the above requirements.

Claim unless it shall have first complied with the provisions of paragraph 9 and 10 of this Schedule.

Any claim will be reduced by the extent to which it is covered by insurance or has only arisen as a result of changes in law, taxation or accounting policies by the Company.

No Warranty Claims can be made expect in respect of matters set out in this agreement.

The Sellers have no liability for anything specifically provided for in the completion balance sheet (to the extent of the provision made).

Payment of any Warranty Claim is in full and final settlement of that claim.

The purchaser can only take action for damages in respect of any breach of the agreement and cannot rescind the sale.

Any overpayments of warranties by the sellers (e.g. in respect of tax) shall be repaid promptly once recovered by the Company.

Claims and payments made under the tax deed and warranties may be offset.

Neither the Purchaser or the Company will make any Warranty Claims against the Sellers expect on accordance with this Agreement.

In assessing any damages or compensation payable by the Sellers the maximum value that can be put on the Company is the sale Consideration.

This agreement does not diminish the Purchaser's or the Company's duty to mitigate their loss.

Schedule 6

Completion provisions

Part 1 – The Sellers' Delivery Obligations – A list if what the seller needs to deliver to the purchaser (e.g. the executed tax deed, disclosure letter, share transfer forms, title documents etc).

Part 2 – The Sellers' Action Obligations – A list of what the seller needs to do (such as the passing of a board resolution to register the share transfers, arrange resignation of pension scheme trustees, arrange that specified directors enter into new service contracts etc)

Part 3 – Purchaser's Delivery Obligations – A list of documents the purchaser has to supply, usually limited to a counterpart Tax Deed, acknowledgement of receipt of the Disclosure Letter and a counterparty Power of Attorney.

Part 4 – Purchaser's Action Obligations – A list of what the purchaser needs to do including most importantly pay the consideration!

Schedule 7

Deed of Tax Covenant

Dated 200[ ]

[*Details of Selling Shareholders to be Inserted*] and [*Details of Purchasing Company to be inserted*]

wardhadaway

Sandgate House
102 Quayside
Newcastle Upon Tyne NE1 3DX

This Deed is made the day of 200[ ]

Between **the Sellers and the Purchaser**

Recital – This Tax Deed is entered into pursuant to the Agreement.

Operative provisions

Definitions – Definitions of the terms used.

Covenant – That the Sellers undertake that they will pay the Purchaser the amount of the Company's outstanding tax liabilities as at completion.

Exclusions – That the Sellers will not be liable to pay the Purchaser tax paid or provided for before completion or arising as a result of actions by the purchaser (such as failure to claim appropriate reliefs).

Mitigation – If the Sellers have to pay the Purchasers under this agreement where there may be a right to reclaim such money, the Purchaser is obliged to pursue such a claim.

Conduct of claims – Details as to how the Purchaser notifies the Seller of a claim, the conduct of any claim by the purchaser and responsibility of the purchaser to deal on a timely basis to avoids unnecessary interest or penalties as well as to keep the seller advised.

Dates for and quantum of payments – Period within which the Seller has to pay any claims.

Deductions from payments – Payments are to be made gross and without any set-offs.

Savings – If it is found that the Company has made a saving on the taxation, the purchaser will pay over the saving to the Seller.

Recovery from third parties – If the Company is entitled to recover funds from third parties that reduce the seller's liabilities then the company will act to recover this (at the seller's expense).

Over-provisions – If the auditors certify that any tax has been over provided for in the Accounts then the purchaser will reimburse the seller.

Purchaser's indemnity – The Purchaser gives the Seller an undertaking that it will ensure that the Company pays its taxation liabilities.

General – That any payment by the Sellers under the Tax Deed will be treated as a reduction in the sale Consideration and general terms about the agreement (e.g. that it is governed by English law).

Schedule 8

Completion balance sheet and the net asset statement – The completion balance sheet and the net asset statement prepared by the Sellers Accountants in accordance with normal accounting standards.

Schedule 9

Profit earn out – Details as to how any profit earn out is to be calculated (as it will normally be based on an adjusted net profit figure with specific exclusions), the amounts to be exceeded before any sum is payable and how and when it is to be calculated and paid.

Signature page

Document supplied by Ward Hadaway.

Index

accounting policies 131, 135, 207, 264, 280, 281, 292

acquisition plan 20, 63, 71, 104, 197, 299, 321, 323

acquisition strategy 55, 63, 287, 407

administrator 107, 407, 410, 412

administrative receivership 398

agriculture 36

annual accounts 129

annual return 62, 87, 92, 129, 272

articles of association 63, 128, 271

assembler 35

asset valuation 191, 203, 217

bank loan 241

basic multiple 192

Belbin 21, 56, 298

beta 209

block discounting 240

book value 131, 203, 204, 217, 234, 283

bootstrapping 222, 223, 403

break-even 136, 140–143

bridging 230, 231, 240

British Venture Capital Association (BVCA) 104

business angel 103, 104, 111, 221, 227, 228

business angel network 103, 104, 105, 109, 110, 112, 405

business database 114

business life cycle 49

business plan 63, 93, 224, 233

business service 39, 42, 113

Buy In Management Buy Out (BIMBO) 60

CAMPARI 225

capacity utilisation 142

capital gains tax 325, 326, 327

cashflow forecasting 212, 283, 381, 382, 389, 415

cashflow management 381

cashflow statement 151

Client Handles Own Customers (CHOCs) 238

closure 319

commercial due diligence 296, 297

Companies House 62, 92, 113, 114, 128, 131, 132, 272, 275

Company Directors Disqualification Act 25, 412

Company Voluntary Arrangement (CVA) 398

Confidential Invoice Discounting (CID) 238, 240

confidentiality agreement 178, 275

conflict of interest 117, 309, 413

construction business 40, 41

consultation 361, 362

contingencies 135, 295

contingent liabilities 193, 273, 278, 285, 293, 295, 326

contract hire 242

corporate finance 6, 65, 66, 68, 98, 100–102, 106–108, 110, 160, 187, 190, 191, 321, 405

corporate owner 77

corporation tax 63, 294, 325, 327, 388
cost drivers 136, 142
cost structure 139, 140, 220
Costs of Sales (CoS) 133, 140, 377
covenants 196, 277, 290, 293, 307–310, 318, 319
Creditor's Voluntary Liquidation (CVL) 398
current liabilities 134, 237
current ratio 145

deal structure 168, 214, 265, 266
defined benefit 136, 276
Designated Professional Body (DPB) 111
direct fixed costs 140
directors loans 243
discounted cashflow 191, 208–212, 214, 217
drop-dead price 188, 205, 256
Department of Trade & Industry (DTI) 25, 233, 361

earn-out 40, 196, 215, 222, 236, 264, 303
Earnings Before Interest and Tax (EBIT) 215
exclusivity 267, 268, 307, 410
executor 77, 79
external shareholder 89

factoring 222, 234, 238, 239, 240, 289, 395
family business 76, 87, 88, 89, 91, 337
financial assistance rules 248
financial information 113, 114, 123, 124, 128, 130, 153, 155, 159, 160, 164, 281, 282, 291, 301, 369, 370
Financial Promotions Order (FPO) 104, 110
Financial Services and Markets Act 2000 (FSMA) 110
Financial Services Authority (FSA) 110

financial stability 136, 145
financial target 33, 130, 341, 373, 374
fixed assets 131, 134, 135, 283, 293, 373, 375, 395
fleximortgage 230
forced sale value 203, 205, 217
franchise 15, 38, 43, 118, 119, 120

gearing 137, 146, 147, 207, 223, 224, 247, 305, 374
Generally Accepted Accounting Practice (GAAP) 129, 132, 280
going concern 101, 203, 204, 205, 217, 322, 324, 327, 407
Goods Received But Not Invoiced (GRNI) 285
goodwill 189, 204, 246, 259
grooming (the business) 98, 197, 200, 270, 305, 368
gross margin 38, 133, 281, 282, 292, 378

heads of agreement 258, 266
heads of terms 258, 266
healthcheck 169

income tax 325, 326, 327
increasing margins 377
increasing turnover 377
indemnities 66, 273, 307–310, 312–317
Insolvency Practitioner (IP) 25, 77, 101, 316, 326, 366, 368, 399, 410
Institute of Chartered Accountants (ICAEW) 111
integrated manufacturing business 36
Intellectual Property (IPR) 158, 170, 275, 316, 320, 366, 395
Internal Rate of Return (IRR) 191, 212
internal review 297
investment business 111
investments 33, 77, 79, 104, 110, 111, 134, 228, 236, 284, 288, 395

invoice discounting 222, 234, 238, 240

key staff 107, 176, 340
key suppliers 175, 285, 318, 332, 350

Land Registry 127
lead adviser 20, 28, 65, 66–68, 106, 108–110
leasing 222, 242
leisure and consumer service 40
letter of engagement 68, 69
licensing 20, 270, 274
lifestyle business 14, 29, 30, 31, 32, 39, 42, 93
limited liability company 62, 63, 192, 258, 365
Limited Liability Partnership (LLP) 60, 62, 128
liquidity 137, 145, 146, 155, 180, 283, 374
long-term liabilities 134

management accounts 128, 144, 170, 236, 281, 291, 294, 301, 369, 370, 401
Management Buy In (MBI) 22, 60
Management Buy Out (MBO) 59, 60
management information 270, 280, 341, 364, 369, 370, 372
management team 60, 163, 169, 176, 216, 225, 236, 262, 298, 404
managing people 352, 353
market valuation 191, 206
memorandum of association 63
mortgage 2, 23, 86, 129, 222, 224, 227, 230, 231, 234–236, 241, 245, 277, 384

net asset 14, 134, 135, 203, 204, 289, 293, 308
net present value 208, 210, 212, 213
net profit 134, 138, 152, 154, 181, 374
Non-Disclosure Agreement (NDA) 177

notes to the accounts 124, 131, 135

Open Market Value (OMV) 203, 204, 230, 245
operating lease 242, 283
Original Equipment Manufacturer (OEM) 35, 37
overdraft 129, 134, 145, 149, 151, 193, 194, 222, 224, 234, 238, 243, 295, 389, 401
overtrading 150, 220, 239, 295, 400
owner manager 77–79, 84–89

package lender 234
partnership 32, 60, 62, 128, 271, 273
PAYE 134, 145, 286, 294, 375, 383, 384, 387, 390
PBIT 215
Personal Guarantee (PG) 24, 79, 80, 150, 194, 226, 243, 244, 262, 401, 412
post-acquisition 6, 33, 197, 287, 298, 299, 321, 323, 334, 367, 381, 393, 407
PPA 21
pre-pack 101, 107, 108
Price/Earnings (P/E) ratio 192, 206–208, 213, 304
process of change 352
Profit and Loss account (P&L) 130–133, 135, 137, 140, 141, 159, 292, 299, 302, 388
profitability 37, 62, 76, 135–137, 139, 143, 151, 158, 201, 211, 270, 281, 296, 374, 375, 394, 403
psychometric test 21, 58, 298, 300, 361
Public Limited Company (PLC) 63

raw materials 36, 41, 139, 141, 284, 378, 394, 412
receiver/receivership 77, 107, 205, 220, 262, 316, 324, 398, 404, 407, 410, 412
reducing overheads 377

redundancy 159, 219, 233, 277, 301, 339, 344, 345, 350, 361, 362, 378, 380, 388, 403, 416, 417
Redundancy Fund 233
regulatory approvals 20
representations 66, 77, 307–313
Reservation of Title (RoT) 273, 411
retained profits 135
return on investment 137, 152, 192, 213, 218
risk management 365, 368
Royal Institute of Chartered Surveyors (RICS) 206

sale and leaseback 234, 235, 242, 245
scale of operation 185, 207
Selective Finance for Investment 232
share capital 63, 135, 209, 271
signatories 284
Small Firms Loan Guarantee Scheme (SFLG) 226, 233, 244
Society of Turnaround Professionals (STP) 417
sole trader 24, 60, 61, 128
stakeholder 88, 89, 276, 302, 337, 340, 347, 348, 403, 417
stamp duty 324, 327
Standard Industry Classification (SIC) code 113
stapled finance 222
Statement of Source and Application of Funds (SSAF) 151
statutory compliance 272
subcontractor 35, 36, 41, 42
sustainable earnings figure 206

target price 188, 189, 268
term loan 241
trade associations 44, 114, 124
trade creditor 134, 145, 194, 237, 295, 375, 383, 384, 386
trade partner 229
Transfer of Undertakings, Protection of Employee Regulations (TUPE) 170, 259, 277
Turnaround Management Association (TMA) 417

underperformance 38, 43

VAT 133, 134, 145, 286, 294, 322–324, 358, 367, 375, 383, 384, 386, 390
venture capital 5
Venture Capitalist (VC) 14, 21, 56, 60, 65, 77, 78, 93, 104, 109, 221, 227, 278, 337

warranties 66, 77, 135, 170, 183, 259, 271, 273, 307–317, 319, 321, 411, 413
Weighted Average Cost of Capital (WACC) 209, 211, 213
whitewash 248, 408
wholesaler 37, 38
working capital cycle 137, 148, 149, 220

zero based budgeting 143